STEREOTYPES AND SOCIAL COGNITION

STEREOTYPES AND SOCIAL COGNITION

Jacques-Philippe Leyens,
Vincent Yzerbyt and
Georges Schadron

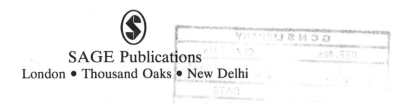

SAGE Publications
London • Thousand Oaks • New Delhi

First published 1994

SAGE Publications Ltd
6 Bonhill Street
London EC2A 4PU

SAGE Publications Inc
2455 Teller Road
Thousand Oaks, California 91320

SAGE Publications India Pvt Ltd
32, M-Block Market
Greater Kailash – I
New Delhi 110 048

British Library Cataloguing in Publication data

A catalogue record for this book is available from the
British Library.

ISBN 0 8039 8583 5

ISBN 0 8039 8584 3 (pbk)

Library of Congress catalog card number 94-067832

Typeset by Photoprint, Torquay, Devon

Printed in Great Britain by The Cromwell Press Ltd,
Broughton Gifford, Melksham, Wiltshire

Contents

Acknowledgements

Several friends and colleagues succeeded in finding time to read and to comment upon a draft of this book: we are very grateful to Richard Bourhis, Olivier Corneille, Benoit Dardenne, Susan Fiske, Chris Goodwin, Alex Haslam and Russell Spears, all of whom provided us with very helpful remarks, criticisms and suggestions. The content of the book also benefited greatly from discussions with Jean-Léon Beauvois, Daniel Gilbert, Dario Paez, Glenn Reeder, James Uleman, Jorge Vala and Eddy Van Avermaet – we thank them wholeheartedly. It was a pleasure to share ideas and to discuss data with our students: Fanny Bellour, Antonio Caetano, Pascal Denhaerinck, Bernard Geeraerts, Gabriella Gonçalves, Pascal Morchain, Stephen Rocher, Anouk Rogier and Dominique Vilain.

Finally, we dedicate this book to those who had to bear with us during the evolution of this work: our wives, Françoise, Isabelle and Pascale, and our children, Gregory and Sophie, Simon and Mathilde, Johanne, Martin and Lucie.

Jacques-Philippe Leyens
Vincent Yzerbyt
Georges Schadron

Preface

What do you expect from these authors? Perhaps you know the authors, maybe a little, maybe a lot, maybe not at all. They are social psychologists, Belgian, French-speaking, Catholic, male, of certain ages, trained at Louvain, writing in English, internationally known. If you know where they come from, maybe you know where they are going. What do you expect from this book, based on what you know?

Your thoughts and judgements, or your decision not to decide, based on your understanding of the authors, illustrate the subject of this book. The extent to which you used any social categories to decide whether or not to pick up this book in the first place, and whether you now, before reading it, expect merely to glance through it, actually to read it, truly to talk about it, maybe to teach from it, or perhaps to keep it on your desk next to the dictionary, depends in part on your social cognitions about the authors, and maybe on stereotypes about the categories they fit.

As I write, on the front page of the *New York Times Book Review*, Brent Staples comments on V.S. Naipaul's work, 'A strictly racial reading amounts to no reading at all' (May 22, 1994, Section 7, p. 1). Staples contests criticisms of Naipaul for not writing 'what he *ought* to write, given that he is a brown man (of Indian descent) born into the brown and black society that is Trinidad' (Ibid.). Instead, his writing has a wider historical reach, a universe of grim truths we might rather not confront.

In a similar way a strictly stereotypic reading of this book would amount to no reading at all. Some might interpret this book on the basis of stereotypes they hold for the three authors. Whereas who they are has certainly influenced what they write, those interpretations reveal our own naïve theories, the stuff of stereotypes. This book reaches beyond any single perspective and any expectations you might have had for these authors. Reaching beyond even their own international reputations, the authors make the broadest social psychological reach to understand stereotypes and stereotyping. They review all our major theories and provide a new one of their own to understand this phenomenon. This theory integrates previous theories and opens new avenues for research. These authors take us a considerable distance along the road towards understanding stereotypes and stereotyping. It is an important undertaking crucial to our survival and the quality of our human lives.

The impact of stereotypes on social cognition is everywhere. Here is a spontaneous sample from the periodicals arriving at our house today, but any day, any house, would do: The *New York Times Magazine* cover article profiles 'an unrepentant fascist, filled with hate,' who 50 years ago 'ordered seven men killed solely because they were Jews' (May 22, 1994, cover). Moving from mass killing to children's television, the cover of the *Sesame Street Magazine* features Burt and Ernie, its exemplars of friendship, but elsewhere they are criticized by homophobic groups for depicting two males who share a bedroom. The *Daily Hampshire Gazette*'s front page announces 'First women graduate from St Hyacinth's' Roman Catholic College and Seminary and next to that headline, under Sports, proclaims 'The woman is an umpire.' And these are only the covers of the periodicals. The interiors contain articles on ethnic cleansing, civil rights litigation, the urban underclass, women's schools, Haitian refugees, as well as stereotypes about sex and the elderly.

The most pressing human problems of today and yesterday involve people's judgements against each other, some of which merely humiliate and some of which lead to violence. This book deals with the root causes, psychological and social. Social psychologists have studied stereotypes for decades, and others are writing new books on the subject. So what's new here?

The authors take seriously the pragmatic position that thinking is for doing. People stereotype in part because it is efficient; stereotyping is useful. The authors take this now mainstream position to make a provocative and original stand: stereotyping smoothes social interaction. If stereotypes have social validity (especially if both parties agree), then stereotyping can facilitate mutual understanding, in this view. Contrary to the American instinct that stereotyping is evil, the authors suggest that the process of stereotyping is necessary to interaction. Some of the contents of stereotypes might be changed, in a better world, but the process is intrinsic and perhaps adaptive in human interaction.

Moreover, people are no fools about the process of stereotyping, according to these authors. People have naïve meta-theories about their own judgement processes. The authors' Social Judgeability Theory proposes that people make judgements only when they feel entitled to judge. People rely on their stereotypes only when they feel it is appropriate, according to their naïve meta-theories. The naïve meta-theories specify several conditions that define adequacy to make a judgement: the judgement must fit reality (the focus of previous social cognition research). The judgement must protect the integrity of one's self and one's group (bringing in motivation factors). The judgement must respect social rules, defined by the culture, about who is entitled to judge whom, and when (highlighting social roles, settings, and historical times). Finally, the judgement must constitute a satisfying, enlightening theory that gives meaning (emphasizing the cognitive glue that makes an explanation stick together).

The authors have done us a favour by writing a book and a theory that not only integrate cognition and motivation (the new wisdom), but also tie in the social rules that guide judgement processes, reviewing classic and current work in stereotyping, attribution, and impression formation under this unifying theme. It is an impressive enterprise.

A strictly stereotypic reading of this book would be no reading at all. The authors, like Naipaul, take the risk not to write what they ought to write, based on someone else's preconceptions of their defining categories. Instead, they write about broader human truths, from the best knowledge we have. Leyens, Yzerbyt, and Schadron faithfully describe a universe of truths, some of which we might rather not confront. But they are wise and interesting guides. Read on.

Susan T. Fiske
University of Massachusetts at Amherst

Introduction

'If I differ from you, far from wronging you, I enhance you', wrote Saint-Exupéry in *Lettre à un otage* (Letter to a Hostage, 1944). We thoroughly concur with Saint-Exupéry's statement. We would agree even more had he written: 'If you differ from me, far from wronging me, you enhance me.' In contrast to this praise of difference, we could also add one for similarity, because we feel enhanced if others are like us and we like them. Indeed, sociability accords with an equilibrium between differences and similarities.

In Western culture, differences between people are preferred to similarities, presumably because of the importance given to individualistic values. This phenomenon may explain why stereotypes are ill-liked. People can't afford, however, to do without stereotypes: were humans all unique, it would be impossible to describe only one of them. Indeed, to think about others is to categorize them – or to particularize them vis-à-vis a category. Categorization implies homogenization and this is partly what the stereotyping process does. For example, if people did not have a category for beauty-spots, clothes or behaviours, they would be speechless about others and themselves. Does this mean that stereotypes function through errors? And, first of all, should stereotypes be essentially regarded as errors?

The issues of accuracy and error have a long history in social psychology. Social psychologists have diligently examined the accuracy of person perception. Studies about who was best at recognizing affinities in groups or at unmasking friends' or foreigners' personalities flourished in the greenhouses of laboratories, schools and military squadrons. When, however, researchers discovered that either they were unable to pinpoint the characteristics of good judges or that there were no altogether good judges, they decided that people were lousy at perceiving others and that accuracy was not a theoretically interesting phenomenon.

Social psychologists then drew their attention to the processes of impression formation and causal attribution. Accuracy was absent from that concern. Asch (1946), who started the studies on impression formation, asked his subjects to describe fictitious persons. Heider (1958), who pioneered attribution studies, was attracted by naïve psychology, the reasoning of laypersons in their everyday dealings.

In the footsteps of Asch and Heider, researchers imagined theoretical models that accounted for the processes of impression formation and causal attribution. They then compared these models with people's actual answers. Two outcomes were possible: the models correctly predicted those reactions, or they didn't. If they didn't, it meant either that the models were inappropriate or that people did not reason well. Actually, experimental subjects deviated from some aspects of the models in systematic ways and researchers concluded that people biased their judgements. In other words, from descriptive the models became prescriptive. Under a novel disguise, accuracy was again a concern in social psychology.

The 1970s and 1980s witnessed an abundance of research showing that people were illogical or irrational. Most often, social psychologists explained this characteristic of human reasoning as the result of a lack of cognitive capacities or a lack of motivation to overcome the 'cognitive miser'. From time to time, a solitary voice would claim that, despite the usual interpretations of the experimental data, people are logical and rational. More recently, there has been renewed interest in accuracy and some researchers have contended that people are actually quite good perceivers of others.

The study of stereotypes is only incidentally linked to the history of research in person perception. When they were first measured, stereotypes were considered errors, abusive generalizations and, thus, marginally related to a field concerned with accuracy. Later on, as interest in the measurement of stereotypes waned and was not replaced by theoretical improvements, the study of stereotypes almost disappeared from social psychology. It is only recently, with the advent of social identity theory and social cognition, that stereotypes have regained their status with researchers.

Maybe it was the sudden interest in errors and biases that prompted curiosity regarding stereotypes. Indeed, although social identity theorists only reluctantly speak of errors, it was an experiment by Tajfel and Wilkes (1963) on categorization and accentuation of similarities within and differences between categories that created a renewed theoretical interest in stereotypes. These were now considered, at least in part, the result of a normal cognitivo-perceptual process. Similarly, to the extent that social cognitivists (e.g. Hamilton, 1981) studied faulty information-processing, it was also natural that they researched stereotypes. For instance, these authors realized that people often resort to stereotypes and neglect useful individuating evidence. At other times, people overlook stereotypes but pay attention to worthless individualized information. A blatant error – the abuse of stereotypes – topples on a congenial one – the undue neglect of stereotypes.

What injected stereotypes into the study of person perception is that researchers saw the latter as a question of balance between social categories such as ethnicity, gender, age, personality and nationality, and individuating information such as behaviours, personal characteristics and situations. Given that stereotypes correspond to social categories, they became an inherent part of person perception.

The usual perspective taken by social psychology is that the good social perceiver correctly weighs categorial and individuating information as if confronted with an intellectual problem. For us, however, person perception is more of the domain of the action than of the intellect. It attempts to make intelligible something which is not immediately and specifically intellectual.

Therefore, the point of view that we adopt in this book is not that people are good or poor perceivers. Neither do we defend that people are rational or irrational when they form an impression of others, and logical or illogical when they attribute a cause to a given behaviour. Our perspective is a pragmatic one. What is pragmatic is often considered useful, and person perception is useful for interacting with others. Assuredly, we adhere to this view of pragmatism. We do not stop there however; for us, social perception is action. This is where pragmatism joins pragmatics. As much as thinking is for doing, doing is for thinking. This is not some kind of activist and anti-intellectual stand. The French philosopher Blondel uses an illuminating metaphor to convince his readers that knowledge precedes, accompanies, and follows action. He writes that 'so in a wheel that moves forward by turning, the spokes at times precede, at times dominate, at times follow, at times are level with the axle; some go back to the rear while the others go to the head' (1902/1962, p. 1250).

It is in this pragmatic spirit that we undertake this book. In our opinion, social perception is an action that explains other people, and this explanation feeds further perceptions and actions. Furthermore, we agree with several authors that *stereotypes are shared beliefs about person attributes, usually personality traits but often also behaviours of a group of people.* Yet, we insist upon distinguishing stereotypes – the social content – and stereotyping – the individual process that takes place in a social context and is moulded by it. People can do without some of the specific contents but they cannot do without the process.

Some of the literature gives the impression that a single stereotype lays in wait behind every person, ready to ambush and to rape people's judgement. This single stereotype becomes the tyrant of their perception; they can't see but through its eyes. Although such a view is still popular, it is a partisan interpretation of the person perception process. Early theories about categorization were in fact more balanced and they recognized that the environment sometimes lacks crucial information. To be sure, categories allow people to sort out the data, but to do the job properly, people need more than just data and categories; they need to take into account factors that constrain their choice of categories. As noted by Medin,

> categorization is less attribute matching than it is an inference process. . . . A concept may be invoked when it has sufficient explanatory relation to an object, rather than when it matches an object's attributes. This means that, when encountering another person, people can count on a vast repertory of categories. They can even create categories on demand. (1988, p. 124)

In our view, there is much more flexibility with categories than with individuating attributes. As Smith wrote:

A 'Black person' is never just that, but also young or old, male or female, a professor or a lab technician, well or poorly dressed, tall or short, friendly or hostile, from the South or the North. Therefore, the first question involving stereotypic perceptions of an individual must be: Which category is used, when? (1989, p. 33)

In her discussion of the role of intent in stereotyping, Fiske (1989) also defends the idea that people are not obliged to use a particular negative stereotype. They have plenty of alternatives. They may, of course, individuate the target, treat that person as a unique person, or they may resort to less negative stereotypes.

Given this flexibility with categories, how do people make a selection? We propose that the way people conceive of the world, and more specifically, the way they conceive of the judgement situation, determines the kind of categories and data they will use. In other words, we stress a pragmatic approach. Referring to pragmatics leads us to inquire about other aspects than just the data and the categories, or the theories about these data. When people enter situations, they are sensitive to the kind of interaction they are involved in and to the kind of goals they are pursuing. We argue that the types of interactions and goals present in a situation will most likely determine the constraints on the categories and the data used in that situation. The same behaviours will probably not trigger the same schema when you speak about your brand new girlfriend or about the one who just dropped you. In the same vein, if a respected psychologist says that you are good at telling stories, it makes a huge difference if it is said about the novel you are writing or about the research paper you just submitted for publication. In our view, when action is at stake, when goals are operant, impression formation becomes an explanation, ratings become judgements. Now the question is: 'When is it OK to express a judgement about a person?' 'When is the explanation good enough to warrant a judgement?'

One obvious answer is that the judgement should correspond to reality. Actually, according to the majority of research, it is the only factor that matters. Of course, no one with good sense would deny that reality does not matter. If it didn't, and if judge and target did not share the same delusion, their interaction would be a disaster. However, to go back to Smith's (1989) example for the categories of a Black person, reality is not restrictive enough to account for all the choices of categories. At the same time, this reality is insufficient to encompass all possible categories. Indeed, the number of possible categories is infinite. While people and behaviours do not vary much over time and space, categories can change enormously. Another way to express ourselves is to say that reality can never constitute the ultimate criterion for judgements. To blame judgements because they do not reproduce reality would be the equivalent of reprimanding painters because they do not replicate exactly the objects of their inspiration. However, because people have to interact, they have to work with the assumption that there is a common reality that can be attained and trusted.

There are other criteria of adequacy besides objective reality that need to be considered when examining a judgement. We label these other criteria: the cultural, integrity and theoretical levels; they are at the heart of what we call the *social judgeability theory*. Before we introduce them, readers should have clearly in mind the differences that we see between the reality level and the social judgeability levels. First, at the level of reality, the problem or the aim is to adequately integrate categorial and individuating information so as to match reality as well as possible. That is, the final judgement should, in some way, reflect objective reality. With the other levels, the problem is to find a useful fit with rather than an exact match with reality. The aim, therefore, is not only to reflect reality but to find a solution that allows people to function socially as well as possible. Second, whereas the reality level concentrates on data and theories about data, the other levels deal with the theories that judges hold about their judgements. Hence, we call this approach the social judgeability theory.

Person perception bears upon the personal and social integrities of the perceivers. In other words, people form impressions but remain attentive so that their self or the group they belong to is not endangered by their judgements. This concern for maintaining an adequate level of integrity shows that motivational factors effect more than just the cognitive process. Motivational factors also taint the conclusions reached by perceivers. Let us illustrate the social part of this level by a recent remarkable Belgian movie, *Daens*. The movie's eponymous protagonist, a priest, starts a kind of socialist and Flemish movement in Flanders (Belgium) at the end of the nineteenth century (most readers know of course that the Flemish identity is very important for many people in Belgium). The bad characters are from all origins: French, Walloons, Italians, Germans and Flemish. However, the good characters are only Flemish! Probably without being aware of it, the movie director set the stage so that only members of his group are the good people. As if doing otherwise, in the context of tricky group relationships, would endanger the social integrity of the group.

When making a judgement, people do not just attempt to match categorial and individuating information, and they do not just endeavour to preserve their personal and social integrity. People also respect social rules. This is the cultural level of adequacy. These rules vary with time and culture. Gould (1983) reports how great scientists like Broca and Lombroso followed the social rules of the nineteenth century to prove the inequality between human beings. They both favoured facts over theories, but they retained as reasonable facts only those that conformed to the then current standards of thought. Like Gould, Katz and Braly (1933) also discovered a judgemental social rule when they measured stereotypes. They found that, at that time, that it seemed legitimate for Whites to publicly express negative stereotypes about Blacks in the United States. At present, and in many cultures, there is a rule that one does not judge only on the basis of a mere categorial information. That is to say that people will judge a person only to the extent that they feel they have received enough information about that person. Several factors may make a target – Mr Clindeye, for example – judgeable. Obviously, diagnostic information about the real Mr Clindeye constitutes the main factor. It is not, however, the only factor, and it is not even a necessary one. People may be deluded about being specifically informed about Mr Clindeye. They may rely on information which is not diagnostic but looks like it is. They may trust the amount of information conveyed about Mr Clindeye rather than its content, or they may feel entitled to judge Mr Clindeye because of their status. Often, the amount of information is related to the richness of the information. Only people who read a lot are knowledgeable – right? Often, also, having status implies having knowledge, even if the basis for that status is unrelated to the content of the knowledge. Because we are professors of psychology, we know better about soccer, Clindeye, and politics – don't we?

We call the last level of adequacy the theoretical level. When people arrive at a judgement, either in terms of a category or in terms of specific behaviours, we presume that this judgement explains the integration of the different pieces of information that have been taken into account. This judgement should also function as a theory from which it will be possible to derive predictions for the future. In a recent paper, Rothbart and Taylor (1992) brilliantly argued that people infuse some kind of essence into otherwise arbitrary social categories. Assuming that psychologists as a group differ from mathematicians, people try to understand this difference by attributing a different essence to the psychologists than to the mathematicians. This essentialism corresponds to naïve theories about the world to use Medin's (1988) terminology. In this book, we defend the idea that people express a judgement about someone to the extent that this judgement corresponds, in their mind, to some theory about the world. Their judgement is their theory. Therefore, an adequate impression of someone should not only match reality, respect certain social rules, and protect people's identity, it should also constitute an *enlightening gestalt* that gives meaning to the world and allows communication.

Traditional models of person perception in general, and of impression formation in particular, focus mainly on epistemic validity. In sharp contrast, the pragmatic dimension that we stress with the different levels of adequacy, relates to *social validity*. Here, the focus is no longer the relation between the object to be judged and the knowledge basis of the judges, but the relation between the judges and their judgement at the service of behaviour; judges bring into the situation theories about inferences, about judgements, that colour the match between the data and the theories about these data. As we said earlier, there is no ultimate truth in person perception, even if there are correct answers. If Julio plays American football, and if Amanda plays badminton, one correct answer is that he is a football player and she is a badminton player, but it does not mean that it is the right perception. One does not even know whether one should speak of sex or gender differences between these two persons. A socially valid response, however, will allow people to interact smoothly with others when speaking about Julio and Amanda.

This book is not a treatise about stereotypes. We do not try to be exhaustive. Rather, we defend a pragmatic stance about stereotypes and stereotyping by presenting our social judgeability theory with its different levels of adequacy. By reviewing definitions, measures, classic theories and empirical evidence, we try to show the relevance of social judgeability.

In the first chapter, we define the concept of stereotype and review its different measures. We insist upon several components that we deem essential for the specificity of stereotypes: description, evaluation, homogeneity and distinctiveness of the targets, as well as consensus of the judges. Throughout the chapter, we launch the distinction between stereotypes and the stereotyping process. Working with stereotypes is not only applying a label; it requires participation in a process. Stereotyping is not just producing or resorting to stereotypes. Also, the labels available and the stereotyping process cannot be held responsible for the use a person makes of them. They serve an interaction. It is the interaction that has to be questioned and, maybe, condemned.

The next three chapters deal with theories about stereotypes. Chapter 2 is devoted to classical approaches to prejudice and stereotypes. Very succinctly, we outline the psychodynamic theories, that is, the authoritarian personality, the open and closed mind, and the scapegoat theory. The social conflict perspective is also presented, along with the realistic conflict theory and the contact hypothesis. Finally, we summarise the socio-cultural approach as a choice between reality and naïve theories for grounding stereotypes. Since Tajfel's social identity theory (SIT) has greatly contributed to the renewal of interest for stereotyping we discuss it next. Chapter 3 presents this theory without neglecting current developments such as the self-categorization theory and the behavioural interaction model. We do not only insist upon cognitive and motivational factors, as does SIT, but we also take into account social norms. The fourth chapter is the last one to be devoted to the theoretical accounts of stereotypes. It deals with social cognition, which has revitalized the field. We illustrate two particular approaches – person memory and impression formation – by presenting representative research concerning three topics: inconsistency management, saliency and spontaneous inferences. Looking back at these different theories, we cannot resist noting that they have tackled and highlighted, at one moment or another, one or the other of the adequacy levels we claim are important in the production of social judgement.

We confront SIT and social cognition in the fifth chapter where we review selected intergroup phenomena such as ingroup and outgroup homogeneity, illusory correlations and ingroup overexclusion. We also launch the issue of social judgeability: people rely not just upon data and theories about data, but also upon theories about judgements. For the perceiver, groups and instances of members do not exist in a theoretical vacuum; it may be that the homogeneity of groups does not only depend on perceptual and mnesic phenomena, but also, and mostly, on the theories held about these groups. The same is true of the classic illusory correlation paradigm. We question its relevance for the comprehension of stereo-typing. Finally, we present our own research on the social part of the integrity level.

Impression formation has been the bedrock of stereotypes. In Chapter 6, we deal with the different models that describe how people achieve a fair balance between categorial and individuating information. The review of the literature on hypothesis confirmation and desirable conclusions gives us the opportunity to present the personal part of the integrity level from a pragmatic viewpoint. We also show that classic explanations in terms of cognitive and motivational factors are not sufficient, and insist upon the importance of social rules in the judgemental process. In other words, we focus on the cultural level of adequacy. The dilution of stereotypes is discussed in the seventh chapter. This dilution is usually considered a nice cognitive error because, for once, perceivers somewhat neglect stereotypes and rely too much on individuating information. Again, we propose that social rules and strategies override cognitive explanations.

Since stereotypes are an integral part of person perception, they are not alien to the field of attribution. Chapter 8 reviews relevant research concerning causal attributions. We focus our attention on the distinction between internal and external causes of behaviours as it applies in the intergroup context, and especially in the overattribution bias. We attempt to show that the ultimate attribution error as well as the overattribution bias are not signs of cognitive deficiencies but expressions of naïve – and fundamental – theories about the world. We stress the importance of this theoretical level as well as of the reality, integrity and cultural levels of adequacy in the Conclusion.

1
The Concept and Measure of Stereotypes

The waves of scandal provoked in some countries by the movie *Basic Instinct* are relatively small when compared with the tide of indignation raised a few decades earlier by Bertolucci's *Last Tango in Paris*. In an almost empty apartment in Paris, a middle-aged American man, Marlon Brando, sexually prowls on a very young French girl during the entire picture. To ridicule the ire of his compatriots, the famous American editorialist Art Buchwald summarized the film as follows: it is the story of an American who finally finds an appartment in Paris. Unfortunately, a French girl wants it too. To discourage her, he sexually assaults her in every possible way. No luck for him; she is French.

Everyone, whether they have seen *Last Tango in Paris* or not, would recognize in Buchwald's interpretation a stereotype about French people and Parisian life. When asked why this is considered a stereotype, these cinephiles would say that it is a general belief commonly held by the majority of Americans about the sexual life of most French. Not only has it a strong affective tone but it is a negative one. Finally, it consists partly of an erroneous perception because, mind you, not every Parisian is a French lover and not every French woman is a sex machine. Such a lay conception (no pun intended) almost completely agrees with Webster's definition of stereotype: 'A standardized mental picture held in common by members of a group and representing an oversimplified opinion, affective attitude, or uncritical judgment.' This definition lacks a direct reference to the negative tone towards the target of the stereotype, but the dictionary does add that people use stereotypes 'to dismiss divergent groups'. This view of stereotypes is not the original one introduced into the social sciences. However, the definition is so generally shared and utilized that one wonders which term people used when 'stereotype' belonged exclusively to the vocabulary of printers.

When the word was coined in 1798, a stereotype referred to a plate cast from a mould of a surface of type. A number of such plates can be cast from the original mould and they serve to make the layout of a document. The term stereotype actually consists of two Greek words: *stereos* and *túpos*, meaning rigid and trace respectively. Before social psychologists, psychiatrists used a similar term, stereotypy or stereotypie, in a metaphorical way. For them, the term described the frequent and almost mechanical repetition of the same gesture, posture or speech common in such disorders as dementia praecox. Ethologists and clinical psychologists still use the term stereotypy to refer to routine, rigid, repetitious behaviours. In *Psychological Abstracts*, this meaning corresponds to the entry 'stereotyped behaviors', whereas the social psychological meaning of the concept corresponds to the entry 'stereotyped attitudes'.

Walter Lippmann (1922), a famous American editorialist and political thinker, introduced the concept of stereotype to the social sciences. He never gave a precise definition of stereotypes in the social psychological sense. For Lippmann, stereotypes were 'pictures in our heads', a quasi-environment quasi-made by humans. According to him, people do not respond directly to objective reality but to a representation that they have created in their minds. 'The real environment is altogther too big, too complex, and too fleeting for direct acquaintance. We are not equipped to deal with so much subtlety, so much variety, so many permutations and combinations. . . . To traverse the world men must have maps of the world' (pp. 10–11). Stereotypes are such maps; they clarify people's itinerary in the windings of social reality but they will prove erroneous if used wrongly or with gullibility (p. 60). Lippmann's conception is very close to recent concepts in social cognition (Chapter 4). His is not, however, a purely cognitive view of the world. For Lippmann, stereotypes also contain affective ingredients. These will later be emphasized by psychoanalysts (Chapter 2) and proponents of social identity theory (Chapter 3).

While Lippmann was speaking about a simplifying device, he himself did not oversimplify reality. He also did not give way to the fashion of behaviourism, which, in the 1920s, was blossoming in academic circles. In his view, people did not merely react to objective stimuli, they constructed them in some way. 'For the most part, we do not first see, and then define, we define first and then see' (pp. 54–55). Stereotypes thus play the role of a double filter: one of perceptions and one of actions. Subsequent researchers concentrated on how the social perceiver constructed reality (e.g. Katz & Braly, 1933; Rice, 1926–1927). However, whereas Lippmann concluded that this was not necessarily a faulty process, his successors described the social perceiver as an almost hallucinating perceiver. According to these theorists, defining before seeing, or in addition to seeing, could only mean that the definition was wrong. These first authors to investigate the problem therefore focused their attention upon its supposed erroneous aspect; they also concentrated their efforts upon the negative content of stereotypes. Subsequently, stereotypes were apprehended in a purely cognitive manner and were regarded as cognitive shortcoming. To the contrary, Lippmann also suggested that stereotypes both originate in society and provide justification for its current state, thereby anticipating the socio-cultural perspective (Chapter 2).

If we insist upon Lippmann's conceptualization of stereotypes, it is not only because of its historical importance and richness, but especially because of its actuality. Indeed, it is striking how Lippmann anticipated many of the current ideas about stereotypes. For him, people are active perceivers of reality; they are not simply moulded by it, they mould it too. This filtering process is not abnormal and not necessarily erroneous. It also conveys values. Following Lippmann's lead, recent investigators have attempted to integrate cognition and motivation, error and truth, good and bad in a somewhat unified perspective.

Ours is a pragmatic point of view. Instead of presenting stereotypes as awful spectres projecting huge shadows on the world, we defend the idea that stereotypes are the result of a process that aims at regulating, as efficiently as possible, people's social interactions.

Definitions of stereotypes and the stereotyping process

Miller (1982) noted that definitions of stereotypes are almost as numerous and diverse as the authors who formulate them. While the various definitions all share central characteristics, their idiosyncrasies have important implications We will not review these various definitions here; such detailed analyses have been excellently done elsewhere (Ashmore & Del Boca, 1981; Brigham, 1971; Miller, 1982). Rather, we propose to draw a distinction between stereotyping and stereotypes. We will not be creative as far as stereotypes are concerned; we hope to be more innovative in our look at the stereotyping process.

Let's agree on a very general definition of stereotypes: they are *shared beliefs about person attributes, usually personality traits, but often also behaviours, of a group of people.* This definition represents only a very small part of the stereotyping process. The process goes far beyond the content of a stereotype, exactly as theorizing does not restrict itself to the formulation of a theory. Stereotypes are only an end-product or a point of departure of the process. To use a given stereotype is to consider that all members of a category such as an ethnic group share the attributes embedded in the stereotype; for instance, the Germans are orderly, industrious and intelligent. On the other hand, *the process of stereotyping individuals is the process of applying a – stereotypical – judgement such as rendering these individuals interchangeable with other members of the category.* For example, Yanelia is an introvert and thus possesses all the behaviours that are typical of introverts.

We will now elaborate on the different points raised by the general definition of stereotypes. Specifically, we will look at the consensus among the judges, the homogeneity of the targets considered members of a group, the distinctiveness of the attributes reckoned as stereotypical, and their evaluative and descriptive components. By the same token, we wish to differentiate stereotypes from neighbouring concepts such as prejudice, bias and attitude, as well as to describe our distinction between stereotypes and the stereotyping process.

Shared versus individual beliefs

According to some authors (e.g. Fiske & Pavelchak, 1986; Hogg & Abrams, 1988; Katz & Braly, 1935), the consensual nature of stereotypes is a necessary ingredient in their definition. Other researchers, on the contrary, do not insist that stereotypes need to be shared. Some of them even defend the idea that they may be held individually. Secord and Backman (1974), for instance, speak of personal versus social stereotypes. In the same vein, Ashmore and Del Boca claim that 'the term "stereotypes" should be reserved for the set of beliefs held by an individual regarding a social group and [. . .] the term "cultural stereotype" should be used to describe shared or community-wide patterns of beliefs'.

The justification for making a distinction between individual versus socially shared stereotypes borrows from several arguments. One is the question of degree of consensus among raters. It is true that stereotypes are unequally shared, but which degree of consensus must be reached before an individual stereotype becomes a cultural stereotype? In our view, it would be foolish to insist that attributes must be shared by everybody before becoming a stereotype. If it were so, many studies concerning stereotypes would lose their rationale because they specifically aim to study the strength or dilution of stereotypes, or to examine who is particularly prone to stereotyping. A second justification for distinguishing personal from social stereotypes is that these two concepts exist. Again, such reasoning seems to us very weak. When we say that the Jews, the Scots and the Dutch are penny-pinching, and when we want to tease the Jews, denigrate the Scots and describe the Dutch, should we therefore distinguish the teasing stereotype, the nasty stereotype and the incorrect stereotype because these different adjectives exist and can be applied to stereotypes?

It remains of course that, historically, a stereotype is first stammered by a few individuals before being shouted by crowds. In its present acceptation, the word stereotype was first proposed by a single person, Lippmann, before being widely used, overused and misused. When does an attitude held by a small group of persons about other persons become a stereotype? When does an idiosyncrasy become a technical term? The answer to such a question cannot be more precise than the response to: 'When does psychology become social psychology?' Stereotypes may be widely shared but the stereotyping process is, by definition, an individual one. Obviously, like any process, stereotyping is greatly influenced by social factors. Still, the confusion between the process and the end-product is in all likelihood responsible for the controversy between personal and social stereotypes. In our opinion, though, the individuality of the stereotyping process does not eliminate the need for a social sharing dimension to the definition. We agree, however, that what some authors call a personal stereotype, as opposed to a social or community-shared stereotype, is actually a weak stereotype. This weak stereotype is nevertheless a stereotype.

Descriptive and evaluative components

It is not original to say that stereotypes have a descriptive aspect. They usually refer to personality attributes and behaviours. Moreover, each description also has an evaluative component (Osgood, Suci & Tannenbaum, (1957). As we said earlier, the studies of the descriptive and evaluative components of stereotypes rapidly restricted themselves to negative aspects.

For Gordon Allport (1954), an influential psychologist, stereotype meant an exaggerated, rigid, bad and oversimplified belief that was equivalent to prejudice. However, stereotype is not the same as prejudice. Stereotypes can be positive. In our view, the term prejudice should be restricted to purely negative, derogatory judgements and discriminatory predispositions towards certain ethnic groups (Aboud, 1988). To further distance stereotypes and prejudice, Devine (1989) distinguishes between stereotypes and the personal beliefs that endorse or do not endorse the stereotypes. Stereotypes are very spontaneous, or quasi-automatic, whereas personal beliefs are under cognitive control. Personal beliefs are mainly responsible for prejudice.

People are experts at reformulating the same description with a different evaluative connotation. This expertise is very handy when they have to 'honestly' describe their group and another group very similar to theirs. 'We' are bold, 'they' are rash; 'we' are determined, 'they' are aggressive; 'we' are confident, 'they' are conceited (Deboeck, 1978; Peabody, 1967). Also, stereotypes of a given group are often a mixture of favourable and unfavourable components (Anderson & Sedikides, (1991).

Ehrenfels (cited in LeVine & Campbell, 1972) provides a fine example of this interplay between descriptive and evaluative aspects of stereotypes. This author conducted a study about the stereotypes between North and South in 20 countries above the Equator. In general, the Northerners see themselves as strong, industrious and serious. The Southerners, on the other hand, perceive themselves as artistic, intelligent and generous. Table 1.1 gives the perception of the outgroup. The self-perception of both groups descriptively corresponds to the perception by the outgroup. Nevertheless, the overall evaluation is quite different in the two cases. This does not mean that the stereotypes of the outgroup are all and completely negative.

The evaluative component of personality traits can be defined from two perspectives: self-profitability or other-profitability. Intelligent and stupid, for instance, have positive and negative adaptive consequences for the self, i.e. the self profits or does not profit from being described in these terms.

Table 1.1 *Stereotypes of the Northerners by the Southerners and of the Southerners by the Northerners*

Southerners see Northerners as	Northerners see Southerners as
Powerful economically	Economically weak
Powerful military	Military weak
Hard-working, energetic	Lazy
Physically strong	Weak
Slow and heavy	Quick and fast
Rough and dirty	Amiable and oily
Egocentric	Unreliable
Stingy	Wasteful
Pessimistic	Optimistic
Hard-hearted	Light-hearted
Serious	Crafty
Stupid	Clever
Fanatic	Spineless

Source: adapted from LeVine & Campbell, 1972

Generous and mean, on the contrary, have adaptive consequences for the other person who interacts with the owner of these traits. How do stereotypes of ingroups and outgroups relate to these two perspectives? Peeters (1992) presented his subjects with 108 national stereotypes drawn from 14 studies. Traits composing each stereotype were rated for self- and other-profitability; they were then weighted according to the number of persons agreeing that the trait pertained to the stereotype and according to the number of traits in the stereotype. Interestingly, positive self-profitable stereotypes involved both stereotypes of ingroups and stereotypes of outgroups (e.g. Black Americans perceiving White Americans in 1942; Americans judging Japanese or Germans before the Second World War and in 1967). Negative other-profitable stereotypes, on the other hand, always corresponded to threatening groups (e.g. Americans stereotyping Germans during the Second World War or the Russians during the cold war).

Ehrenfels' and Peeters' research nicely illustrate that people use stereotypes as explanations like scientists use theories. A scientific theory is not true or false, but useful or not useful. In the same manner, one should not consider stereotypes as correct or incorrect but as useful or harmful. Social psychology contains more theories about antisocial or negative phenomena than about pro-social or positive ones. This bias contradicts people's fundamental optimism (Czapinski, 1985). In the same way, most stereotypes focus on the dark side of humanity, but they need not.

Precisely because social psychologists usually favour the dark rather than the bright side of human behaviour, they have concentrated their attention upon a negative end-product – stereotypes – rather than upon a normal process – stereotyping. If you will permit the comparison, it is as if atomic power was considered only in terms of atomic bombs, and not in terms of atomic fission and energy. Likewise, most psychologists have considered the stereotype a nasty categorial judgement disguising singularities and they have neglected anything that preceded it. A stereotype is a categorial judgement whose content may be negative. However, insisting only on this aspect leads one to consider the stereotype mainly or exclusively as a lazy and unfriendly gimmick used to deal with the world when it could be conceived of as a creative device giving meaning to this world.

The kernel of truth controversy

Most of the time, stereotypes are disliked. They are confused with prejudice, and are also considered errors in perception. Stereotypes are abusive generalizations: every American eats hamburgers and only hamburgers. To be sure, stereotypes are generalizations, but this does not mean that the stereotyping process is a pathological way of thinking.

What is the 'kernel of truth' in stereotypes? 'Are French males indeed more romantic than English males?' worry Hogg and Abrams (1988, p. 67). Are stereotypical judgements purely and merely an error, without basis in reality? Of course not; many stereotypes are grounded in reality, even if they constitute an exaggeration of reality or were outdated by the reality that contributed to their expression. Going back to the study by Ehrenfels, one may ask oneself if there is something true in the stereotypes between North and South above the Equator. The temptation to give a positive answer is increased by the observation that the stereotypes are reversed when one goes below the Equator. For instance, Brazilians from Rio Grande do Sul consider themselves clean and industrious whereas they think of the North-East Brazilians as lazy and thieves. No great imagination is needed for what the North-Easterners claim about the Southern states of Brazil.

Indeed, Levine, West and Reis (1980) tackled an unconventional problem when they asked people for the time in Brazil and in the USA. The answers were more correct and more precise when given by a North American than by a Brazilian. Just on the fringe of caricaturing, the latter would say: 'a little bit over 6' whereas the other would state: '6:12 p.m.'. This was not a question of using a wristwatch (of better quality, digitalized, etc.); the researchers also controlled for the time displayed by public clocks. Brazilian clocks showed more flexibility than their American counterparts. We are unsure whether the citation of such research is useful other than to tease our Brazilian friends. What would certainly be futile would be to tease out the part of the stereotype due to reality and the part which is abusive. Some efforts have been made in this direction with regard to other problems, but, as one can easily imagine, they have not proven very helpful, either practically or, especially, theoretically.

We claim that reality and truth are not the only criteria used to judge the adequacy of social judgements. Again, we plead for the distinction between stereotypes and stereotyping process. The content of stereotypes may be pleasant or unpleasant, praising or derogatory, based on correct or inaccurate observations. The process of stereotyping is, by definition, a generalization and it may be helpful as well as detrimental depending on the conditions of its use. In other words, generalizing is not per se a bad thing, to the same extent that individualization is not necessarily the appropriate line to follow.

Distinctiveness of the targets

Is a stereotype a category that characterizes a group or a means of distinguishing one group from another? For example, suppose subjects have to rate the extent to which personality attributes apply to comedians, musicians, psychoanalysts and engineers. Comedians, who have to keep in good shape, are judged to be significantly more athletic than psychoanalysts, who spend long hours in an armchair behind a couch. Also, engineers are rated as much more dull than musicians. Does that mean that athletic is stereotypical of comedians and that dull is counter-stereotypical of musicians? In other words, are distinctive attributes separating groups in a particular context part of a general stereotype? Conversely, suppose that a vast majority of the judges perceive comedians and psychoanalysts to be cultivated, and that many rate engineers and musicians as industrious. Is culture part of the stereotype for comedians and psychoanalysts? Can the engineers and the musicians be stereotyped as industrious? These traits may characterize the professions in general, but they don't help to distinguish between them.

Both uses of traits for characterization and distinctiveness have served to isolate stereotypes. The difference may not matter much when the two groups are on opposing poles of the same dimension, such as men versus women, or introverts versus extroverts. However, the difference may be important when the two groups are not usually defined by mutual reference, such as in the case of comedians and psychoanalysts. All the attributes that distinguish these two groups may not be relevant for their definition and may therefore not follow the rules of the stereotyping process (Denhaerinck, Leyens & Yzerbyt, 1989; see also Hilton & Fein, 1989; Nisbett, Zukier & Lemley, 1981).

These latter remarks insist once more upon the fact that the categorial label expressing the stereotype is not only a summary of reality, but an explanation of it (Yzerbyt & Schadron, 1994). As an explanation of a given entity, it may differentiate this entity from others. In other words, there is an infinite number of possible distinctions between two groups depending, among other things, on the interaction in which the expression of the stereotype takes place. However, distinctiveness will be informative only if it articulates what this entity is for the subjects involved in the interaction. In other words, what is stereotypical of the musician, or of the comedian, will depend upon the context: who is expressing the stereotype of the comedian, or of the musician, to whom for what? Haslam, Turner, Oakes, McGarty and Hayes (1992), for instance, showed not only that the stereotype held by Australians about Americans changed as a function of time (before and after the Gulf War), but that it was also affected by the countries the Australians were comparing the Americans to (Australia and Britain, or Australia, Britain, Iraq and the Soviet Union). Had the experimenter in that study not been British, but American, the results could still have been different.

Individual versus categorial level

Do stereotypes only apply to groups, such as the Belgians, or are they also applicable to an individual, such as Paul? According to Schneider, Hastorf and Ellsworth, 'our impressions of another person are also a form of stereotype; we abstract certain aspects of his or her behavior, organize them around certain disposition, and develop a picture of the person' (1979, p. 15).

This quotation may be understood in two ways. On the one hand, it could mean that we stereotype a given individual, rather than a group, because our impression about that individual generalizes over time: John is always extroverted. We would not apply the term stereotype to this meaning because it is only John who is referred to and his characteristics are individual ones: he is extroverted in the same manner than he is also nice-looking and has a beauty-spot in the middle of his right cheek. On the other hand, it may mean that John is an extrovert or, in other words, that John is one exemplar of all those people who form the extroverted category. This latter meaning corresponds to our definition of a stereotype, that is, a category-based judgement. We argue that stereotypes are generalizations based on the membership to a category, i.e. beliefs that derive from the inference that all members of a given category share the same properties and are, therefore, interchangeable.

When does a category lead to a stereotype? Do certain categories differ from others in this respect? Andersen and Klatzky (1987) distinguish between what they call personality traits, which are adjectives, and social stereotypes, expressed by nouns. Politicians, comedians and used-car dealers correspond to social stereotypes – we would prefer to say social roles – whereas extroverted, hysterical and hypocritical are personality traits. Andersen and Klatzky have shown that social roles are associatively richer, more visual and more distinctive than traits. In this sense, social roles constitute a more basic level of categorization than personality traits (Cantor & Mischel, 1979). It follows that roles should be more efficient for information-processing than traits. Indeed, Andersen, Klatzky and Murray (1990) have verified this. Their subjects had to respond as quickly as possible, 'yes' or 'no' to sentences where the subject was either a role-type or a trait-type and whose action was unrelated to the content of the type. As predicted by the authors, the subjects reacted more rapidly to the sentence 'The daddy's girl type closed the door' than to 'The immature type closed the door'. Moreover, later on these subjects were better able to recall what the daddy's girl had done than what the immature person had done.

A difference between categories seems to exist: all of them are not created equal. Even if some categories share the same content – 'being immature' in the present case – another aspect must be added to this content before it is a stereotype. This aspect is process-oriented. This process, stereotyping, implies that all members are alike, that they are homogeneous and predictable on the basis of their membership to the category. One could say that stereotypes concern beliefs (derived from content information) about members of a group, implying that the behaviour of these members is determined by their membership (derived from the process of stereotyping). This statement completely agrees with the essentialist thesis defended by Medin (1989) and by Rothbart and Taylor (1992). Indeed, to the extent that groups are explained by some kind of essence, all members participate in this essence and are, thus, interchangeable.

Summary

This historical overview of the concept of a stereotype reveals that controversies and ambiguities around the concept stem from a neglect to distinguish between stereotypes and the process of stereotyping. Whereas stereotypes are shared evaluate and descriptive beliefs about members of a category, stereotyping is an intra-psychic process whose main function is to make sense of the world. When the targets of stereotypes share the same category, they are thought to be similar, and the attributes selected to describe them are consensually conceived as informative because of a given context. By definition the person who stereotypes generalizes. This question brings up the issue of accuracy but accuracy is not the main problem. What matters is the reason for stereotyping. There is no pathology in stereotyping, but the content of stereotypes may be pathogenic.

Measures of stereotypes

When Lippmann gave a new meaning to the word stereotype, social psychologists were quick to adopt the concept despite its imprecisions. Still, no ready-made operationalization of the concept came with the package. The concept of stereotype had close links with what social psychologists called an attitude, but the overlap was not such that the measures were interchangeable. In the remaining part of this chapter, we trace the main efforts at operationalizing the concept of stereotype. For the sake of clarity, we focus our illustrations on ethnic and gender stereotypes.

Not surprisingly, a concern with the prejudicial aspect of stereotypes has occupied centre-stage. For about forty years, the main goal of researchers was to uncover stereotypes' descriptive and evaluative aspects. In so doing, they stressed the consensual nature of stereotypes, on the side of both raters and ratees. Later on, new methods were proposed which were atuned to more sophisticated views on stereotypes. Researchers questioned consensus as a built-in feature of the measures of stereotypes. First of all, they believed consensus among raters was not an essential component of stereotypes. Additionally, researchers minimized the importance of homogeneity, that is, consensus among ratees, and turned instead to notions of distinctiveness and heterogeneity. These changes reflect the evolution in the definitions of stereotypes. Also, it is clear that the trend in research over the years corresponds to an increasing concern with processual issues. Stereotypes are more and more conceived of as important variables regulating person perception. When appropriate, we will attend to the processual aspects implied or vindicated by the different methods.

Pictorial material

Remember that for Lippmann, stereotypes are 'pictures in our heads'. Rice (1926–1927) took this suggestion quite literally and reasoned that if stereotypes really shape our perception, they could be measured via the recognition of pictures of persons belonging to different social groups. If these persons are recognized at a rate above or below chance level, a stereotype must be at work. Rice presented 141 Dartmouth undergraduates and later a group of farmers with nine photographs taken from the *Boston Herald*. He told his subjects that the photographs represented a bootlegger, a European Premier, a labour leader, two manufacturers, an editor-politician, a Bolshevik, a US Senator and a financier. The first six persons on the list were recognized at a rate well above chance with the bootlegger on top of all; he was the only one in outdoor costume with a cigar firmly gripped between his lips. The Bolshevik was the least recognized; only 9 people identified him correctly. He did not have a long beard and a smoking bomb clutched in his fingers as the contemporary stereotype wanted it. Instead, he was a man with a wing collar, a Van Dyck beard and moustache, well-dressed and distinguished in appearance. The man on the photograph actually was the Soviet ambassador in Paris.

Clearly, the problem with Rice's recognition measure is that it doesn't tell much about the actual content of the stereotypes. If the recognition matches reality as in the case of the bootlegger, is it because of the costume, of the cigar, of the particular face and the grip of the cigar? If, on the other hand, the recognition fails as with the Bolshevik ambassador, one doesn't know for sure what the stereotype really is: is it really a long and dirty beard hiding a bomb? As a matter of fact, this technique did not meet with great success. It regained popularity, however, immediately after the Second World War in response to some new questions. Why is it that so many Jews, who tried to hide their ethnic origin during the war, were recognized and thus victims of denunciation? Did they have a recognizable Jewish face? Were antisemites better than non-prejudiced persons at recognizing Jewish faces? (See Chapter 5 for a detailed analysis of this question.)

Another line of research dealt with pictures as means to measure ethnic preferences (Brand, Ruiz & Padilla, 1974) and confusions within in- and outgroups (Secord & Backman, 1974). The latter approach is particularly relevant for research on eyewitness testimonies: are eyewitnesses as reliable when the defendant is of the same race as the witness (Brigham, 1986; see also Zebrowitz, 1990)? Because the method did not provide much information in terms of content, it never became a hit among students of stereotypes. Still, one advantage of using pictorial material in the study of stereotypes is that it avoids verbal codes which are open to higher levels of control on the part of the respondents. Because of these characteristics, pictorial material is often utilized to activate a supposedly known stereotype rather than to measure it. Building upon a long tradition of research on the psychology of rumours (Allport & Postman, 1965; Rosnow, 1991), researchers used visual information to uncover biases in the encoding, storage or retrieval of information relevant to stereotyped targets. Sagar and Schofield (1980), for instance, showed films of ambiguously aggressive behaviours to their subjects. The behaviours were interpreted as more hostile and threatening when performed by a Black person than by a White person (see also Darley & Gross, 1983; Duncan, 1976).

Lippmann's idea of 'pictures in the head' is sometimes in use today, at least indirectly. Thanks to the availability of flexible statistical tools that can handle large numbers of data, researchers can use new methods to test specific hypotheses about the structure of stereotypes. Work carried out by Marylinn Brewer is a clear example of the use of a methodology that does not rely on verbal descriptions. According to Brewer (1988), physical characteristics play a key role in the appraisal of other people. In particular, age and sex are two crucial dimensions of interpersonal differentiation, and, as such, they stand as universal features of implicit social categorization. These two dimensions help partition the social world into specific person types (Brewer, Dull & Lui, 1981; Brewer & Lui, 1985; Deaux, Winton, Crowley & Lewis, 1985). Brewer and Lui (1989) found evidence for this hypothesis by giving subjects a set of 140 photographs of Caucasian adults varying in age and sex. The experimenter asked them to sort the photos according to similarity in character or personality type, similarity of specific physical characteristics, or similarity of psychological traits or states. Subjects were told to choose as many categories as they saw fit within the constraint that they select no fewer than 6 and no more than 12. Age and sex were good predictors of the final sorts made on the basis of person types and physical appearance. Quite a different arrangement resulted, however, when subjects were asked to group the pictures on the basis of psychological traits and states.

Bogardus' Social Distance Scale

Since stereotypes are often confused with signs of prejudice, it is not surprising that measures of the latter have served to tally the former. Bogardus' (1925) Social Distance Scale is a good example of such a strategy. Typically, subjects are asked to express the intimacy they will tolerate from people of a different nationality. The original scale provided the subjects with the following steps:

1   would admit to close kinship by marriage;
2   would admit to my club as personal chums;
3   would admit to my street as neighbours;
4   would admit to employment in my occupation in my country;
5   would admit to citizenship in my country;
6   would admit as visitors only to my country;
7   would exclude from my country.

One could, of course, imagine other sequences. This type of scale has a crucial feature, however. Once subjects reject one level of intimacy, admitting other nationals as neighbours for example, they should also reject all steps involving a higher degree of intimacy, such as marriage. Obviously, the distance between the different steps is not always the same. This causes a problem when the scores of a given sample must be averaged.

Other techniques have been proposed to measure prejudice: Thurstone's equal interval scales, Likert-type scales, Gutman's scalogram, Osgood et al.'s semantic differential. These scales all constitute psychometric refinements (for reviews, see Dawes & Smith, 1985; Himmelfarb, 1993). They do not, however, change anything about what is really apprehended. First, by themselves, these measures of stereotypes do not imply a consensual view of the raters. Second, the descriptive component, that is, the content of the stereotypes, is often left out of such measures to the profit of the evaluative aspect. In other words, the stereotype is reduced to its prejudicial dimension.

Typical traits assignment

Probably, the best known measure of stereotypes is the personality trait checklist, first proposed by Katz and Braly (1933). According to authors like Ashmore and Del Boca (1981), checklists are responsible for having shaped the field (see also Brigham, 1971). The method is extremely simple and aims at documenting shared stereotypes.

In the first part of their study, Katz and Braly asked Princeton students to rank in order of preference 10 ethnic groups: Americans, Blacks, Chinese, English, Germans, Irish, Italians, Japanese, Jews and Turks. This first step was an adaptation of the Bogardus scale (see Table 1.2). They then instructed a sample of subjects to write down the adjectives that they believed characterized these 10 nationalities or groups. Katz and Braly secured 84 personality traits this way and calculated their score of favourability, from which they obtained a composite score of desirability per group. As Table 1.2 shows, the correlation (r = .89) between these composite scores and the ratings of preference is quite high. Finally, another group of 100 students was asked to select the five most typical traits for each group. A trait chosen at random should only be given by 6 per cent of the subjects (100 × [5/84]). A quick look at Table 1.2 indicates that the actual data are far above this chance level. In other words, there is a clear consensus among judges about the kind of characteristics that typically belong to each of these groups. The content of these stereotypes as obtained by Katz and Braly in 1932 lend themselves to comparisons with two exact replications, one conducted by Gilbert (1951) in 1950, and the other by Karlins, Coffman and Walters (1969) in 1967 (see Sigall & Page, 1971, for a critical evaluation of these data).

Katz and Braly (1933) also computed a measure of homogeneity, which they called uniformity, for each ethnic group. They defined homogeneity as the lowest number of traits needed to account for one-half of the total selections, that is, 250 (5 traits × 100 raters). They counted the number of times the most popular trait was attributed to a given group, added this number to the frequency of the next item in popularity, and then continued in this manner until they reached the total of 250. The number of traits involved in this addition forms the homogeneity index. It could thus vary from 2.5, if the 5 selected traits for a given group were given by all subjects, to 42, if all 84 traits were mentioned as equally characteristic of the group. The results for this homogeneity/uniformity index appear in Table 1.2.

Several aspects of these results deserve comment. To appreciate them fully, however, one has to remember that, in the early 1930s, few Black students attended Ivy League universities. Moreover, privileged-class White students were barely acquainted with Blacks at all. The first interesting conclusion is therefore that the homogeneity component of the stereotypes and the prejudice remain unrelated. Indeed, Blacks and Turks were equally disliked; still, these two groups stand at the opposite ends of the homogeneity scale. Second, familiarity does not seem to be the guiding criterion for homogeneity. The best-known group to the subjects, the Americans, falls near the middle of the scale. This pattern is quite surprising in light of recent models of stereotyping. According to the familiarity/complexity hypothesis (Linville, 1982; Linville & Jones, 1980), for instance, people should have a more nuanced view of the ingroup than of other groups because they know more instances of the former than of the latter. This means that Americans should have been last on the continuum of homogeneity.

At the time of Katz and Braly's investigation, other researchers suggested that homogeneity or consensus occurs for those groups with which the ingroup is or has recently been in conflict, and least for those who are far and alien (Murphy, Murphy & Newcomb, 1937). In other words, ethnocentrism and conflict might be at the core of stereotypes.

Table 1.2 *Descriptive traits, degree of consensus, level of prejudice, desirability and uniformity for 10 different ethnic groups*

Ethnic groups	Traits	Consensus (%)	Prejudice	Desirability	Uniformity
Americans	Industrious	48	1.15	6.77	8.8
	Intelligent	47			
	Materialistic	33			
English	Sportsmanlike	53	2.27	6.26	7
	Intelligent	46			
	Conventional	34			
Germans	Scientifically minded	78	3.42	6.02	5
	Industrious	65			
	Stolid	44			
Irish	Pugnacious	45	3.87	5.42	8.5
	Quick-tempered	39			
	Witty	38			
Italians	Artistic	53	5.64	4.4	6.9
	Impulsive	44			
	Passionate	37			
Japanese	Intelligent	48	5.78	5.89	10.9
	Industrious	46			
	Progressive	25			
Jews	Shrewd	79	7.1	4.96	5.5
	Mercenary	49			
	Industrious	48			
Chinese	Superstitious	35	7.94	4.52	12
	Sly	30			
	Conservative	30			
Turks	Cruel	54	8.52	3.05	15.9
	Very religious	30			
	Treacherous	24			
Blacks	Superstitious	84	9.35	3.55	4.6
	Lazy	75			
	Happy-go-lucky	38			

Source: adapted from Katz & Braly, 1933

Another explanation, however, could be that conflicting groups are more salient or distinctive to the judges. As a result of having exchanged more information, and having looked for more explanations to account for the salience, judges reach a greater consensus than they would otherwise.

Surprising as it may seem, Katz and Braly were not especially interested in the measurement of stereotypes as such. Their concern was a theoretical one rather than a methodological one. They reasoned that the global measure of prejudice obtained with the previous instruments, such as the Bogardus Social Distance Scale, was due to the traits that were evoked by the different nationalities. If only very undesirable traits were elicited by the Turks and mildly negative ones by the Irish, one should expect prejudice to be greater for the first group than for the second one. (As a matter of fact, some decades later, this issue of 'facts' combining into a broad and single evaluation became the central concern of the information-integration approach; Anderson, 1981.) This is the reason why Katz and Braly measured the desirability of the traits in addition to prejudice, consensus and homogeneity.

Katz and Braly's methodology set the stage for future research and moulded the theoretical analyses for many years (for a recent use of checklists, see Eagly & Kite, 1987). For decades, many investigators have compulsively established dictionaries of ethnic stereotypes. It may be fun to learn that Americans are ambitious, Germans scientifically minded, Italians artistic and Thais sensual, but the fun fades away when there isn't anything else. And there wasn't for a long time.

Percentages of shared attributes

Authors using Katz and Braly's typical traits assignment method often met with problems. They were often confronted with individuals reluctant to attribute stereotypical traits to ethnic groups. Gilbert, for example, reports that a good number of his subjects voiced 'a protest against the unreasonable task of making generalizations about people – especially those they had hardly ever met' (1951, p. 251). In other words, subjects did not feel in a position to judge some groups of people when using Katz and Braly's method. Brigham (1971) circumvented that difficulty by asking his subjects to give the percentage of members of a given group who had such and such traits. He provided possible answers in the form of a Likert-type scale, ranging by 10s from 0 per cent to 100 per cent. Whereas the delivery of typical traits do not allow exceptions, percentages do: to say that many Portuguese, say 90 per cent, are friendly is to recognize that some are not.

Katz and Braly's method raises another problem by not allowing researchers to calculate individual scores of stereotyping for the judges. Brigham's technique does. According to Brigham (1971), stereotypes are unjustified generalizations. It follows that any extreme percentage assigned by an individual can be considered a stereotypical response. For instance, an experimenter may decide that any percentage above 70 or below 30 represents an unreasonable generalization. The number of such generalizations given by individuals provides a fair estimator of the degree of stereotyping. When averaged at the group level, the percentages tell us which attributes are stereotypical for a particular sample. Brigham notes that so-called typical traits, as obtained by Katz and Braly's method, are not necessarily considered as being possessed by many people. In a study comparing the typical traits assignment method and his (Brigham, 1971), the percentages of typical traits ranged from 10 to 100, with an average of 55. Thus, according to Brigham, Katz and Braly did not uncover stereotypes in the sense of erroneous generalizations about the targets. Rather, they focused their attention upon consensus among the raters. Brigham, instead, deals with the homogeneity of the ratees as it is mistakenly perceived by the raters.

Gardner, Wonnacott and Taylor (1968) proposed another method that they called the stereotype differential.

> This technique [. . .] defines the stereotype in terms of extreme polarity of semantic differential ratings. Subjects are asked to rate ethnic group labels on a series of semantic differential scales having bipolar trait descriptive adjectives at the endpoints. [. . .] An item is identified as being part of the stereotype when the mean deviates significantly from an assumed neutral mean [i.e. the middle of the scale], given the variability in the ratings as indexed by the standard deviation. (Gardner, Lalonde, Nero & Young, 1988, p. 41)

This method, which corresponds to the classical Student's t-test, retains the extremity dimension of Brigham's approach and at the same time takes into account the consensus among the raters through the measure of dispersion.

The diagnostic ratio

Some authors criticized the preceding measures because the percentages of or extremity judgements about a trait in a given population do not take into account the probability that the attributes may be as prevalent in other groups as in the target group. To say that 90 per cent of the Portuguese are friendly does not necessarily mean that friendliness is solely a part of the Portuguese stereotype. After all, Spanish, Italians, Americans and many other nationalities are also very friendly, and maybe more so than the Portuguese.

To address this issue, McCauley and Stitt (1978) developed a measure, inspired by Bayes' theorem, called the diagnostic ratio. The diagnostic ratio is the probability that someone has a particular trait given his or her group membership divided by the probability that this person has the trait regardless of group membership. To put it simply, it consists in dividing the proportion of friendly Portuguese by the proportion of friendly humans in general. Deviations from a ratio equalling 1 correspond to stereotypes. If the ratio is less than 1, the trait is counter-stereotypical. The greater the deviation, the more the trait is (counter-)stereotypical of the group under consideration. It is possible to calculate a general individual index of stereotyping, first, by translating the ratios inferior to 1 into their reciprocals, and, second, by averaging all the ratios obtained by a given judge for the different traits. To get a measure by attribute, the averaging is done over the individual ratios per attribute.

The diagnostic ratio measures what subjects think are typical characteristics of a group. Typical here is not used to mean that all members of the group possess a given characteristic. Rather, it refers to the salience or distinctiveness of the targets. Members of a group are said to have stereotypical attributes to the extent that, for these attributes, they deviate from what is normally expected. One special feature of the diagnostic ratio method is that it can be used to assess individual stereotypes as well as shared stereotypes. In line with Brigham's concern, the diagnostic ratio also de-emphasizes consensus among raters.

Implicit theories of personality and subtyping

The richness of data measuring the attributes assigned to people and the progress in statistical methods allowed researchers to verify whether people have a structured view about persons. In other words, do the characteristics sustain meaningful relations among them, or do these characteristics just constitute a salmagundi of personality traits? Are there specific views about kinds of people, and if these views are structured, are the structures reliable over different samples of judges?

One such structure corresponds to what has been called an implicit theory of personality, that is, general beliefs about the distribution and relationships between personality traits (see Chapter 4.) According to Rosenberg (1988), people tend to share an implicit theory constituted by two almost orthogonal dimensions: socially good/socially bad and intellectually good/intellectually bad (these two dimensions are not alien to Peeters' [1992] distinction between self- and other-profitability). For instance, people perceive a close relationship between warm and reliable and between cold and unreliable. The social perceiver may thus believe that warm people are also more reliable and that cold persons tend to be unreliable. Rosenberg and Jones (1972) also tried to uncover idiosyncratic implicit theories. They analysed Theodore Dreiser's book *A Gallery of Women*. In this autobiographical novel, the writer succeeds in attributing at least one stable personality trait to no less than 241 persons. A multidimensional analysis found three dimensions that fit what is known about Dreiser's life. The first dimension of conformism/anti-conformism corresponds to Dreiser's reactions to literary successes. The other two dimensions are very close to each other; they oppose soft and feminine on the one hand and hard and masculine on the other. This also fits with Dreiser's reputed relations with women. There were two kinds of women for him: the vertical and the horizontal. The former were intelligent and accompanied him as his public relations; the latter were more sexually attractive and his mistresses.

This example implies that gender stereotypes can be approached through implicit theories of personality. However, it seems that people do not have just one theory about men and another single theory about women (Amancio, 1991; Ashmore, 1981; Huici, 1984). A refinement of the implicit theory of personality approach is thus to identify the many male and female subtypes. Several theorists have suggested that global attributes such as sex and age may be too large and that researchers should turn their attention to more restricted, basic-level categories. In other words, people differentiate among the many members of a broader social category by creating a manageable set of subtypes. These subtypes constitute, then, the appropriate level to examine people's perceptions, evaluations and behaviours towards each other. This perspective led researchers to rely on techniques aimed at measuring subtypes as opposed to general stereotypes.

Starting from the Roschian approach, Cantor and Mischel (1977, 1979) were first to provide evidence of the hierarchical nature of personality types. This line of research opened the door for similar suggestions within the realm of stereotypes. A series of studies by Brewer et al. (1981) constitute one good example of the subtype approach. The authors first verified that people distinguished elderly persons in 'grandmotherly', 'elder statesman'. and 'senior citizen' types. Their subjects were then handed six sets of three photos taken either from the same cluster, e.g. grandmotherly, or from the three different clusters. They had to assess attributes of the sets of pictures by checking adjectives on a list. In general, trait attributions for subtypes proved to be richer and more consensual than those for the general category of elderly persons. In other words, sub-types allow better communication than the more encompassing categories. Not only do subtypes induce more inferences, but also, these inferences are more widely shared by people.

The idea that people function with subtypes is intuitively appealing. Nearly everyone has clear pictures of the punk type or of the career woman type. It also has much to say about strategies that aim to change prevailing stereotypes or to keep them (Hewstone, 1990). The availability of a variety of subtypes allows people to protect stereotypical beliefs from disconfirm-ing information by dividing a category into any number of subgroups (Allport, 1954; Fiske & Neuberg, 1990; Pettigrew, 1981; Taylor, 1981). Whereas people can modify their stereotypes by gradually integrating new information (the 'bookkeeping' model, as Rothbart, 1981, calls it) or change their conception in a more dramatic way (the 'conversion' model, in Rothbart's terms), the subtyping model seems particularly relevant when incongruent information is concentrated in a few targets (Weber & Crocker, 1983).

Associationistic, dimensional and typological perspectives

Most people have no difficulty accepting the idea of subtypes. To what extent, however, do subtypes compare to other more traditional approaches of person perception in general, and of stereotypes in particular, such as trait intercorrelation matrices or implicit theories of personality? In a fascinat-ing study, Anderson and Sedikides (1991) tackled the relative merits of what they call the associationistic, dimensional and typological models of personality. Simple traits covariations (e.g. open and friendly) are at the heart of the first, associationistic, model of person perception. In contrast the dimensional model states that people are perceived in terms of a limited number of dimensions (e.g. extroversion and introversion) and that corresponds to the implicit theory of personality approach described above. Finally, the typological view claims the existence of subtypes (e.g.

the used-car dealer, the politician) and the importance of the relations among traits within any given subtype.

Anderson and Sedikides asked subjects to evaluate two different target persons on a series of 108 traits, allowing the computation of a 108 × 108 intercorrelation matrix. Using multidimensional scaling, the relations among these 108 traits were examined. Two dimensions emerged: general evaluation and dynamism. The authors also performed a hierarchical cluster analysis. Specifically, all 108 traits were initially considered as their own cluster and then iteratively combined with other traits or sets of traits having the largest similarity scores until all traits ended up in one large cluster. Based on a specific set of criteria, the authors retained eleven clusters from the analysis. The description data thus provided associationistic relations among the traits (the trait intercorrelations), dimensional information (the two dimensions) and typological information (the clusters).

In order to uncover the unique contribution of the typological information, Anderson and Sedikides identified the weakest and the core traits that were members of each cluster by looking at the average intercorrelations among the traits comprising a cluster. For instance, the 'extroverted' cluster had ambitious, enthusiastic, energetic and outgoing as core members and confident as the weakest member. The authors also identified strong non-members, that is, traits that were not members of the cluster but had higher average intercorrelations with the core members than did the weakest member of a given cluster. For example, pleasant and friendly were strong non-member traits of the 'extroverted' cluster. The authors then showed a second group of subjects the core members of each cluster. For each cluster, subjects had to write a description of a target person who possessed the core traits, to indicate to what extent strong non-members and the weakest member belonged to the target person, and to evaluate the probability that the target person would also possess the strong non-members or the weakest trait. As expected, results indicated that the weakest member performed better than the strong non-members on spontaneous generation, on belonging scores, and on conditional probability ratings. Thus, an ambitious, enthusiastic, energetic and outgoing person is more likely to be confident than pleasant or friendly.

The typological approach is very akin to stereotypical descriptions. Athletic and lazy, or creative and superficial, are traits people rarely consider as compatible unless they think of the stereotype that White Americans hold about Black Americans for the first couple of traits, and of the stereotype Belgians hold about the French for the second couple of traits.

Homogeneity of the ratees

Many early attempts at measuring stereotypes gave the impression that no exceptions to the stereotypes were allowed. For instance, all Belgians were bon vivant and serious. More recent work, however, acknowledges the existence of many exceptions to the dominant trend in a group. Moreover, a correct interpretation of Bayesian measures of stereotyping means accepting the idea that a given group may, for example, be stereotyped as serious even though the majority of its members are not serious. Simply, serious has to be perceived more frequently in the group under scrutiny than in the general population. Obviously, a lot more is known about groups than simply what seems prevalent in one particular group as compared to other groups. People definitely have a sense of how much the members of a given group vary among themselves with respect to a specific attribute. For instance, we, the authors of this book, are quite confident that the Portuguese are friendly. Nevertheless, we also have some knowledge about how much variability in friendliness is to be expected among Portuguese people.

The recent emphasis on subtypes reflects this concern for within-group variability. Still, it is the perception of homogeneity that has been investigated more thoroughly over the last decade. Quattrone (1986) distinguished among three different aspects of variability: general variability, dimensional variability and taxonomic variability. General variability is probably the simplest index of the degree of homogeneity among members of a given group. Intuitively, everyone has personal views about the diversity among members of a particular group. Thus, the crudest way to inquire about the homogeneity of group members is to explicitly ask people to rate the group's overall variability (Park & Rothbart, 1982). As Quattrone notes, one obvious problem with this measure is that it presents the targets in terms of their group membership and may thus inflate the level of perceived homogeneity. One way to avoid this problem is to ask people to make inferences about members of a group on the basis of one specific individual's behaviour (Quattrone & Jones, 1980). Dimensional variability corresponds to beliefs about how people of a particular group are distributed along given dimensions (Jones, Wood & Quattrone, 1981). For example, depending on their particular sport, athletes' weight range from very light to quite heavy. In contrast, the range is more restricted if the same attribute applies to cover girls. An indirect way to measure dimensional variability is to look at the scale position of the average member of the target group. The more variable the group is, the more average member deviates from the stereotypic end of the scale (Denhaerinck et al. 1989; Park & Rothbart, 1982). Taxonomic variability adds a crucial aspect to the dimensional index by allowing researchers to gauge the relatedness of the various attributes under scrutiny. Suppose a group is characterized by three distinct attributes each with three different levels. If a rater sees no relation whatsoever among the attributes, then there are nine subtypes in the group. In contrast, if a rater considers the three attributes perfectly correlated, then there are only three subtypes. Clearly, there is less variability in the group for the second type of rater than for the first (Linville, 1982; Linville & Jones, 1980). In fact, subtypes emerge nomothetically only to the extent that a consensus exists among raters.

Whatever index of variability is used, a key question concerns the bases for people's beliefs about the degree of variability to be expected in a group. According to Linville, Fisher and Salovey (1989), every time people encounter members of a group, they store feature combinations and build up their knowledge basis about this group. When questioned about variability, people retrieve the exemplars they have stored in memory and perform the necessary computational work. In this perspective, the number of known exemplars becomes the key determinant of people's inferences concerning variability. Whereas exemplars may include both specific instances of the category (e.g. Madonna) and abstracted types of subtypes (e.g. female singers), Linville and her colleagues only take into account instances. They propose this measure to gauge sensitivity to the differentiation among members of a group:

$$Pd = 1 - (p_1^2 + p_2^2 + \ldots + p_i^2 + \ldots + p_m^2)$$

where p_i represents the perceived proportion of group members described by level i of a given attribute whose levels can go from 1 to m. Pd is defined as the probability of attribute differentiation. Thus, if all members of a group fall in the same level, $Pd = .0$; if 10 per cent of the members fall into each of the 10 possible levels, $Pd = .90$, etc. This measure is at the core of a computer simulation model called the PDIST model. The model aims at simulating the exposure to group exemplars and indicates that differentiation (the Pd index) and variability (the variance) within a group increase as a function of the number of exemplars. Because people generally know more ingroup than outgroup members, Linville uses the PDIST model to account for a very important finding in the realm of intergroup relations: the outgroup homogeneity effect, i.e. the fact that less variability is perceived among outgroup than ingroup members (see Chapter 5).

Summary

It is not our intention to compare all of these measures to each other. They all have their advantages and shortcomings, and need to be weighted by the researchers in the light of what they are investigating. What matters to us is that measurement of stereotypes has focused on description, evaluation, consensus, homogeneity and distinctiveness, that is, on the different components of stereotypes. However, there is not yet a method able to encompass all these aspects. The aspect privileged by a given method usually stems from the definition of a stereotype held by the researchers. Sometimes, however, users of a given method are not quite aware of the implications of their choice for the picture they will get about stereotypes.

Conclusions

In our synopsis of the concept of stereotypes, we have insisted upon description, evaluation and homogeneity of the targets, upon consensus of the judges, and upon distinctiveness of the information. Stereotypes are not hallucinations; they want to say something meaningful about human beings. They want to say it quickly, that is, economically, in a nutshell, but at the same time they want to say as much as possible, as if the nutshell was Ali Baba's cavern. This is for description. As for evaluation, nobody would deny that this aspect is vital. In all possible studies on the components of meaning, evaluation comes first. Apparently, ours is not a world of indifference. Frequently, stereotypes are also confounded with prejudice. We certainly do not dispute the fact that stereotypes are often used to justify prejudice, since they are explanatory devices. We contend, however, that they do not necessarily have to be linked to prejudice, to the same extent that biology is not to be excommunicated because it participates with racist ideologies. Consensus of the judges, homogeneity of the ratees and distinctiveness of the information are also important if one adopts a pragmatic point of view. It is to people's advantage to express their beliefs in harmony with others, that is, without discordance between what they say and whom they say it about. Insisting upon the consensus among the judges and the homogeneity of the targets makes clear that we consider stereotypes generalizations. They are often also mandatory, useful and efficient. Also, if stereotypes are social explanations, then people should react to what is distinctive and what differentiates specific targets. This aspect of distinctiveness nuances the idea of homogeneity of the targets. Homogeneity is helpful only to the extent that it highlights distinctions between targets. Keep in mind, though, that how a person distinguishes between groups depends on the context of the judgement and the goals being pursued by that person.

If stereotypes are to play an efficient role in people's everyday dealings with the world, they have to be flexible. People should be able to dispose of a lot of possible stereotypes and not be prisoners of some. Flexibility is also present in each of the components of stereotypes. For instance, homogeneity of the ratees is an important factor in the perception of outgroups and ingroups, but do people always perceive their own group to have more variability than an outgroup? Also, do they build a picture of a social category as a whole and forever, or do they collect individual pictures and go through their album when necessary? Related to these questions of flexibility are questions about which information is likely to have an important role when people have to make a global judgement. Furthermore which groups are most likely to be stereotyped on which attribute? The answers to these questions rely heavily on the concept of distinctiveness. Other questions concern evaluation, which refers both to extremity of judgements and to affective reactions. What are the conditions likely to attenuate a stereotypical attitude? Can a stereotype be diluted? Is it possible to switch from a categorial judgement – a stereotype – to an individuated one? Is this switch linked to affective reactions both at the inception of the information and at the outset of the judgement? How is it possible that people agree on these judgements? Can't the consensus among judges be explained by the theories that they share? Can't the theories change in their importance as a function of the interaction? Finally (and most importantly?), is stereotyping a necessity, a utility or a vanity?

These are some of the questions we will address in the forthcoming chapters, but, first, we discuss the scientific theories that have been elaborated to account for the use and abuse of stereotypes.

2

Classical Theories about Stereotypes

We will review the main approaches to stereotyping primarily from two recent traditions. One, social identity theory, which eventually gives way to self-categorization theory, has a European tradition. The second is mostly an American tradition labelled social cognition. In our opinion, these two approaches pose the best, most intriguing questions.

Stroebe and Insko (1989) observe that past and current theories of stereotyping may be analysed according to two dimensions: whether or not there is a conflict implied, and whether the focus is on the individual or the group. We will blend this grid of analysis with the historical trend of the theories. First, we will glance at psychodynamic explanations, that is, conflictual theories with a focus on individual processes. Second, we will survey the socio-cultural approach, which implies no conflict but does acknowledge societal influences. Third, conflict at a social level will be presented with the realistic conflict theory, the contact hypothesis and the social identity theory. Finally, we will address the social cognition approach where the individual is not considered as ethnocentric but as processing different levels of information. Special chapters will be devoted to social identity theory and social cognition.

The psychodynamic approach

The psychodynamic approach peaked in the 1940s and 1950s when several social and experimental psychologists aspired to build a bridge between psychoanalysis and behaviourism. In this venture, three main psychoanalytical concepts – repression, catharsis and projection – were somewhat brutalized by being forced into behavioural strait-jackets.

The authoritarian personality

The Institut für Sozialforschung was inaugurated on 3 February 1923 in Frankfurt, Germany. It is now known as the Frankfurt School (Jay, 1973; Zima, 1974). At that time, it attracted philosophers with an interest in sociology and psychoanalysis. Almost all of them were Jews craving for freedom, equality and human rights. They were Marxists of a special kind who, in the 1930s, developed the 'Kritische Theorie'. These philosophers, who came from rich entrepreneurial families, saw in a socialist, proletarian revolution the salvation of the individual from the monopolistic capitalism that had eroded free entrepreneurialism. For them, the liberal individual was the focus of attention and interest. Theodor Wiesengrund Adorno (Adorno being his mother's maiden name) was one of the main figures of this group. Other important members included Max Horkheimer – who wrote the Preface to *The Authoritarian Personality* (Adorno, Frenkel-Brunswik, Levinson & Sanford, 1950) – Walter Benjamin, Herbert Marcuse and Erich Fromm.

The country in which the Frankfurt group dreamed of their revolution eventually succumbed to fascist collectivism. Adorno and the other members of the Institute saw in this change of society the disintegration of paternal authority as a source of autonomy and one that led instead to conformism and submission. In 1936, they collectively published *Studien über Autorität und Familie* (Institut für Sozialforschung, 1936) where they analysed the links between paternal authority and repression at a philosophical level. Because of the rise of fascism, they left Germany in 1933 for Geneva, Paris, London and finally the United States. In the United States, Adorno met other Jews with a positivistic psychological background, and together they further developed their theory and measurement of the authoritarian personality. The team was comprised of another immigrant from Austria, Else Frenkel-Brunswik, a psychologist trained in Vienna and the wife of Egon Brunswik, as well as Nevitt Sanford and Daniel Levinson, both from Berkeley. Before being joined by Adorno, the latter three authors had already undertaken a project on the link between personality and prejudice.

Their ideas and investigations went into print in the classic 990-page volume *The Authoritarian Personality* (Adorno et al., 1950). In this book, they contend that ethnocentrism, fascism and antisemitism are all part of an authoritarian syndrome. Individuals with such a syndrome have been raised in families where they could not express their opposing views, where the authority – usually the father – was always right, and where values were once and forever defined. This climate of repression prevents any expression of hostility, which is supposed to accumulate in a kind of Papin's pot. For the pot not to explode, the pent-up energy has to be ventilated towards outside targets. In other words, the projection of aggression towards people external to the valued and untouchable ingroup has a cathartic value. Also, given that the individuals have been educated in the cult where the authority has defined strict boundaries between good and bad, they become subservient towards their leaders. They think rigidly, with stereotypy, in dichotomous terms. Examining nuances of values and questioning authority is not their lot.

In order to measure the personality of these weaklings, who are anxious to protect themselves by attacking non-threatening minorities such as Blacks and Jews, Adorno and his colleagues developed several scales. The A-S scale gauges antisemitism; the E scale diagnoses ethnocentrism; and the F scale predicts fascism. Items were presented using a Likert-type format. Examples from the three scales are, respectively: 'Jews seem to prefer the most luxurious, extravagant, and sensual way of living', 'There is something inherently primitive and uncivilized in the Negro, as shown in his music and his extreme aggressiveness', 'Homosexuals are hardly better than criminals and ought to be severely punished'. Less well known than the former ones, a fourth scale concerned politico-economic conservatism and presented items representative of either a conservative or liberal orientation.

As one can easily imagine, the book attracted a lot of attention and many of the proposed scales, such as E and F, are still in use today, albeit under revised forms. It attracted criticisms, too (for excellent summaries, see R. Brown, 1965; Deutsch & Krauss, 1965). A minor one has to do with the construction of the scales. The items were always worded so that a yes response would mean being prejudiced. In other words, authoritarianism was confounded with acquiescence (if the psychologists delivering the items are regarded as authority figures, this confusion is a clever one). A second criticism has to do with the validating technique of the instrument. Validation was obtained by conducting thorough interviews with people having low or high scores on the scales. The problem is that the interviewers knew the scores in advance and may therefore have influenced the persons they interviewed. Knowing that a man was high on authoritarianism, for instance, the interviewers might have induced him to give answers in accordance with their expectations.

More fundamental for our purpose are those criticisms dealing with the link between prejudice and the 'deep' personality. First, in looking only at individual personalities, Adorno et al. neglected, de facto even if not in principle, situational and socio-cultural factors that can be important determinants of prejudice. Several authors have contended that prejudice in everyday life does not necessarily result from an authoritarian personality. One of these researchers, Thomas Pettigrew (1958), worked in South Africa and in the Southern States of the USA. Not surprisingly, his White subjects showed high levels of anti-Black prejudice. On the F scale, however, their results were comparable to those obtained by non-prejudiced subjects coming from other areas. According to Pettigrew, the origin of their racism stems more from the dominant norms of the culture where these individuals live than from their 'deep' personality. Data collected by Minard (1952) also agree with the cultural norm explanation. His subjects were White miners in Virginia. During work, more than 80 per cent of these men exhibited friendship and solidarity towards their Black co-workers. Once out of the mine, however, it was not acceptable to show those feelings. As a result less than 20 per cent of the White miners maintained friendly relations with their Black workmates outside of work.

A second puzzle is that prejudice is almost uniform in some cultures. What about individual differences? How can a personality explain such uniformity? Conversely, a third problem concerns the historical specificity of prejudice and discrimination. Certain recurrent forms of prejudice can appear abruptly. Again, a personality explanation cannot account for sudden changes. These dramatic examples persuasively suggest that attitudes of different groups towards each other depend more on the types of relations they maintain between them than on the family relations within groups.

As one can expect from a Marxist sympathizer, Adorno never denied the force of socio-economic factors on prejudice. 'Psychological dispositions do not actually cause Fascism; rather Fascism defines a psychological area which can be successfully exploited by the forces which promote it for entirely nonpsychological reasons of self-interest', wrote Adorno (1951, p. 298) in a book edited by another psychoanalyst interested in cultural factors – Geza Roheim – Sanford (1973, p. 73) is as explicit about these 'nonpsychological reasons of self-interest': 'nothing we know of personality in relation to racism', he writes, 'contradicts the principle that overt manifestations of prejudice depend on socio-economic conditions'.

Actually, data reported in *The Authoritarian Personality* gave evidence for the role of socio-cultural factors. There was indeed more authoritarianism in lower socio-economic classes. According to Billig (1976), who masterfully studied the psychodynamic approach of intergroup relations, Adorno et al. thought there was an authoritarian 'Weltanschauung'.

> Such an ideological system of beliefs, although shot through with contradictions and inconsistencies, could not have been fortuitously created by each authoritarian solely as a result of his relations with his parents. Cultural and social influences must have inevitably shaped the ideologies of the post-war American authoritarian. The mass-media, schooling, beliefs of parents, etc. must have all gone some way to producing the final belief-system. (Billig, 1976, p. 111)

While this quotation announces the socio-cultural approach, it remains that *The Authoritarian Personality* pleads against a certain kind of family, and, more pointedly, against a repressive father. It is the mother who can salvage the children because she incarnates autonomy and creativity. In fact, Adorno has devoted much of the rest of his life to a philosophy of aesthetics.

The open and closed mind

Even more than Adorno et al., Rokeach (1960) sees in personality the origin of ethnocentrism. He wants to get rid of ideology – the content of the beliefs – to pay attention only to the structure of these beliefs. The study of a right or left authoritarianism is bound to consider historical and social influences; the investigation of authoritarianism per se can restrict itself to personality processes.

This ahistorical point of view, bridging the right and the left, led Rokeach to study dogmatism in his famous book *The Open and Closed Mind* (1960). According to Rokeach, the dogmatic or closed mind has difficulties accepting ideas that do not fit in a pre-existing mould, whereas the non-dogmatic or open mind is more tolerant and does not measure the value of new ideas with reference to old standards. This means that dogmatic persons will be anxious and rely on authority standards. To measure this personality, Rokeach developed two scales: the Dogmatism scale and the Opinionation scale. From even a cursory look at the items composing these scales, it is hard to believe that they are content-free (for example: 'Communism and Catholicism have nothing in common'). The instrument does not measure up to the theory, and as for the latter, the same criticisms apply as those raised by the work of Adorno et al. In addition to these criticisms, here is an illustration of another general weakness of the psychodynamic approach.

In the British *Sun* newspaper of 1 November, 1990, the following question was posed: 'Which is the thinnest book in the world?' The answer: 'The list of French war heroes.' Actually, that particular issue of the *Sun* devoted three pages to insulting the French people because of the policy of the President of the EC, Frenchman Jacques Delors. Why should the dogmatic British attack another important nation rather than foreign immigrants, or the supporters of a competing soccer team? Was it because their then Prime Minister, Margaret Thatcher, disliked Jacques Delors? Was it because de Gaulle and Winston Churchill did not get along either? Was it because French people eat frogs' legs? We could go on and on with this line of reasoning. The bottom line of our argument is that neither the authoritarian and dogmatic personality theories nor the scapegoat approaches (to which we will turn next) are able to predict which target will be chosen or when. There are a great many facts that these theories can explain but few outcomes they are capable of predicting.

The scapegoat theory

In 1939, Dollard, Doob, Miller, Mowrer and Sears published *Frustration and Aggression*, which used an integrative view of psychoanalytical and behavioural processes concerning aggression. This theory is too well known to need an in-depth discussion here. It is sufficient to remember that any frustration, i.e. 'interference with a goal response', leads to aggression, and that any aggressive reaction has frustration as an antecedent condition. Displacement of aggression was part of the original formulation. As the frustrations build up and aggression cannot be expressed towards their sources because of the fear of negative reinforcement for instance, a substitute or scapegoat for the source will be found. The classic example is the increase of lynchings of Blacks in Southern States as the price of cotton went down and provoked an economic crisis.

In the original formulation of *Frustration and Aggression*, any frustration contributed to aggressive reactions. Later authors modified this view and insisted upon relative frustrations. They mean that frustrations are subjective; frustration will arise to the extent that the goal is highly desired and its prevention is resented. In other words, people have to think they are deprived of something they were entitled to have. To be the first victim of a suddenly new policy is much more frustrating than suffering the same losses when the new policy has become an integral part of the system. To see a cut in your salary is much more devastating if your profession is the only one to be hurt.

This reformulation is known at the relative deprivation theory (Berkowitz, 1972; Crosby, 1976, 1982; Davis, 1959, 1971; Guimond & Tougas, 1994; Gurr, 1970). The above examples illustrate two different kinds of deprivation. The first example refers to egoistic deprivation, the second to altruistic or fraternal deprivation (Runciman, 1966). In both cases, there are expectations, but their origins are different. The first victim of the new and sudden policy, for instance, did everything that was routinely expected for promotion. The expectation is target-based. The decrease of salary in the second example is unexpected compared to the other professions. The expectation is category-based. Therefore, egoistic relative deprivation involves comparisons between a given individual and other members of a group. Fraternal relative deprivation, on the other hand, concerns the comparison between groups, mine and yours.

There are numerous situations where either category-based or target-based expectations have led to unrest and aggression. Analysing archival data, Turner, Cole and Cerro (1984) found relations between socio-economic wealth, birthrate, and homicides. The curves for each are cyclical and almost identical to each other except that there are gaps between them. After some time of wealth, the birthrate increases, but when an economic crisis arises, many more young people than usual are relatively deprived; they do not get what they thought they were entitled to given their parental standards. When these young people arrive at the age of about 20, the common age for committing homicides, there is an increase in these crimes. The data are reported in Figure 2.1 and support the egoistic version of relative deprivation.

Another example illustrates the dictum: 'give them an inch and they'll take a mile'. Various studies have shown that an increase in education without accompanying improvements in other domains leads to open conflicts from the part of the newly educated. Not because of better education per se, but because this progress increases other hopes that were frustrated within the group, which could compare itself to other groups. This cycle of vindicative ingratitude is a classic case of fraternal relative deprivation.

To compare the two kinds of deprivation, Guimond and Dubé-Simard (1983) worked with French Canadians engaged in the labour force. They measured and manipulated the perception of inequality of salaries among English- and French-speaking Canadians. They also obtained measures of dissatisfaction about the gap between either the French- and English-speaking Canadians (fraternal deprivation), or between individual subjects and each of these two groups (egoistic deprivations towards the in- and outgroup). Finally, they asked for political endorsement of the Quebec nationalistic movement, which at that time sought complete autonomy from the rest of Canada. The perception of inequality does not correlate

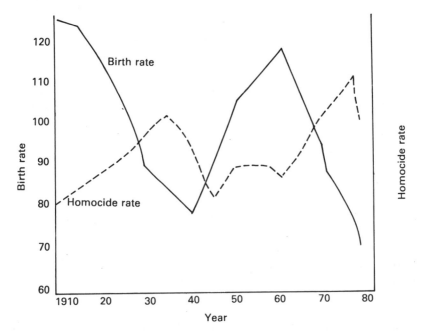

Figure 2.1 *US birth rates per 1000 females aged 15–45 and homicide arrest rates per 100,000 males aged 15–34 from 1910–1977 (Turner, Cole & Cerro, 1984, p. 330)*

with, or induce, discontent. However, both kinds of relative deprivations, fraternal and egoistic, combined with perception of inequality significantly correlate with a wish for autonomy. When the different elements are partialled out of the correlations, however, only fraternal deprivation is significantly related to nationalism. Does this mean that dissatisfaction about the status of one's French-speaking group relative to the English-speaking group produces a wish for autonomy, or does allegiance to a separatist party makes the group's inferior status more salient and more unsatisfactory?

We could go on and on with examples supporting relative deprivation, but it would be as easy to come up with many counter-examples. According to Pettigrew, a major problem with the theory, is that 'Relative deprivation as an explanatory concept has often been invoked in *post hoc* fashion, its causal relationships left ambiguous, its measurements varied and questionable, and its application confused by the failure to specify precisely its operation at both the individual and social level of analysis' (1978, p. 32). This means that explanations have been provided after the facts and that the power of the theory may be due to hindsight. Neither the original frustration hypothesis nor its reformulations can predict who will be the scapegoat. Among the reformulations of the frustration–aggression hypothesis, the one advocated by Berkowitz (1993) is the most encompassing and empirically sound. Berkowitz contends that aversive stimulation (which includes frustration) produces a state of arousal that may lead to aggression and anger. Also, the target of aggression often must be associated with the idea of violence for the aggressive reaction to take place. This last precision of the theory somewhat narrows down the possibilities for the choice of victims. It may explain, for example, why frustrations or aversive treatments sometimes lead to positive rather than negative feelings towards a potential target: the suffering subject may associate the target with common misery instead of aggression.

The socio-cultural approach

Authors within the socio-cultural approach, also called the social learning perspective, primarily focus on society. This means they look at the evolution of stereotypes within a given cultural system and at the modes of transmission. Katz and Braly (1933) initiated this line of work. They were first to explicitly use the concept of consensus in the definition of stereotypes. In so doing, they considered the stereotypes as a phenomenon that needs to be studied at the level of groups or societies. Following this early path, 'A voluminous amount of research effort has been directed toward the assessment of stereotypes held by members of one national group about the members of selected other national groups. Most researchers have used the Katz and Braly experimental framework in toto, often using the identical 84 adjectives' (Brigham, 1971, p. 20).

In general, this research concluded that large numbers of observers share similar representations of a given target group, and that this general image lasts through time. Gilbert provided the best example through direct replications of Katz and Braly's study carried out on the campus of Princeton University. In 1951, he found that the Second World War influenced stereotypes about the Germans and the Japanese. In 1933, Princeton students thought Japanese were intelligent, industrious and progressive. In 1951, they saw Japanese as sly and shrewd (Gilbert, 1951). In 1969, Karlins, Coffman and Walters showed that the stereotypes had basically returned to what they were in 1933. Katz and Braly's replications, then, not only show a relative stability of stereotypes over time, but they also indicate that stereotypes are – adaptive? – pictures of the relations between groups.

In fact, the socio-cultural approach makes no assumptions whatsoever as to why stereotypes exist. Supposedly, stereotypes either derive from the direct observation of the differences among various groups in a given society or are a consequence of exposure to media and other channels of information, most notably via social learning and social interaction. A large quantity of research (see Rajecki, 1990) has thus been devoted to the modes of learning stereotypes and the modes of transmission of stereo- types such as TV programmes, commercials, periodicals, peer groups or interactions. These studies mainly conclude that stereotypes are indeed part of the environment. Moreover, they found a wide consensus about the characteristics belonging to the various target groups of nationalities. However, these studies say little about the mechanisms that turn these shared images into stereotypes. To put it briefly, 'most researchers seem to assume that the members of the mass media audience simply "absorb" what is portrayed in the media' (Ashmore & Del Boca 1981, p. 25).

A recent example of the social learning approach can be found in Alice Eagly (1987) and her colleagues' work (Eagly & Kite, 1987; Eagly & Steffen, 1984; Eagly & Wood, 1991). Eagly is concerned with the way stereotypes get to have a specific content. In line with the socio-cultural perspective, stereotypes are formed through the observation of behaviours performed by members of the stereotyped group. According to Eagly, the role the members of a given group occupy is a crucial factor. Take the example of national groups. If observers know very little about a given country, if they have very few occasions to interact with citizens of this country, the only behaviours they will observe are those that attract media attention. Assume that the media concentrates on a hijacked plane, and the aggressive behaviour of the hijackers is the only sample of behaviour the audience has to build up a mental representation of the hijackers' nation. For other nations, which more often attract the media, the citizens of the observed country will appear in a wider variety of roles. For example, for a long time, Palestinians were reduced in Western media to the role of terrorists and hardly anyone knew about Palestine's intellectuals. Israelis, on the other hand, appeared in the media in a larger variety of roles than just bigots.

It remains, however, that the nature of the roles most often encountered are influenced by the economy and the social structure of the depicted nations. According to Eagly, the beliefs concerning racial differences in a country derive, at least in part, from the observation that racial groups are unevenly spread over social classes and roles in society. Thus, in the USA, the socio-economic status of Blacks is lower than that of Whites. In Belgium, the socio-economic status of North Africans is lower than that of natives. In Great Britain, Indians and Pakistanis have a lower status than the Queen's European subjects. This means that US Blacks, North Africans, Indians and Pakistanis can be observed more often than Whites in roles that imply less competence, less power, etc. To the extent that stereotypes about persons are based on the observed behaviours, the negative stereotypes about Blacks, Pakistanis, etc. thus come from a confusion between the characteristics of the people themselves and the characteristics of the social roles they typically occupy in those countries.

The same argument holds for sex stereotypes. Interestingly, research on the content of sex stereotypes (e.g. Deaux & Lewis, 1984; Williams & Best, 1982) shows that women are perceived to be altruistic and caring for others, whereas men are seen as willing to impose themselves and wanting to control their environment. Inspired by Bakan's (1966) terminology,

Eagly and Steffen (1984) use the concept 'communal' to label the behaviour typically attributed to women and the concept 'agentic' to label the behaviour typical of men. The general idea is again quite straightforward: sex stereotypes arise because, in Western societies, social roles are ascribed differently to men and women. Everyday experience convincingly shows that the roles typically assigned to male and female persons are different. The 'communal' tone of the traits attributed to women highly depends on our having many more occasions to see women be 'homemakers' and occupy low-status hierarchical positions. In contrast, men more often find themselves in the roles of white-collar workers and executives, inducing observers to attribute 'agentic' traits to them. As in the case for ethnic stereotypes, observers mix up the person and the roles. In other words, role-specific behaviours are associated with the persons most often performing these roles. These observations, then, are used as diagnostic information about the internal characteristics of the persons, not the roles.

In order to test this hypothesis, Eagly and Steffen (1984, expt 3) provided their subjects with brief descriptions of either 'an average man' or 'an average woman' that they introduced either as an employee, a homemaker, or without further information. Among other things, subjects had to estimate the likelihood that the target would be working. Estimates were much higher for a male than for a female target when it was not specified if the person was working or not. On the other hand, the sex of the target had no impact on the perceptions of the homemakers and employees. Evaluations of the male and female homemakers were in line with the stereotype of women: communal and not agentic. Conversely, evaluations of the female and male employees corresponded to the stereotype of men: agentic and not communal. In sum, beliefs about men and women are quite similar to those about workers and homemakers, respectively. Moreover, beliefs about social roles seem more important than the beliefs about the sexes. It is important to notice that Eagly's perspective rests upon the 'kernel of truth' assumption: sex stereotypes do indeed correspond, in some way, to reality.

On the basis of results like those presented above, Eagly developed a 'social role theory' of actual sex differences. These differences are the consequence of people's conformity to social role expectations. This implies an objective correspondence between actual behaviour of both sexes and their typical stereotypes. There are two common criticisms of this approach. First, the social learning approach cannot account for the almost universal derogation of the outgroup, that is, for ethnocentrism (Sumner, 1906). Indeed, if stereotypes more or less reflect actual social differences, positive representations of both the ingroup and the outgroup should be as frequent as negative ones. In other words, if stereotypes are learned like any other piece of knowledge, they should be based on direct observation and objectively reflect reality. However, we know that true representation of reality is seldom encountered in the present context

(Brewer, 1979). At a minimum, the social learning perspective appears incomplete.

A second criticism has been raised by Hoffman and Hurst (1990) and concerns the use of stereotypes to explain and rationalize reality. These authors disagree with Eagly about the kernel of truth assumption partly because people are actually very bad at detecting covariation (Nisbett & Ross, 1980). Moreover, pointing to another weakness in the social learning approach, they argue that

> The major problem with the notion that gender stereotypes are primarily the result of observed differences in the personalities of homemakers and bread-winners is simply that it fails to explain convincingly how or why the stereotypes come to characterize males and females in general. In other words, why do we have gender stereotypes in addition to homemaker and breadwinner stereo-types? (Hoffman & Hurst 1990, p. 198)

Hoffman and Hurst agree that the distribution of men and women into distinct roles ('homemaker' and 'breadwinner') is responsible for the stereotypes, but they propose another underlying mechanism: gender stereotypes are fictions that serve to justify the sexual division of labour.

Here is the experimental test of their hypothesis. Subjects had to imagine two fictitious groups, the 'Orinthians' and the 'Ackmians', living on a distant planet. For half of the subjects, the distinction between the groups is said to be biological; the two groups are, in fact, two different species. For the remaining subjects, the distinction is said to be culturally based; these are really two different subcultures within one species. Subjects then received information about members of each group. Most members of one of the groups were city workers and the majority in the other group were child-raisers. However, there were no personality differences between the two groups. After having received these different pieces of information, half of the subjects were immediately asked to rate the 'Orinthians' and the 'Ackmians' on agentic and communal traits. The other half of the subjects had to first think about and write down a reason underlying the group-role relation observed on the planet. As shown in Figure 2.2, the most important result is that stereotypes were strongest when the basis for the distinction between the two groups was biological rather than cultural and when the subjects had been induced to find an explanation for the differences. Interestingly, reasons collected in the explanation condition most often referred to personality differences to justify the distribution of roles.

Hoffman and Hurst's (1990) experiment shows the impact of explanation in stereotyping. Indeed, their subjects felt entitled to apply stereotypical traits to the 'Ackmians' and 'Orinthians' to the extent that they had an explanation for the differences in behaviours of these two groups. Moreover, the differences between groups given biological or cultural explanations imply that the underlying theories people use to account for group differences moderate the impact of stereotypes in individual judgements. This nicely illustrates the importance of the 'theoretical' dimension of stereotypes.

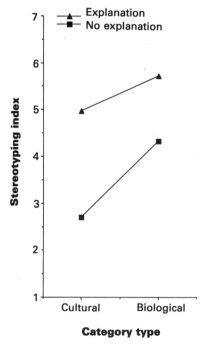

Figure 2.2 *Stereotyping index as a function of category type and explanatory set (Hoffman & Hurst, 1990)*

Such a perspective linking the content of the stereotypes with their explanatory function and the subjects' general systems of explanation opens new avenues for research. This early attempt elegantly suggests that stereotypes cannot solely be conceived of as the consequences of a kernel of truth.

The social conflict approach

With the social conflict approach, we again change the level of analysis. The focus is still on social actors, as opposed to individual persons, but now the scenario includes good and bad characters, winners and losers.

The realistic conflict theory

The work of Sherif on intergroup conflict is probably the best and most well known example of realistic conflict theory (Sherif, Harvey, White, Hood & Sherif, 1961). Together with colleagues, Sherif organized special summer camps for 'normal' WASP adolescents in three different years (1949, 1953 and 1954). The groups at the camp went through four phases. The first phase consisted in the creation of two independent groups each with their specific norms, the emergence of leaders, as well as networks of affinities, etc. For one of the camps, the two teams were created without awareness of each other's existence. In all other cases, the researchers led the children to interact freely and establish friendships before composing low cohesiveness groups by separating good friends. Very quickly, within five days, the newly formed groups were again highly cohesive (ready to attack and defend themselves as testified by the names they chose for their groups: Bull Dogs and Red Devils, Panthers and Pythons, Eagles and Rattlers).

During the second phase, the two groups were brought into contact by ways of competitive games quite common in such camps. Invariably, this introduced a high number of conflicts between the groups: fights, calling each other names, raids against each other's camps, and even the change of a leader to better lead the men to combat. In other words, Sherif and his colleagues created what Golding (1954) had simply fantasized in his *Lord of the Flies*. Because of the special competition introduced by Sherif, this approach has come to be known as 'the realistic conflict theory'. Indeed, in most competitive summer camp games, the outcome is all or none, win or lose. In other words, the resources or prizes were real, they were scarce, and they could not be distributed to both groups. The conflict takes place over these real and scarce resources.

Before discussing the third phase, it is interesting to note how new behavioural norms developed during the conflict between the two groups of adolescents. There were runaway norms for example. Those members who tried to continue friendships across the groups' boundaries were treated as traitors. We already said that a conciliatory leader was replaced by a more 'bullish' one. Also, communication between groups was avoided or prohibited, except for calling each other names. This phenomenon has been labelled autistic hostility by Newcomb (1947) and can only lead to self-fulfilling prophecy, that is, in this case, escalation of conflict. All these phenomena necessarily lead to a distortion of perception where the same behaviours or values are seen completely differently depending on whether one adopts the glasses of the ingrouper or of the outgrouper (e.g. 'We are loyal but they are ethnocentric'). To illustrate this double standard in group perception, we can't resist quoting a dialogue imagined by Osgood. It is during the cold war and Socrates questions American Man.

'Suppose,' says Socrates, 'that Russian Man were to decide that war under present conditions is intolerable and were to publicly junk all his weapons – would you, American Man, leap to destroy him in a nuclear holocaust?' 'Of course not,' replies American Man – 'we are only concerned with protecting ourselves, not destroying others.' 'Would you overrun the Soviet Union,' asks Socrates, 'and make slaves of the Russian people?' 'For goodness sake,' American Man replies with a grin, 'we have no imperialist ambitions – and in any case, a world unified under our way of life would be as good for them as for us. To tell the truth,' he adds, 'we'd welcome the chance to get rid of our weapons and live in peace.' 'All right, then,' says the wise Socrates, 'do you think that Russian Man would leap to destroy you with his nuclear missiles if you were to lay down your weapons and render yourself defenseless?' Here there is a long pause. Finally American Man replies that maybe the Russians wouldn't, but he certainly can't take a chance on it – and in any case, he adds, they would certainly take advantage of our helplessness by over-running the world and making Communists out of everybody. 'All I can conclude,' says Socrates, shaking his head with puzzlement, 'is that Russian Man must be somehow intrinsically different from American Man'. (Osgood, 1960 pp. 35–36)

In the third phase of the summer camp, Sherif and his group of researchers implemented activities they hoped would reduce conflicts. First, they supplied each group with positive information about the other group, but this information was refused or not listened to. They tried individual competitions instead of intergroup ones, but the former were always treated as if they were the latter. They asked leaders to intercede to reduce antagonisms, but the leaders refused since their power rested upon the conflict. They organized nice activities (movies, fireworks, special dinner) to promote contact, but these were transformed into competitions. (The implications of this approach at resolving conflicts will be discussed in the next section.) In the final and decisive phase of the camps, Sherif and his co-workers introduced what they called superordinate goals. These superordinate goals could not be achieved without interdependence and cooperation between the two groups. These types of goals arise when there is a common enemy coming from outside or when a crucial problem comes from the inside. These new activities greatly altered the network of friendships and ended up bringing harmony to the summer camp before the adolescents were restituted to their parents.

Other researchers have extended Sherif's studies on groups of adolescents to groups of adults (Blake & Mouton, 1962), religious groups (Diab, 1970), etc. At the core of this approach is the assumption that people struggle over scarce material resources. This competition causes antagonisms, ethnocentrism, discrimination and prejudice (LeVine & Campbell, 1972). According to some authors, Sherif's solution to group tensions, super-ordinated cooperation, actually creates interdependence between people who used to be members of two groups but are forced, by necessity, to mould themselves into a single entity.

The contact hypothesis

Although it originated at an earlier time than Sherif's publications and in a somewhat different theoretical context, it seems appropriate to speak here of the contact hypothesis. This hypothesis is at the heart of one of the most glorious pages in the history of the behavioral sciences and, maybe, one of its most disappointing ones. In 1954, the Supreme Court of the United States ruled that school segregation was unconstitutional. This judgment relied mainly on the implications of the contact hypothesis. Unfortunately, school desegregation often did not meet the expectations of the hypothesis. Although the rate of intergroup conflicts never declined, the contact hypothesis continues to make people dream and to bring them disillusion.

At the core of the contact hypothesis is the phenomenon of faulty ignorance. According to the hypothesis, substituting knowledge for ignorance should reduce conflict. Ardent supporters of the contact hypothesis describe the process this way:

> This approach generally assumes that the development of stereotypes and attitudes stems from the absence of sufficient information and/or the existence of erroneous information held by one group about the other one, and that contact situations provide the opportunity for clarifying erroneous perceptions and for relearning by supplying new information. (Ben-Ari & Amir, 1988, p. 51)

All those who live where there are religious, ethnic, national, linguistic, class or whatever intergroup conflicts, know very well that contact is not enough to bring correct perceptions and peaceful relations. Quite on the contrary, contact may exacerbate problems as it did in Sherif's camps. Those psychologists (Clark, Chein and Cook) who testified for the Supreme Court knew that reality very well, and they stated under which circumstances contact had to be introduced to induce the desired effects. Here are those conditions recommended by Cook (as listed by Miller & Brewer, 1984, p. 2):

1   Contact must occur in circumstances that define the status of the participants from the two social groups as equal.
2   The attributes of the disliked group members with whom the contact occurs must disconfirm the prevailing stereotyped beliefs about them.
3   The contact situation must encourage, or perhaps require, a mutually interdependent relationship, that is, cooperation in the achievement of a joint goal.
4   The contact situation must have high acquaintance potential; that is, it must promote associations of a sort that reveals enough detail about the member of the disliked group to encourage seeing him or her as an individual rather as a person with stereotyped group characteristics.
5   The social norms of the contact situation must favor group equality and egalitarian intergroup association.

Although these conditions were not explicitly manipulated by Sherif in his summer camps, they correspond to the fourth phase in his field experiments (it is amazing that Sherif is not often quoted in books on the contact hypothesis: see Hewstone & Brown, 1986; Miller & Brewer, 1984). Interestingly, Sherif (1979) is well known for his opposition to contact per se as a means to bring harmony between conflicting groups.

A substantial amount of research on the contact hypothesis has accumulated (see Amir, 1969; Brewer & Miller, 1988; Gaertner, Dovidio, Anastasio, Bachman & Rust, 1993; Vivian, Hewstone & Brown, 1993). During that time, several new models have been proposed that constitute either sharper insights into some of the points raised by Cook, or redirections of some of these points. Here, we will simply try to illustrate some of the arguments.

Extremely prejudiced female students from Tennessee were selected by Cook (1979, 1984) and randomly assigned either to an experimental or to a control group. Supposedly recruited for a part-time job, you can imagine the surprise of the experimental subjects when they realized that they would have to work for 20 days with a White and a Black co-worker. These subjects were not even ready to go into a swimming-pool polluted by the presence of Blacks, and now they had to collaborate, share responsibility, assist each other, eat together, and be taught by the Black co-worker. This Black person was, of course, an accomplice of the experimenter as was the other, White, co-worker who made plain her integrationist views. With few exceptions, the Southern prejudiced students behaved friendly towards the Black confederate and, at the end of the 20 days, expressed highly favourable evaluations about her. Several months later, almost half the experimental participants still maintained drastic reductions of their earlier prejudice towards Blacks. As impressive as they are, the results obtained by Cook must be gauged according to the extent that they generalize outside the perimeter of the experimentation, for example to other real as opposed to questionnaire-type members of the prejudiced group. Often this generalization doesn't take place. One is reminded here of the study by Minard (1952) on White Pocahontas coal-miners. Whereas these men entertained the best possible relations with their Black colleagues under the ground, they often ignored each other and lived without much contact when they came out of the mine. We already alluded to this study in reference to the authoritarian personality.

We are also acutely aware that the five crucial conditions proposed by Cook and his colleagues were often not met in the US desegregated schools (see Gerard, 1983), or in a similar case where Israelis mixed Jews of African-Asian and European-American origin (Schwarzwald & Amir, 1984). The question is whether these conditions can ever be met (Gerard, 1983). For instance, students and parents are not often completely free about the choice of schools. Stroebe, Lenkert and Jonas (1988) reasoned that many difficulties could be alleviated if the integrated populations had previously expressed the desire to experience contact with another country. They investigated the development of stereotypes among American students who had volunteered to spend a year of study in France or Germany. Assuredly, in this context, the authority in charge of the exchange programme was supportive of the contact. Equal status between students of the different universities could be presumed, and the problem of competition was excluded since the grades obtained by American students could not interfere with those of the host universities' students. Jumping immediately to the main results, it appears that the image of Germans slightly worsened among the students who remained in Germany for one year. The deterioration was dramatic for comparable students in France. No generalization to Europeans took place, however, since Stroebe and his colleagues verified that the image of British people had not been altered.

These results could be heart-breaking for proponents of the contact hypothesis if the authors did not mention two facts. First, although the picture of the visited country deteriorated, the number of spontaneous stereotypical traits emitted by the visitors about their hosts diminished. Second, and most important, it seems that the opportunities for informal contacts outside the classrooms were rare, especially in France. It could well be that the American students in France ended up living in a kind of ghetto, partly by choice and partly by necessity. One can imagine them brooding together on their misfortune and finding relief in food – the only French item to meet approval in their eyes! From this study on exchange students, one could be tempted to conclude that, although American students frequented restaurants, they didn't chat enough – in French – with the cooks. (Another obvious alternative is, of course, the kernel of truth, but we do not consider it because this explanation is not theoretically interesting in the present context.)

The inference about the lack of interpersonal contact is partially countered by a study conducted by Hamilton and Bishop (1976). These authors measured the impact of the arrival of a Black family in 8 'pleasant, middle-class residential neighbourhoods' and contrasted this with the arrival of a White family in 10 other comparable neighbourhoods of the Eastern coast. At first, the purchase of a house by Blacks aroused fears. This intrusion was very salient and remained so during the year of investigation. By the end of this year, however, the residents of the 'desegregated' neighbourhoods showed less prejudice than their control counterparts. This result happened irrespective of the number of contacts with the newcomers. Also the fear of seeing the neighbourhood over-flowed by Blacks disappeared because the threat was not confirmed. The authors explained the lessening of prejudice as resulting not through personal contacts, which didn't seem to mediate anything, but by the disconfirmation of expectancies. Obviously, the White residents expected the new Black family to function as a rotten orange in a basket but then they realized that the orange was not even rotten. Amazingly, their attitude, formed from a single new family insulated in their only neigh-bourhood, generalized to Blacks as a whole.

These different sets of results pose a problem. At which level does the contact have to take place: at the interpersonal or intergroup level? The investigations of Stroebe et al. or Cook give the impression that the contacts have to be interpersonal. Indeed, Cook's successful study involved contacts that were clearly interpersonal. Moreover, Stroebe et al. attribute the worsening of attitudes to a lack of interpersonal contacts and, possibly, to the fact that the contacts took place at an intergroup level. The experts called upon by the US Supreme Court most certainly had in mind the interpersonal level. Allport (1954) is also well known for his focus on individuals. As for Cook and Chein, they were part of the Human Relations movement started at the National Training Laboratories (De Visscher, 1992). The enemy for them was the boundaries between groups, e.g. Blacks versus Whites, Jews versus Gentiles, etc. Their heaven, too, would be crowded by individuals and not by members of groups. Miller and Brewer (1984) share the interpersonal viewpoint that outgroup members must be de-categorized for intergroup conflicts and stereotypes to diminish. Gaertner et al. (1993) promote re-categorization rather than de-categorization. Not unlike Sherif, they advise that the 'we' and 'them' categories be replaced with the 'us' category. However, while Sherif posited that intergroup conflict was directly influenced by the perceived interdependence between groups, Gaertner and his co-workers assume that the influence is indirect and mediated by the cognitive representations of the groups; that is, the perceptions that the groups have evolved in one single group.

If the contact has to be interpersonal, how do you explain Hamilton and Bishop's (1976) results? Their research is a clear example of intergroup contact: the Black newcomers were experienced not as individuals – people hardly knew their name – but as representatives, and potential forerunners, of a foreign threatening group. It was sufficient that these few outgroupers acted normally, they didn't misbehave, for the outgroup as a whole to be perceived more benevolently. In a laboratory context, Brown and Wade (1987) also showed that clear group boundaries, or roles, led to greater friendliness towards a cooperative outgroup than did ambiguous boundaries. To account for these data and contrary to Miller and Brewer's arguments, Hewstone and Brown (1986) defend the idea that the abandonment of group boundaries can threaten people's social identities (see Azzi, 1994, for related ideas about the importance of identity in intergroup conflicts). They therefore advocate contacts between groups, rather than between individuals, in cooperative settings that offer each group the opportunity to give an equally flattering view of itself. How do you reconcile this view, however, with the data obtained by Stroebe et al. or by Minard?

Intergroup contacts often correlate with anxiety. This anxiety could well lead to negative stereotypes of outgroup members (Dijker, 1987; Islam & Hewstone, 1993; Stephan & Stephan, 1985). This is actually a very old psychodynamic explanation of stereotypes: they are defence mechanisms against anxiety. One does not need to agree with that explanation to concede that meeting foreigners may provoke fear, suspicion and irritation. These aversive affects can lead people to consider these foreigners as typical of their group ('Be careful, they are all alike'). From there, it is a short distance to abusive stereotypes ('Be careful, they are all aggressive'). In the neighbourhoods studied by Hamilton and Bishop, the original anxiety was not fuelled by any misbehaviour on the part of the newcomers, or by the massive arrival of other Blacks. Over the period of the study, this anxiety had time to fade. Vivian, Hewstone and Brown (1993) are presently developing a model that combines the different approaches summarized above together with negative affects. The challenge is immense as the number of group conflicts never seems to diminish.

Conclusions

The psychodynamic and the social conflict theories are more concerned with prejudice than stereotypes, with discrimination rather than stereotyping. The psychodynamic theories are unable to predict who will be the target of prejudice and discrimination. The conflict theories presuppose a competitor for scarce material resources. Moreover, the contact hypothesis postulates that the competition rests upon an error: Were people more knowledgeable about each other, they would not need to compete or be afraid of each other. The socio-cultural or social learning approach delivers quite a different message than the psychodynamic and social conflict theories. It directly tackles the problem of acquisition and transmission of stereotypes. The social learning theory implicitly links stereotypes and behaviour. Presumably, the type of behaviour perceived will depend on the evaluative meaning of the stereotypes.

It is interesting to examine these early (albeit often updated) theories with the four levels of adequacy of social judgements: reality, integrity, cultural and theoretical. Obviously, they do not have much to say about reality, but this observation should not come as a surprise. Remember what we said in the Introduction: at first, stereotypes were considered almost exclusively as errors deviating from objective reality. The integrity level is nicely represented by the psychodynamic perspective as well as by the realistic conflict views on stereotypes. When groups compete with other groups for scarce and valued resources, people not only treat the other groups as enemies, but they also enforce strict norms (the runaway norms, or the autistic hostility to use Newcomb's terms) for their own group members. According to the psychodynamic approaches, in order to be 'cured' of their problems, people project them outside, find scapegoats, discriminate against them, and justify these actions through negative stereotypes. In other words, their individual integrity is safe to the extent that they perceive others are endangering them. The idea of prejudiced personality was undermined with the finding that people sometimes behaved quite differently depending on the historical moment or the particular setting they were in. This limitation is totally compatible with the view that people rely on social rules in order to make judgements. These rules change with place and time; a function of the cultural level. This level is also useful for looking at the socio-cultural approach to stereotypes. Parents, friends and mass-media teach people which information they should take into account, what kind of judgement is appropriate in which context, etc. The fourth level, the theoretical level, is present in every approach. Whatever the 'deep' reason for their stereotypes, people use them to explain the behaviour of others, to justify their own actions, to communicate, and to give meaning to the world (Bruner, 1957).

3

Social Identity Theory

Sherif, and other researchers after him, clearly demonstrated that ethnocentrism and intergroup conflict can simply arise as a consequence of putting groups in a situation of competition. This approach, which Campbell (1965) labelled 'realistic group conflict theory', showed that competition or negative goal interdependence is a sufficient condition for intergroup discrimination to appear. But is competition also a necessary condition?

In one of the summer camps that he organized, Sherif (1966) observed discriminatory behaviours as soon as groups became aware of each other's existence, that is, before they engaged in actual competition. Several studies have replicated this phenomenon. For instance, Ferguson and Kelley (1964) studied the factors influencing the overevaluation of group products in a non-competitive situation. Two groups worked simultaneously in the same room. They performed three different tasks, allegedly because experimenters wanted to observe how efficient and motivated groups work. Ferguson and Kelley were very careful not to give the impression that one group was expected to perform better than the other. Members of the groups were asked to judge the groups' products, but there would be no winner and no prize offered. Before the two groups started a task, one member of each group was to leave the room. Such non-participation would supposedly guarantee the objectivity of the judgements. In fact, the products of all three tasks were rated by both the absent and the active members. As it turns out, people overevaluated ingroup products even if they did not participate in the production. The debriefings, however, revealed that many subjects experienced a strong tendency to compete in spite of the experimental scenario. Apparently, the presence of another group working on the same task was sufficient to drive people to compare group products, to compete in other words. As Ferguson and Kelley concluded: 'It appears that the foundations of intergroup conflict are exceedingly easy to lay' (1964, p. 228).

Still more surprising, from a realistic conflict perspective, this ingroup bias has been observed even when groups were expected to cooperate (Brewer, 1979; R.J. Brown, 1984). Quite clearly, then, negative goal interdependence is not a necessary condition for ingroup bias to occur. Which conditions are necessary? Social identity theory (SIT) gives the most elaborate answer to this intriguing question. According to this theory, symbolic rather than material resources are the keys to conflict. Status, self-esteem and beliefs override objective benefits in importance. This theory focuses less on individuals within groups, as was the case with realistic group conflict theory, than on groups within individuals (Capozza, 1994).

This approach was pioneered by the late Henri Tajfel and his Bristol group. Since Tajfel (1969) first expressed his views, things have become more complex, and

> strictly speaking, there are now in fact two social identity theories: the original intergroup theory, which is an analysis of intergroup conflict and social change and focuses on individuals' need to maintain and enhance the positively valued distinctiveness of their ingroups compared to outgroups to achieve a positive social identity (Tajfel, 1972b, 1981; Tajfel and Turner, 1979, 1986; Turner, 1975), and the more recent self-categorization theory (Turner, 1982, 1984, 1985; Turner et al., 1987), which represents a general theory of group processes based on the idea that shared social identity depersonalizes individual self-perception and action. [. . .] The fundamental hypothesis shared by both theories is that individuals define themselves in terms of their social group memberships and that group-defined self-perception produces psychologically distinctive effects in social behaviour. (Turner, 1988. pp. x–xi)

Given the importance of SIT in the field of stereotypes and stereotyping, we will devote this entire chapter to appraise it.

Paradigms in search of a theory

To put into perspective the work conducted by Tajfel or inspired by him, it is necessary to examine the experiments which preceded those of the Bristol group and which were conducted within another framework.

The minimal social situation

Jaap Rabbie conducted the first studies that tried to determine the minimal conditions under which a discrimination between in- and outgroups would arise (Rabbie, 1966; Rabbie & Horwitz, 1969). To introduce them, we cannot resist mentioning an anecdote that illustrates how personal events can influence the quest of a researcher (Rabbie, 1991). As a young Jewish boy, Jaap lived through the dramatic events of the Nazi occupation in the Netherlands. Up to then, he had been more interested in childhood games than in religious matters. However, that changed when the Nazis ordered all Dutch Jews to wear a distinctive sign. The first day people had to wear it, little Jaap went to school like he did every day, only he wore his sign. On his way, he passed an old man. The man did not know Jaap but lifted his hat to salute him. Jaap then realized that the sign he was wearing had been used by the old Dutch man as a means of identification. For the first time, he really identified himself with the Jews and he felt that his lot was highly dependent on that of all other Jews. Many years later, in order to study intergroup relations, Rabbie adopted Lewin's theoretical approach: people form a group when they are aware of the interdependence of their destiny.

Rabbie and Horwitz (1969) told teenagers of both sexes that they were studying the way people build up first impressions. Upon their arrival at the laboratory, eight subjects were separated for administrative reasons into two groups of four: the 'blues' and the 'greens'. In three experimental conditions, subjects learned that only half of them would be rewarded for their participation. The prize was a radio and, because there were only four radios left, only one group would receive them. In each of these three conditions, there was a different mechanism for selecting the group to be rewarded. The choice was either random, based on an arbitrary decision, or based on the votes of one of the two groups. In a control condition, there was no reward. After the radios were distributed, subjects were asked to give their impressions about the other persons, and they had to choose those persons with whom they would like to work further. In the control condition, sociometric choices and judgement scales revealed no bias at all in favour of the ingroup. In contrast, ingroup bias was found in all the other three conditions for both groups, the frustrated one and the rewarded one. Apparently, the mere fact that people shared the same fate, no matter how this came about, was sufficient to create a bias in favour of one's own group. This conclusion is totally in line with Lewin's views concerning interdependence.

In another experiment, Rabbie and Wilkens (1971) separated high school students into groups of three persons each. Again, the study allegedly concerned first impressions. There were three experimental conditions: groups competed against each other, they worked together but independently, or they worked separately. Subjects in the competition condition learned that the group with the best performance would receive money. In the non-competition condition, people were told that both groups could be awarded the money if the products conformed to certain criteria. On the basis of people's impressions, Rabbie and Wilkens concluded that members of the 'separate' groups displayed less ingroup favouritism than members in the 'competition' or 'non-competition' groups. Contrary to the authors' expectations, these last two conditions did not differ significantly from each other. However, a post-experimental questionnaire revealed that people in these two conditions felt the same amount of competition.

In sum, factors such as shared fate or objective competition can induce ingroup favouritism. Tajfel and colleagues (Tajfel, Billig, Bundy & Flament, 1971) tried to create an even more minimal social situation than the one imagined by Rabbie and Horwitz (1969). In their plan, this minimal social situation would serve as a base-line against which they could gauge the impact of different variables. This innovation created a famous paradigm which seeded the field for a new theory.

The minimal group paradigm

Here is a sketch of how researchers commonly set up the 'minimal group paradigm'. Subjects are classmates and the experiment takes place in their

Matrix 1 (allows for ingroup favouritism, fairness or altruism)													
Member 74 of Klee group 1	2	3	4	5	6	7	8	9	10	11	12	13	14
Member 44 of Kandinsky group 14	13	12	11	10	9	8	7	6	5	4	3	2	1

Matrix 2 (allows for fairness, maximizes group differentiation or joint profit)												
Member 12 of Klee group 7	8	9	10	11	12	13	14	15	16	17	18	19
Member 50 of Kandinsky group 1	3	5	7	9	11	13	15	17	19	21	23	25

Figure 3.1 *Examples of allocation matrices used in the minimal group paradigm*

school. They are shown a series of slides of abstract paintings, two at a time, one from Klee and the other from Kandinsky. The names of the painters are not attached to the slides. For each pair of slides, adolescents have to write down on a special sheet which painting they prefer, the one on the right or the one on the left. When all slides have been shown, the experimenter collects the sheets and corrects them with ostentatious zeal. When this is finished, he calls each student, one by one, and whispers in his or her ear: 'You are in the Klee group'. The students are warned that they should not share their secret with their neighbours. When this whispering session is terminated, Tajfel distributes a booklet to each student. It contains matrices of points designed by the French psychologist Claude Flament; the points represent pennies that the students have to distribute to members of their ingroup, Klee, and or to the outgroup, Kandinsky.

Figure 3.1 shows two examples of such matrices. Subjects have to select one of the columns. The rows express the number of points or pennies afforded to either anonymous ingroup or anonymous outgroup members, depending on the instructions delivered with each matrix. Both rows may correspond to allocations for ingroup or outgroup members. The upper row may represent the ingroup and the lower one the outgroup, or the reverse. The adolescents are explicitly told that giving points to their ingroup members does not contribute to what they themselves will receive. Their own reward will depend on the responses of the other participants. The matrices appearing in the booklet and the instructions allocating the different rows are designed so as to investigate the strategies adopted by the subjects. For instance, matrix 1 allows researchers to observe ingroup favouritism, fairness or altruism. Suppose the upper row stands for the ingroup members and the lower one for the outgroupers. Selecting a column in the middle of the matrix means fairness; the gains for both groups are about equal. Choosing a column towards the extreme left is generosity to the outgroup. Choosing the extreme column on the right symbolizes complete ingroup favouritism. For that particular matrix, subjects usually tend to choose a column towards the right, that is, they choose an ingroup favouritism strategy. It is very rare that they pick the extreme right case because the norm of fairness is also at play, but they clearly do not select the generous columns on the left.

Matrix 2 is designed to test two other strategies besides fairness. This time, the matrix is not symmetrical like the preceding one and the total of the various columns is no longer identical. Subjects are actually using the strategy 'Maximum Joint Profit' if they choose a column towards the right. The middle section represents fairness and the more they move left from it, the more they elect to use a 'Maximal Group Difference' strategy. As you might have already guessed, subjects do not follow a Maximum Joint Profit strategy but a Maximal Group Difference, in favour of the ingroup, strategy. In other words, they prefer to give, for example, 9 points rather than 17 points to their ingroupers because, choosing 9 puts them 4 points ahead of the outgroup's 5 points, whereas choosing 17 puts them 4 points behind the outgroup's 21. Again, because the norm of fairness is present, the subjects tend not to choose the extreme cells. When both rows are devoted to ingroup members, subjects will take more extreme right columns than when both rows are devoted to the outgroup. This difference shows ingroup favouritism.

These are just two examples of matrices. The calculation of the different strategies is quite sophisticated (for a review, see Bourhis, Sachdev & Gagnon, 1994). Also, the matrices designed by Claude Flament may not be ideal, according to some authors (for a discussion, see Bornstein 1983; Turner, 1983). However, results obtained with this paradigm in various countries, with different populations and experimenters using modified operationalizations, have proven to be very reliable. More important, these results seem protected from artifacts and demand characteristics, and they tell a lot about spontaneous human reactions. Do not forget that these adolescents belonged to the same classroom for quite a long time. They probably did not know Klee and Kandinsky and couldn't care less about abstract paintings. Nevertheless, telling them explicitly: 'You are in the Klee group' and implying: 'There are Kandinsky members, even though you do not know who they are' is sufficient to create discriminatory behaviour. Remember also that Tajfel and his team did not expect such a result. The situation was supposed to create a base-line condition where no discrimination would occur and to which other variables could be added to obtain the desired differentiation. Therefore, the experimenters' expectancy does little to explain the results.

The minimal group paradigm reminds one of the 'in the eye of the storm' experiment. In a third grade American school, the teacher divided her pupils according to whether they had 'brown' or 'blue' eyes. On the first day of the experiment, the blue eyes are given a higher status than the brown eyes; the reverse occurs on the second day. The same experiment was later conducted with adults, and the same results ensued. Although these children and adults knew each other for quite some time, making an arbitrary division in terms of biological factors was sufficient to produce and legitimize strong discriminatory behaviours.

First explanations: norms of 'groupness' and 'fairness'

Simply placing people in a category on an arbitrary basis appears to cause discrimination against the other category, even despite a total lack of objective competition. Rabbie explained these data as resulting from an interdependence that reminded subjects of a group's norms. Tajfel's first explanation (1972b; Tajfel et al., 1971) also refers to norms, or, more precisely, to a compromise between two norms. On the one hand, a generic norm of 'groupness' tells subjects that it is right for them to favour their ingroup members. On the other hand, if ingroup favouritism is not absolute, it is because of a 'fairness' norm which reminds people to be fair towards every person present. The finding that levels of discrimination observed in minimal groups vary whether children are Europeans, Samoans or Maoris supports this explanation (Wetherell, 1982). All these groups displayed ingroup favouritism, but it was especially the case for the European kids.

Variations in cultural norms may partially account for these differences even though every culture tested showed ingroup favouritism. Data from a study by St Claire and Turner (1982) also bring into question the role of norms as the only determining factor. These authors found that schoolgirls who were not themselves categorized but simply had to guess the responses of categorized subjects did not show ingroup favouritism. If norms are at work in the minimal group paradigm, they do not seem to apply to predictions made by observers. In that same experiment, post-experimental interviews asked categorized subjects whether they had followed a particular rule and to describe that rule. Most subjects declared that they had no rule in mind during the experiment; some thought they had simply tried to be fair. A small minority acknowledged that they relied on ingroup favouritism. In fact, ingroup favouritism was present for all subjects. In a third condition, researchers presented the study to the subjects as an investigation about prejudice. Subjects in this condition said that the strategy to be used was an unfair one. Nevertheless, they didn't discriminate more than the subjects of the control condition.

Given the apparent insufficiency of norms as an explanation for ingroup favouritism, Tajfel's data were still in search of a theory. He solved his problem by linking the minimal group paradigm to his previous research on perception and stereotypes. The result was the social identity theory (SIT). In the next paragraphs, we summarize Tajfel's early work, sketch the main proposals of SIT and of its descendant, self-categorization theory (SCT), propose some current challenges to SIT and SCT, and link the preceding arguments with the field of stereotypes.

The basic concepts of SIT

Henri Tajfel (1972a) first enunciated SIT in his contribution to a French handbook of social psychology edited by his friend Serge Moscovici. Very soon, John Turner (1975) joined him in Bristol. Turner contributed greatly to the first formulations of SIT and later expanded it into self-categorization theory, or SCT. In this chapter, we will speak only of SIT, encompassing under this single label both Tajfel's and Turner's perspectives.

As Hogg and Abrams (1988) point out, SIT is both a metatheory and a theory. As a metatheory, it corresponds to a psychological Marxist's view of the world. First there is society, and 'society comprises social categories which stand in power and status relations to one another' (Hogg & Abrams, 1988, p. 14). The need to refer to power and status relations explicitly implies that it is a conflictual society. Its structure constantly changes because of conflicts. Social categories become human groups (almost the title of Tajfel's auto-ergobiography, 1981) because the individuals who compose them come to realize that they share a common identical plight. Essentially, SIT 'explores the psychological processes involved in translating social categories into human groups' (Hogg & Abrams, 1988, p. 17). In a very fundamental way, SIT focuses upon the groups within the individual as opposed to other approaches that study the individuals in the group. SIT is also a theory and posits a set of interrelated propositions with falsifiable hypotheses. It is composed of three parts: *social categorization*, *social comparison* and *social identity*, the latter being a metonym when serving as a generic term in the title. We will examine each of these fundamental bases in turn.

Social categorization

When the Second World War broke out, Henri Tajfel was a wealthy Polish Jew travelling in Europe. He fought in the French Army, was made a prisoner-of-war, and upon his liberation worked for six years with his wife to take care of Jewish orphans. The Allies offered to pay his university tuition. He chose Psychology, rushed through a Ph.D. in the UK, and went on to study at Harvard where he joined Bruner, the founding father of the 'New Look'.

The New Look approach melded motivation with perception. The most appealing illustration of that combination was the propensity of poor children to overevaluate the size of highly valued coins. Before leaving for the States, Henri Tajfel 'replicated' this phenomenon, but his explanation, rather than stressing the overestimation, focused on the accentuation caused by categorization. His main hypothesis of concern here was: 'when a classification is correlated with a continuous dimension, there will be a tendency to exaggerate the differences on *that* dimension between items which fall into distinct classes, and to minimize these differences within each of the classes' (Tajfel, 1981; p. 133; original emphasis). He conducted his most well-known experiment to test that hypothesis with Wilkes in 1963. Subjects saw, in random order, a series of lines of unequal length and then had to estimate their objective length. For some subjects, each line was matched at random to one of two letters, A or B. For others, the lines were presented without any accompanying letters. In those two conditions, the subjects' estimations more or less corresponded to physical reality. There was a third group of subjects who received the lines with the letters but this time the matching was not random. The same letter, say A, always accompanied the shorter lines; the other letter, B, the longer lines. Since a concept or category is defined as two or more elements holding together, the combination of a letter and the length of a line is probably the crudest operationalization one can think of. Similarity being one way to hold together, the lines sharing the same letter should look similar, and they should look different from those lines with a different letter, lines thus belonging to another category. In other words, Tajfel and Wilkes expected that their induction of categorization would accentuate the similarities within the categories and the differences between categories. Only the latter part of the hypothesis was significant. There was a tendency in favour of the first part of the hypothesis, but it was not statistically significant. (For a review, with significant results, see Eiser, 1990.) For Tajfel (1959; Tajfel & Wilkes, 1963), the link of categorization with persons and stereotypes was immediate and obvious. From this research, he wrote his Allport award winning paper (Tajfel, 1969), which influenced the whole field. From there, he conducted and reanalysed several empirical studies on stereotypes.

David Wilder has provided some of the most elegant illustrations of social categorization. In one of his studies (Wilder, 1978), subjects heard a tape of a discussion where the participants supposedly belonged to the same group, to two different groups, or constituted an aggregate of individuals. The tape was stopped after one participant expressed his opinion and the subjects were asked to guess the reactions. As expected, when the participants were thought to be members of a single group, subjects predicted the next speaker would have a more similar opinion than in the other conditions. The least similarity was anticipated and obtained in the two groups condition, although the subjects were not told the reason for the categorization into the groups. In another experiment, Wilder and Allen (1978) categorized their subjects into two groups on the basis of preference for paintings or treated them as aggregates. Before engaging in a discussion, subjects could select to attend to information provided by the other participants. They were told the information would vary in similarity with their own views. No preference emerged in the aggregate condition. In the social categorization situation, subjects elected to see similar information about the ingroup and dissimilar information about the outgroup. This series of experiments nicely illustrates the link between similarity and categorization.

A related question to categorization concerns accuracy. Are the consequences of categorization, i.e. stereotypes, errors? According to Tajfel (1972a), three types of 'errors' are to be considered from the viewpoint of SIT. First, categorization may brutalize reality when one tries to fit an object into a category. Bruner and Potter (1964) demonstrated this aspect with a technique often used nowadays in TV games. The contestants see a picture and have to guess what it represents. The picture is unfocused at first and becomes clearer as time goes by. Those people who quickly, but erroneously, see the object as one thing are less willing than others to correct their perception as evidence appears that they made a mistake. In other words, they have forced the fit and are reluctant to realize that the fit doesn't match reality. The second 'error' occurs once the object has been categorized. If you decide that Miss Blue is gay, you'll probably attribute to her a passionate love for her deceased father because this corresponds to the features of your category of lesbians. However, it might be that her father, or other men, never counted much to her (Snyder & Uranowitz, 1978). The third 'error' is linked to the values associated with categories. Your heart may not be moved very much when it encounters the category 'migratory sparrow' or 'solo yachtsman', but many social categories are heavily attached to values. We know, for example, some female colleagues who value very much the category 'tall American males'. To preserve their John Wayne category, they consider Dustin Hoffman and Woody Allen as not really Americans but Jews and they hardly believe us when we tell them Paul Newman's height.

The question really is: to what extent is it an error to consider Paul Newman as a tall person rather than as a little big man, or to believe that all lesbians love their father?

> . . . Perceptual accentuation need not be considered as a 'maladaptive' phenomenon. The fact that it may represent a departure from 'objective reality' led to a general criticism which consisted of pointing out that in order to survive we must perceive the world as it is, that we usually do, and that therefore the fleeting phenomena of over-estimation are more typical of the specific laboratory situations in which they are demonstrated than of perception under normal conditions. There is, however, a possibility that these shifts in the judgments of magnitude do not interfere with adequate handling of the environment. They may even be of help. (Tajfel, 1981, p. 63)

For SIT, errors of these three types are not necessarily mistakes, overgeneralizations or distortions (Funder, 1987). First, the existence of an error requires the recognition of a criterion for correctness. According to SIT, individuals relate to the social world and not to 'things' (Turner, 1988). The social world is a construction and the criteria for judging its quality are not given once and forever. Second, for SIT, errors may be functional. At the time this chapter was written, Rwanda was suffering internal turmoils between Tutsi rebels and the mostly Hutu governmental forces. In general, Tutsis are taller than Hutus. Anthropologist Maquet (1961) has noted that, within Rwanda, people exaggerate the difference in height between the two ethnic groups. Such an exaggeration may be very useful to both ethnicities during the conflict. This functional view is not to be confounded with Social Darwinism à la Lorenz, for whom inequality between groups is a good thing because it keeps order since everyone knows where they stand. Whereas the latter view is static and linked to a specific content, SIT is interested in the dynamic process. Social categorizations are not 'givens', they change and their implications change as a function of social comparisons. As Oakes and Turner note: 'to apply a social categorization to an individual is to refer to a true psychological as well as social invariance and it is not, in principle, to distort or overgeneralize the "true" properties of the person' (1990, p. 122).

Social comparison and social identity

Why do ingroups get more favourable judgements than outgroups? The reason may be that people like being associated with positive categories. In other words, differentiation helps to establish a positive self-evaluation. Thus, dividing the world into categories does not only simplify and give meaning to the world. Categorization fulfils another important function by defining who people are. According to Tajfel (1981), and Tajfel and Turner (1979, 1986), a person's identity has two components: a personal identity and a social identity. There are as many social identities as there are groups the person belongs to. SIT holds that people can improve their self-image in two ways: by improving their personal identity or by enhancing their social identity (Bourhis & Leyens, 1994; Rijsman, 1983).

If part of who people are is defined by their membership of a series of groups, it seems quite normal that they prefer to see these groups positively rather than negatively. But how do they manage to establish such an evaluation? Tajfel and Turner (1979) suggest that evaluations of groups are essentially relative; people estimate the value of their group by comparing it to other groups. Tajfel and Turner build this idea upon Festinger's (1954) theory of social comparison. It should be noted, however, that social comparison stems from a different origin for Festinger than for Tajfel and Turner. When Festinger proposed his theory of social comparison, he meant that, in the absence of objective information coming from physical reality, people would satisfy themselves by evaluating their opinions and abilities in comparison to those of relevant others. For Tajfel, information is already social, or socially built, and thus social comparison should not be considered an ersatz for physical or objective comparison. The outcome of social comparison is important for SIT because it has direct consequences for people's self-image. In other words, the comparison is most likely to be biased so that the ingroup comes out positive.

The link between social identity and social comparison makes it possible to account for the social competition created in the 'minimal group paradigm'. In the abstract and ambiguous context of these experiments, subjects build up order and assign meaning to the situation by using the categorization provided by the experimenter. The categorization process makes each group perceptually salient and reduces the variability among members of the same group. From there on, social comparison takes place by means of the only available dimension of comparison: allocation of money or points. Finally, the subjects choose a strategy of maximum differences in order to establish a better position for the ingroup than for the outgroup. For Tajfel and Turner (1979), when people engage in social comparison, they are moved by a need to maintain their self-esteem. When they compare their category to others, they will thus privilege theirs so as to give a favourable image of themselves. They will do this for these dimensions that are relevant to their social identity.

Let's go back to the Klee and Kandinsky experiment. The adolescents in this study did not know who exactly was in their group. They probably hardly knew what it meant to be in the Klee or Kandinsky category, but they knew for sure that they were members of a group and that there was another group 'opposed' to them. The only dimension relevant to them for improving their self-esteem was to give their group more points than the other. Conversely, when several dimensions are made available to group members, they may rate the outgroupers as superior on certain dimensions because these do not mean much to them (Mummendey & Schreiber, 1983, 1984; Mummendey & Simon, 1989). Ingroup favouritism appears when the dimensions of measurement are important. If the intelligence of my children is important for me, I may recognize that my neighbour's offspring are better looking, are better at tennis, and are more polite and persevering. Actually, they need all that and much more to beat the intelligence of my children. At the core of social comparison, as viewed by SIT, is the motivational variable of self-esteem.

Self-categorization and metacontrast

According to Turner (et al. 1987), people form self-categorizations at different levels of abstraction, ranging from an abstract conception of the self as a human being, to the intermediate level of ingroup–outgroup representations, to the subordinate level of personal self-categorizations as a unique individual. The self is thus simultaneously part of several levels: humankind, groups, individuality. At each level, the individual is motivated to evaluate the self-categories positively. Depending on which level of comparison is salient, the individual will try to establish a positive distinctiveness either between the self and other ingroup members, or between ingroup and outgroup.

The principle determining which category is salient, or the category's 'goodness of fit', is the following: the most adequate category is the one that most closely corresponds to the data in their specific context – the normative fit – , and that maximizes the differences between categories while minimizing the differences within categories – the comparative fit (Oakes, 1987; Turner et al. 1987). This latter aspect is also defined as the metacontrast principle. The idea, directly borrowed from Rosch (1978), has been operationalized as follows: the metacontrast ratio is the average perceived inter-category difference over the average perceived intra-category difference (Haslam & Turner, 1992). The MCR also allows to appraise the degree to which any member of a group represents his group's norms. If a member differs a lot from outgroup members and, simultaneously, differs very little from ingroup members, he/she will stand out as a prototypical member of the group. For example, imagine three ingroup members embodying three moderate positions on a pro- versus anti-surrealism scale:

Group members:	O_1	O_2	O_3	I_1	I_2	I_3	O_4	O_5	O_6
Scale position:	-4	-3	-2	-1	0	$+1$	$+2$	$+3$	$+4$

In this example, I_2 can be found to be the most prototypical member of the group, I_1 and I_3 being both less representative of the ingroup norm. Importantly, the prototypical position of a group need not correspond to the mean position but only to the one that maximizes differences from the outgroup positions and similarities with the ingroup positions. Imagine now that the above ingroup members occupy the three extreme positions to the left of the surrealism dimension, the most extreme member, I_1, would gain in reletive prototypicality and the less extreme member, I_3, would be become less prototypical.

These few lines certainly do not do justice to the richness of SCT. Obviously, the quantitative translation of the comparative fit, the MCR, does not always makes intuitative sense but the basic idea remains appealing. Our aim was less to introduce SCT than to introduce the challenges facing self-identity and self-categorization theorists (Oakes, Haslam & Turner, 1994).

Unresolved challenges

The role of self-esteem

For SIT, ingroup favouritism leads to an increase of self-esteem, a hypothesis tested in several experiments. Oakes and Turner (1980) conducted an experiment of the 'minimal group' type for half of the subjects: They were categorized and, not unexpectedly, they displayed discriminatory behaviours. The other subjects were not categorized and had just to wait and read a newspaper. These latter subjects, who were not given a chance to allocate rewards, had a lower level of self-esteem than the rest of the subjects. Abrams and Hogg (1988) criticized this study on two grounds. The first is methodological. Three valid self-esteem scales were combined in order to construct the one subjects used. Thus, the validity of the instrument is questionable. Furthermore, some items were extracted from a scale designed to measure global self-esteem whereas the subjects had to describe their current self-esteem. The second and more important problem concerns the interpretation of the difference between the subjects in the two conditions. Abrams and Hogg argue that the results could be due to a lowering of the self-esteem of the subjects who had merely to wait and to read a newspaper article. It also could have been due

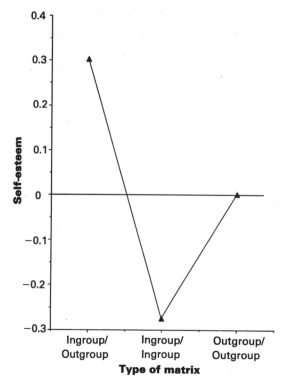

Figure 3.2   *Self-esteem as a function of the type of matrix (Lemyre &*
Smith, 1985)

to the psychological inequity of having been participants in an interesting
experiment against having simply waited and read.

Lemyre and Smith (1985) confirmed the pattern found by Oakes
andTurner. Furthermore, they showed that intergroup discrimination
rather than discrimination per se is really what matters. Their experiment
involved eight conditions varying in different dimensions. Here, we take
into account only these conditions that are most relevant (see Figure 3.2).
Some of their subjects were categorized and were allowed to allocate
money either only to ingroup members or only to outgroup members. They
thus could discriminate but it was not an intergroup discrimination. These
subjects showed a lower level of self-esteem than other subjects who could
allocate money to members of different groups. As Abrams and Hogg
(1988) note, even if this study indicates a link between discrimination and
self-esteem, the results do not explicate the motivating aspect of self-
esteem. Indeed, Lemyre and Smith's experiment does not establish that
categorized subjects discriminate in order to restore their self-esteem.
Actually, categorized subjects who could discriminate against outgroup
members showed the same level of self-esteem as control subjects who had
not been categorized and had not been given the opportunity to discriminate.

Until now, there has been no clear evidence that low self-esteem or threatened social identity induces a motivation for protection and, thereby, for intergroup discrimination. Some studies actually suggest that high-status groups are more likely to discriminate than low-status ones (Caddick, 1982; Crocker, Thompson, McGraw & Ingerman, 1987).

> The relation between self-esteem/social identity threat and intergroup discrimin-ation is a complex one and depends . . . on a multitude of additional factors . . . such as the availability of alternative strategies to restore one's self-esteem (Tajfel, 1981), the permeability of group boundaries, the coexistence of competing motivations (e.g. self-consistency, self-presentational concerns), or the perceived legitimacy of status differences. (Maass & Schaller, 1991, p. 192)

In this 'multitude of additional factors', Turner, Hogg, Oakes and Smith (1984) focused on the engagement of the members towards their group as the crucial factor for group cohesion and group identification. Borrowing an idea from dissonance theory (Festinger, 1957), these authors propose that people will react by increasing their identification with the group assuming that they are accountable for their behaviour (that is, they freely chose to belong to the group) and that the behaviour entails negative consequences (i.e. the group fails). 'I chose to enter in this group that seemed OK and attractive, but it failed. Why did I after all go for such a group? My attraction for this group must have been more important that I first suspected.' To test this hypothesis, Turner and his colleagues asked groups of schoolgirls to compete in problem-solving. The most important variable was that the girls either thought they chose to belong to their group or that the experimenters decided the group membership for them. Of course, none of the girls had a choice but, in half of the groups, subjects signed a form that they accepted to stay in the group. At the end of the competition, subjects filled in various scales measuring self-esteem and group cohesiveness. For those subjects who thought they had no choice about their membership, the usual results were obtained (Myers, 1962; Worchel, Lind & Kaufman, 1975). In other words, winning groups were more cohesive than losing ones and their members also displayed higher self-esteem than the others. The results were totally different when the schoolgirls thought they were free to choose their group. More cohesive-ness and higher self-esteem was found when the group lost than when it won.

Globally, the role of self-esteem in discrimination against other groups remains a problematic issue. Reviewing the studies pertaining to the 'self-esteem hypothesis', Abrams and Hogg concluded that: 'the evidence for self-esteem as either a basis for or a consequence of minimal intergroup discrimination is mixed. This may be a result of methodological problems or may be because self-esteem is only indirectly associated with discrimin-ation. A number of other mediating motives may exist' (1988, p. 328). Similarly, Messick and Mackie (1989) argue that the causal relation between self-esteem and discrimination has not yet been adequately tested and that, in fact, an adequate test of such a relation is difficult to imagine.

Norm and interdependence

Early in his research programme, Tajfel wondered whether categorization alone was sufficient to create 'a group'. Do the adolescents in the minimal group paradigm studies, for instance, show discriminatory behaviours because of the categories they belong to or because of the interpersonal similarity – sharing a preference for Klee – induced by the experimental scenario? An experiment by Billig and Tajfel (1973) attempted to disentangle the operationalization of the two concepts.

There were four conditions in the study. The first condition (categorization and similarity) was the usual one where subjects are assigned to one of two groups on the basis of their preference for Klee's paintings. Categorization was removed from the second condition (no-categorization and similarity) and subjects were just told that, like some subjects and unlike others, they had preferred a certain kind of painting. In the third condition (categorization and no-similarity), subjects were assigned to a group by the toss of a coin without reference to aesthetic preference. Finally, no references to either group or preferences were made in the fourth condition (no-categorization and no-similarity). Thus, in this experiment, categorization was manipulated by treating subjects as group members or aggregates. Similarity was operationalized by the preferences for the Klee or Kandinsky paintings versus a random basis. Subjects had to allocate money through the usual matrices. Results showed ingroup favouritism in the categorization conditions but not in the no-categorization conditions. Similarity also produced ingroup favouritism. More important for Billig and Tajfel, however, is the comparison between the second and third conditions. Similarity without categorization led subjects to respect fairness. In contrast, categorization alone was sufficient to generate ingroup favouritism. In other words, similarity per se is able to increase discrimination but not to create it. In sum, even though both concepts effectively produce ingroup favouritism, social categorization is most important.

As far as similarity is concerned, this conclusion agrees with Lewin, who stated that 'It is not similarity or dissimilarity that decides whether two individuals belong to the same or to different groups but *social interaction or other types of interdependence. A group is best defined as a dynamic whole based on interdependence rather than on similarity*' (1948, p. 184; emphasis original). However, SIT does not envisage interdependence between individuals as the required bridge to transform social categories into human groups. It could even be said that categorization, as well as similarity, leads to interdependence. What matters for the psychological existence of a group is the status of the self regarding the social category. SIT says that a group exists when two or more people consider themselves to be members of the same social category (Turner, 1982).

The absence of interdependence among the 'groups' and their members in the minimal group paradigm constitutes a central step in the development of SIT. Indeed, because of the elimination of a motivation for discrimination in that paradigm, social identity theorists argue that the motivation has to be found elsewhere, namely in the fact that social categorizations are internalized to define the self (Turner, 1981) and in the need to maintain or enhance self-esteem (Tajfel & Turner, 1979).

Rabbie and Horwitz (1988; Horwitz & Rabbie, 1989) make an argument based on this elimination of a motivation for discrimination. As faithful Lewinian supporters, they oppose a view of groups as mere categories. Their own minimal group experiments presented above (Horwitz & Rabbie, 1982; Rabbie, 1966; Rabbie & Horwitz, 1969) were based upon the Lewinian perspective that belonging to a group involves concrete, dynamic relations between persons. They claim, as do Abrams and Hogg (1988), that the assumption that subjects' categorization into a minimal group is internalized in order to define their selves has not been sufficiently supported. Moreover, they contend that SIT evolved from a misinterpretation of the minimal group paradigm's results. For them, subjects in those experiments were not reacting to what they perceived as a social category, as defended by SIT theorists, but were actually responding to what they considered a social group, that is 'a locomoting entity, one that actively moves or is passively moved in its environment toward or away from group harms or benefits' (Rabbie & Horwitz, 1988, p. 119).

According to Rabbie et al. (Rabbie & Horwitz, 1988; Rabbie, Schot & Visser, 1989), a perceived interdependence is present in the minimal group paradigm and contributes to the discriminatory behaviour. Even in that minimal context, people have expectations about members of the ingroup and of the outgroup. They entertain norms of reciprocity and fairness as well as generic group norms. To test the idea that ingroup favouritism is built upon subjects' perception of their dependence to ingroup and outgroup members, Rabbie et al. (1989) conducted the following experiment. One condition replicated the standard situation used by Tajfel: subjects were informed that at the end of the experiment, they would receive an amount of money that an anonymous person of their ingroup and one of the outgroup had awarded them. In another condition, subjects were told that the money was allocated only by members of their ingroup. In a third condition, the money came from outgroup members. In other words, the dependence was varied in the three conditions. The researchers were interested in the way experimental subjects partitioned monetary rewards to anonymous members of the ingroup and of the outgroup. Globally, the results showed that the subjects allocated more money to the members of the groups they thought they were more dependent on. In the classical condition, where they believed their outcomes to be dependent on both ingroup and outgroup members, they allocated slightly more money to ingroup than to the outgroup. In the ingroup dependence condition, they gave much more money to ingroupers than to outgroupers. Most importantly, when they perceived their outcomes as dependent on outgroup members only, subjects allocated more money to outgroup members than to ingroup members. In conclusion, people displayed ingroup as well as outgroup discrimination although the category differentiation was constant. The type of discrimination was a function of who was presented as controlling the resources of the subjects. Rabbie et al. interpreted these results to mean that their subjects' strategy was to distribute more money to interdependent others with the expectation that the allocations would be reciprocated, and, thus, leading to a maximization of their own economic self-interests.

Gagnon (1993) attempted to replicate Rabbie et al.'s results. Subjects were assigned to one of two groups by the toss of a coin. Half of them – the so-called interdependent subjects – went through the matrices and also distributed a sum of 100 points to members of the two groups according to the usual instructions. The other half – the autonomous subjects – were guaranteed that they would receive the maximum possible reward from the experimenter regardless of what the other persons, from the ingroup and the outgroup, would give them. When the two allocations tasks were completed, subjects indicated the extent to which they identified with their ingroup. Ingroup favouritism was obtained for the two dependent variables; there was no difference between autonomous and interdependent subjects, but those who identified highly with their ingroup showed significantly more discrimination towards the outgroup than the low identifiers. In still another experiment, Mlicki (1993) not only manipulated the interdependence of his subjects, but also varied the instrumentality of the allocation tasks in order to obtain rewards. The interdependence variable did not affect the non-instrumental task, but it did influence the instrumental one.

We give Messick and Mackie the last word on this:

> nearly 20 years after the discovery that mere categorization produced intergroup bias, an adequate theory of the phenomenon has yet to be developed. Both perceptual accentuation effects and self-esteem maintenance seem likely to be part of the story, but empirical findings have not definitively clarified their necessary or sufficient roles. (1989, p. 62)

In our view, the controversy over interdependence has taken the wrong track. Rabbie and his co-workers trapped themselves in a very crude operationalization of the interdependence concept that the social identity theorists had no difficulty ridiculing. For Rabbie, interdependence boiled down to an egotistic concern for personal reward. To us, the concept of interdependence is intimately linked to the existential coherence of the group for its members. People using brand 'Chutzpah' toothpaste may form a category but are unlikely to constitute a group (Tajfel, 1982), until it is discovered that this specific brand has very toxic side-effects (Rabbie & Horwitz, 1988, p. 119). The sudden discovery that one shares a potential danger gives coherence and meaning to an otherwise arbitrary category. We suggest that going through the very complex task of allocating rewards via Tajfel's matrices helped build this sense of coherence for the subjects. They start the task as category members and they end it being group members. There is no wonder, then, that those subjects who discriminate most also profess the highest identification with what has become their group.

Allocating punishments

In the classical studies on the minimal group paradigm, ingroup favouritism always delivers a greater reward to the ingroup than to the outgroup. In many real-life situations, favouritism also causes avoidance. Think of the stamina of those military officers responsible for enlisting soldiers who spend their time avoiding recruiting their family and their friends' sons for hard or dangerous duties. Mummendey and her co-workers (1992; Mummendey, 1993) simulated this latter conception of ingroup favouritism in the laboratory. Subjects had to allocate punishments of varying intensities (e.g. electric shocks) to other people who did or did not belong to their group. Results proved rather erratic, but it can cautiously be said that no discrimination occurred. Why?

Is it that the alleviation of punishments does not contribute to the enhancement of self-esteem? We are willing to bet that officers drafting discriminatively have as high a self-esteem as philanthropists. Is it that the minimal group paradigm is too minimal a situation, as Tajfel first thought, for this kind of discrimination to materialize? We are tempted to accept this very simple explanation, but it has implications for the justification of categorization. How can one add something to strengthen the categorization without, somehow, giving it substance, i.e. a meaning or a coherence, that goes beyond mere labelling?

There is not much use for experiments in a vacuum (Tajfel, 1972b). Likewise, social categories in a vacuum are probably rare and not very helpful. What preempts the vaccuum is the theoretical coherence, however naïve it is, that is accorded to the categories.

SIT and stereotypes

We extensively discussed the ease of inducing discriminatory behaviour. We also stated that Tajfel had no problem linking his experiments to stereotyping. But what, exactly, do these studies have to do with stereotypes? In the minimal social situation there were no actual groups. In none of the Klee and Kandinsky experiments were attitudes towards the outgroup members measured. These data merely show that in a social situation, especially when groups are involved, it is very easy to discriminate or to differentiate. As a matter of fact, though we spoke of the Klee and Kandinsky groups as distinct entities, there was never a Kandinsky group!

An old experiment (Hartley, 1946) shows that subjects have no problem discriminating even against groups that they do not know, and that sometimes do not even exist! American subjects from eight different universities had to react towards 35 ethnic groups. Hartley used a distance scale that measures, as you will remember, how close you are willing to accept (e.g. to marry him) or to reject a person (e.g. not to allow her in the country). In the list of the 35 groups, three were fictitious: the Danerians, the Pirenians and the Wallonians (we would like to point out that the authors of this book are Walloons, born or living in Wallonia in southern Belgium!). Only a few students refused to rate these three ethnic groups, and of those who did rate them, the vast majority rejected our poor fictitious cousins.

The only dimension that Tajfel's subjects could use to differentiate the in- and outgroup was the distribution of points or pennies. In the case of Hartley's groups, it was a social distance scale. In everyday life, where groups really exist, stereotypes are another dimension by which people can differentiate WE and THEY. Actually, stereotypes are such easy devices that almost no knowledge about the groups is necessary for them to appear. Hearsay and TV series are sufficient. Here is another old experiment that shows that it is easy to apply stereotypes to social categories that we do not know very well. Schoenfeld (1942) asked his subjects to match eight first names with eight personality traits. Among the 120 students who took part in this study, 63 said that Richard was handsome, 58 said that Herman was stupid, and, for 71 students, the Adrians were artists. This investigation has been used to support the thesis that there is no kernel of truth to stereotypes. We prefer to see in it an illustration that stereotypes are extraordinarily effortless devices for categorizing and discriminating.

The functions of stereotypes

Stereotypes are not only the natural result of the categorization process, of the individual need to organize and simplify the environment, but they also fulfil a social function: to explain social events and to justify the ingroup's actions. Tajfel (1981) explored these facets by distinguishing three social functions of stereotypes: social causal explanation, social justification, and social differentiation.

The function of *social causality* is to understand social or non-social events by identifying groups that may be responsible. One well-known and very contemporary example is the tendency to accuse immigrants of causing economic recession. The explanation involves the elaboration of a negative stereotype in relation to the economic events. *Social justification* concerns the creation of a specific stereotype to justify behaviours towards a given group. For example, colonial powers created negative stereotypes of the people they colonized. Similar reasoning holds for slavery or for simpler situations of competition among groups. The function of *social differentiation* aims at clarifying and accentuating the differences among groups in order to establish a positive distinction in favour of the ingroup. Stereotypes will be especially prevalent when intergroup distinction is unstable. Individual members are thus motivated to preserve and strengthen the superiority of their group. One direct consequence of this is the tendency to 'over-exclude' ambiguous members from a positively evaluated group (Leyens & Yzerbyt, 1992; Yzerbyt, Leyens & Bellour, 1994).

According to Tajfel, stereotypes cannot really be understood unless these functions are taken into account. Still, as noted by Condor (1990), these aspects have not been at the heart of the empirical work. It has been generally assumed that stereotypes fulfil these functions, but the processes linking stereotypes to these functions remain obscure. Condor also stressed the important theoretical problem of distinguishing between functions understood as consequences and functions understood as intentions. Social identity theorists do not seem to make the distinction and generally assume that stereotypes result from deliberate intention. For example, Social identity theorists think the stereotype of Blacks was created to justify slavery. The intention of legitimizing some unjustified state of affairs is deduced from the content of the stereotype. However, because there is no independent estimate of such an intention, one cannot be sure that such an intention exists. This criticism reflects the argument raised by Hogg and Abrams (1988) concerning the role of self-esteem in discriminatory behaviour. They argue that discrimination between groups results from the intention to establish or restore members' self-esteem via a positive distinction between ingroup and outgroup. However, this has never been directly tested. For SIT, the establishment of a distinction between ingroup and outgroup is one of the functions generally attributed to stereotypes. This postulate, too, has never been tested.

Stereotypes working as norms

> From the social identity perspective, the crucial feature of the stereotypes is that they are shared. They are not merely idiosyncratic generalizations which are coincidentally or by chance made by a number of people. . . . This sharedness is due to a social process of social influence which causes conformity to group norms, called referent informational influence. (Hogg & Abrams, 1988, p. 75)

According to Turner (1982, 1985), the process of referent informational influence includes three stages. First, people categorize and define themselves as members of a social category. Second, they learn the stereotypical norms of that category. Third, they assign these norms to themselves. Thus, group behaviour is normative behaviour, and group belongingness implies uniformities in behaviour, attitudes and perception. In other words, self-categorization generates social uniformity, intra-group consensus and shared perceptions. That is, when people perceive themselves as group members, they also perceive themselves as possessing the same characteristics as the other members of their group and as sharing the ingroup's perceptions and reactions to other groups.

It appears that self-categorization is indeed a determining factor in social influence. For instance, considering phenomena like norm formation, conformity or group polarization, Abrams, Wetherell, Cochrane, Hogg and Turner (1990) have shown that a source of influence is more powerful when perceived as belonging to an ingroup rather than to an outgroup. In the authors' terms: 'You know what you think by knowing who you are'. More important for our purpose is the fact that perceiving that one belongs to an ingroup can affect one's perception of an outgroup. According to SIT, a person's identity as member of a social group should be particularly salient when other ingroup members are present to cue this identity. This salience should in turn make vivid shared norms or shared perceptions including stereotypes about other groups. The shared beliefs should then have the strongest effect on the ingroup members' perceptions.

Wilder and Shapiro (1991) recently investigated this kind of functioning. These authors reasoned that an audience of students belonging to the same university should facilitate the perception of a person in categorial terms, i.e. his or her college membership, and should also activate the stereo-typical expectations associated with that outgroup. In two experiments, subjects from one university were first presented with patterns of infor-mation about 10 students of another university. This information was arranged to create or to avoid stereotypes about this outgroup. Either six traits appeared repeatedly in the profiles, or they were scattered more widely. In a second stage, subjects listened to a tape-recording of an interview with an outgroup student. Finally, they had to answer a questionnaire about the target person. Subjects listened to the interview alone, in the presence of an 'expert' audience (the experimenter and an observer), or in the presence of two other students of their own university. Results showed that subjects were more likely to judge the target in line with the stereotype when in the presence of ingroup members than when alone or in the presence of experts. A third experiment differed from the first two in that it did not include the expert audience but confronted subjects in the other conditions with specific information about the target person that was either consistent or inconsistent with the stereotype of his group. The presence of ingroup members did not affect the judgements of the target when confirming information was provided. However, an ingroup audience when compared to no audience significantly reduced the power of disconfirming information. Finally, in all three experiments, subjects thought they were more like others from their ingroup when members of the group were present. Also, ingroup identification correlated significantly with the stereotypicality of the judgements.

This pattern of results indicates that stereotypes can work as norms of perceptions. Also, stereotypes appear to be in line with Rabbie's statement that the role of norms was too rapidly discarded from the study of intergroup discrimination. In sum, it could be said that, for social identity and self-categorization theorists, stereotypes are envisioned in a triple perspective. First, stereotypes result from a cognitivo-perceptual process that enhances the similarity of members belonging to the same category. Second, subjects use stereotypes to rationalize, justify, explain and clarify behaviours. Third, stereotypes provide prescriptions by defining what perceptions, behaviours, and attitudes are appropriate given one's allegiance to the group.

Conclusions

Henri Tajfel's talent and his ideas on social identity theory stimulated creative lines of research in the numerous people around him. SIT has alternatively focused on cognitive factors, on social norms, and on a mixture of cognition and motivation. The best known explanation of SIT looked at social categorization, social comparison and social identity. At present, with self-categorization theory, the pendulum is again on the side of cognition. Norms are now seen as consequences. However, they may well again take the role of antecedents, a hypothesis defended since the beginning by Rabbie, a supporter of Lewin rather than of Tajfel. In spite of its temporary and exclusively cognitive bents, what has remained steady is that, for SIT or SCT, stereotypes have never been errors, incorrect overgeneralizations or maladaptive phenomena. In that sense, one could say that this set of theories has always been concerned more with stereotyping than with stereotypes.

From what precedes, it is clear that the level of reality in the adequacy of judgements is neither the only nor the most critical element for SIT. SIT's defenders instead assign a great importance to the context of judgements; this context accounts for what is stereotyped and in what way. Hence, for them, stereotypes are not given forever, but change with the context (Di Giacomo, 1980). The social part of the integrity level is also very much in tune with SIT. According to SIT, people are driven by a positive image of their group. People can achieve this positivity by discriminating against other groups. The integrity is achieved by downgrading other groups as inferior or less privileged. The cultural level, and its concern with social rules of judgement, has not been directly tackled by SIT or SCT. However, as norms are more and more integrated into the theory, and since the context is of utmost importance, there is nothing that impedes social rules from playing a role. With the functions of stereotypes encompassing social causality, justification and differentiation, SIT might have had substantial things to say at the theoretical level. However, the statements about functions did not stimulate much research. In the future, the theoretical level could become influential as the controversy between interdependence and mere categorization brings to the forefront questions about the coherence of the categories or of the groups.

4

The Social Cognition Approach

A few years after the launching of social identity theory in Europe, another approach came to life in the US under the label of social cognition. In the late 1970s, the social cognition wave flooded over social psychology. Ostrom (1984), one of the founding fathers of social cognition, entitled one of his essays 'The Sovereignty of Social Cognition', a title probably less pretentious than true. Social cognition shares one peculiarity with SIT in that it also emanates from a specific area of research but has the ambition to cover the whole domain of social psychology (Devine, Hamilton & Ostrom, 1994; Hogg & Abrams, 1988). Whereas research on intergroup relations gave the impetus to SIT, social cognition was first proposed to deal with person perception and impression formation.

The social cognitivists' dream was to revolutionize the field by bringing in important metatheoretical and methodological changes. Here are those most often talked about:

1   Social cognition emphasizes processes rather than descriptive outputs. Whereas traditional studies of stereotypes focused on outcomes, social cognition further developed the understanding of the dynamics of stereotyping.
2   Social cognitivists use fine-grained analyses of processes involved in person perception. This shift was achieved by borrowing paradigms from the mainstream in cognitive psychology.
3   Most of the processes that are studied within this tradition are purely cognitive and concerned with models of information-processing and memory.
4   More dependent variables are investigated. Researchers are no longer interested only in global evaluations of the targets, but they are using new dependent variables such as reaction times, recall, recognition, etc.

As the reader can infer from the above changes, there are some clear distinctions, not to say antagonisms, between SIT and social cognition. First, remember that SIT treats motivational and cognitive variables equally. Although more recent social cognition approaches explicitly attempt to give motivation and affects a status equivalent to cognition, the balance between these factors is definitely not a property of the original trend. Second, the focus of SIT is deliberately social as opposed to individual. The social cognition approach is unquestionably individual.

We have set several goals for this chapter. In the first section, we define social cognition and identify two rather distinct lines of research that vary by their emphasis given to models of memory: impression formation and person memory. In the second section, we describe our conception of the building blocks of social cognition: categories and schemata. We then devote three sections to substantial questions in social cognition: the management of inconsistent information, the impact of salient information, and the automatic processing of information. For these three topics, we present illustrative research within each of the two traditions of research, namely impression formation and person memory.

What is social cognition?

The expression 'social cognition' was first introduced in social psychology by Bruner and Tagiuri (1954). At the time, the term did not capture the attention of researchers because it too vaguely referred to the knowledge of persons as well as the role of social factors upon knowledge in general. This is not to say that there is now a general and consensual definition of the field. However, those researchers who flock under the social cognition flag are clearly identifiable. In this chapter, we will illustrate two tendencies represented by the following definitions. According to Hamilton, social cognition includes 'a consideration of all factors influencing the acquisition, representation, and retrieval of person information, as well as the relationship of these processes to judgments made by the perceiver' (1981, p. 136). Fiske and Taylor, on the other hand, define social cognition as the study of 'how ordinary people think about people and how they think they think about people' (1984, p. 1).

There is nothing incompatible in these two definitions. In order to think about oneself or others, one obviously needs some information: acquired, represented and retrieved. Still, there are myriads of possible representations of the acquired information; the solutions that researchers pick for investigation depend on how they think people think. The two definitions emphasize, however, different aspects of person perception. Fiske and Taylor's focus on 'how people think' relates to *impression formation* and naïve social psychology as defended by Asch and Heider. Assuming that people behave knowingly or unknowingly according to their beliefs, why not study those beliefs? In contrast, Hamilton's definition is directly concerned with the intake of information and its representation. Followers of this latter perspective have christened it *person memory*.

To speak of a social cognition approach is a euphemism; a tidal wave would be more appropriate. In the last ten years, social cognition theories have influenced and refreshed so much of social psychology that it would be absurd to dream of giving this perspective complete credit in a few pages. In this chapter, we have chosen to present a few concepts that should give the reader a taste of the two perspectives, *impression formation*, on the one hand, and *person memory*, on the other. The next chapter will be devoted to a more extended review of some phenomena related to stereotyping. That will also give us the opportunity to contrast SIT with social cognition.

Categories and schemata

If you listen to, or merely hear, social cognitivists, your attention will be titillated by words such as categories, fuzzy sets, exemplars, features-sets, nodes, scripts, frames, instances, attributes, prototypes, stereotypes, schemata, top-down, bottom-up, pointer plus tag, etc. According to some critics of the social cognition approach, theorists who dispose of such a refined vocabulary sound like Molière's physicians: they believe they possess the truth because they can identify things by using esoteric – and often exotic – names. To be sure, not every concept used in the social cognition literature is defined unambiguously and consensually. Moreover, as research progresses, it appears that certain terms become old-fashioned whereas others regain vitality. Like any other scientific paradigm, social cognition undergoes evolution.

Remember the debate between the Tajfelian and Rabbiean views on minimal groups. A crucial difference between these two lines of work lies in the use of concepts like social categories and social groups. In social cognition, the concept of category is also a central one. It is thus quite important to devote some space to make explicit its meaning in this context. *A category is an abstract structure of knowledge that groups things that hold together on the basis of coherence.* A sparrow and a robin are parts of the category 'bird' because they are similar; a spoon and a pan are parts of the 'kitchen utensils' category because they serve the same function; 100 pounds of ice-cream and an obese person are parts of the 'glutton' category as cause and effect, etc. Moreover, categories are made of structured attributes: the bird sings and flies, has feathers and wings; the extrovert has bulgy eyes and is sociable, etc. Attributes may themselves be categories depending on the level of focus. Feathers, for instance, may be a generic term for tectrices (primary and secondary), remiges (primary and secondary), rectrices and down. An attribute and a category are distinguished by the structuring (organizing) quality at any given moment (Schul & Burnstein, 1988).

Not many categories have necessary and sufficient attributes. They have volatile boundaries and are best seen as fuzzy sets. However, some members of the category are better members than others. They represent the category better and serve as reference points to decide whether or not an intruding element will be considered as a member of the category. The best abstract exemplars are called *prototypes*. To European eyes, someone with his blond hair imprisoned under a Stetson, a soccer-player-stature erected in Tony Lama boots, and a hamburger replacing the cigar is more American than a dark complexioned shrimp with Dior dresses and a weakness for sweetbreads. How does information enter into our categories and how is it represented in memory? Since this is a booming area, you will be hardly surprised if we tell you that there are lots of memory models, too many to review here. Going to the core message instead, we could say that there are two general types of memory metaphors.

According to the *co-existence* metaphor, perceived information is stored in memory and remains there unchanged until it is retrieved. If not much attention was paid at the time of acquisition of this information, if it was not especially striking, if much time elapsed since one last thought of it, this information may be obliterated. Or more exactly, it is available but not accessible. According to a strict co-existence model, people have no guides for the intake of information, they only store *exemplars*, or *instances* of members of categories. When asked to give a judgement about a given category, people review all accessible exemplars and compute what is required under the particular circumstances (for instance, generosity or punctuality).

In contrast to the co-existence metaphor, the *alteration* metaphor assumes that the prototype of the category guides perception and acquisition. What is encoded may be altered to fit the existing elements in memory. For instance, if I think insurance agents are hypocrites, I will perceive the offer of a ride by my insurance agent as ingratiation rather than as generosity. One particular use of the prototype is that it allows perceivers not to bother with all the details of the original information. When asked several years later about my insurance agent, I may well remember that he ingratiated me several times, but I will not recall the actual behaviours that called upon that particular label. When the prototype is used as guide for perception, memory and behaviour, it is often called a *schema* (Bartlett, 1932; Fiske & Linville, 1980).

Now, it would be foolish to think that people function exhaustively with instances, that is, only with data, raw information and without theories about data, without expectations or prejudgements. A human being without prejudgement would be nothing more than biological magma. It is equally absurd to imagine that one only works according to schemata, that people are incapable of taking in raw data for what it is, that they are inept at distinguishing information from expectation. Were it the case, life would be a perpetual status quo. What is not preposterous, however, is to investigate under which conditions people tend to function according to the alteration model or according to the co-existence model, and under which circumstances people blend these two approaches. This is why stereotypes and stereotyping are ideal objects of study for social cognition. Indeed, stereotypes and stereotyping necessarily evoke categories as well as individuating information. As a result, the differences between the two metaphors are best illustrated when people are asked to make a series of judgements about targets. We will examine more specific implications of each metaphor in Chapter 5 when we report on research about a classic phenomenon in intergroup relations: the outgroup homogeneity effect.

In the following sections, we will examine how the blending issue has been researched in the two social cognition traditions defined earlier: impression formation and person memory. We will centre our presentation on three different lines of research: management of inconsistent information, salience and spontaneous inferences. We will illustrate the *management of inconsistent information* first. Actually, the word 'inconsistent' is not neutral. It implies that an expectation exists and the new information is unexpected from the perspective of the already acquired information. Often, researchers examine inconsistencies that alter the views perceivers hold about a particular target person. Sometimes, they have also evaluated the impact of inconsistency on the category as a whole (Johnston & Hewstone, 1992; Weber & Crocker, 1983). It is noteworthy that inconsistent information is also particularly salient because it is unexpected and infrequent. More generally, the issue of *salience* has a privileged place in social cognition research. Fiske and Taylor (1991) define salience as the extent to which particular stimuli stand out relative to others in their environment. Numerous studies, both on person memory and on impression formation, address the issue of the antecedents, mediators and consequences of salience. Finally, we will end our illustrative journey by looking at a third topic of interest to social cognitivists: the *spontaneous character of inferences*. Here again, we can distinguish between the impression formation and the person memory approaches. In the former perspective, the focus is on the nature of the inferential work people do when confronted with information. The question is thus to see whether or not people engage in dispositional explanation. In contrast, researchers in person memory have essentially assumed the existence of these early dispositional inferences and have instead looked at how they may influence the processing of additional information.

Inconsistency management

Inconsistency and impression formation

Work on impression formation dates back to a seminal research by Asch and to the subsequent controversy between Asch and Anderson. This well-known work does not need to be reviewed here in detail (for excellent reviews, see R. Brown, 1986; Fiske & Taylor, 1991; Schneider, Hastorf & Ellsworth, 1979; Zebrowitz, 1990). Let us just restate the main aspects.

Asch (1946, 1952) initiated his research on impressions of personality at a time when disagreements about the criterion for good perception marred person perception studies. Interested in impression rather than in perception, Asch did not need such a criterion. He cared more about the cognitive process involved in impression formation. As he himself said, before we come to like or dislike people, we have to know them. For one, he wanted to see whether people are capable of integrating various 'data of observation into a single, relatively unified impression'. To solve this problem, he

Table 4.1 *Traits inferences as a function of the type of list presented to the subjects (in percentages)*

	Type of list			
	'Warm'	'Cold'	'Intelligent'	'Envious'
1 Generous	91	8	24	10
2 Wise	65	25	18	17
3 Happy	90	34	32	5
4 Good-natured	94	17	18	0
5 Humorous	77	13	52	21
6 Sociable	91	38	56	27
7 Popular	84	28	35	14
8 Reliable	94	99	84	91
9 Important	88	99	85	90
10 Humane	86	31	36	21
11 Good-looking	77	69	74	35
12 Persistent	100	97	82	87
13 Serious	100	99	97	100
14 Restrained	77	89	64	9
15 Altruistic	69	18	6	5
16 Imaginative	51	19	26	14
17 Strong	98	95	94	73
18 Honest	98	94	80	79

Source: Asch, 1946

presented his subjects with the following personality traits that supposedly characterized a fictitious person: 'intelligent, skillful, industrious, warm, determined, practical, cautious'. He then asked subjects to write what they thought about that person. In addition, subjects were invited to characterize that fictitious person on a series of other personality traits. Subjects had no difficulty writing a personality sketch about the fictitious person and they generally agreed on their choice of the other personality traits (see Table 4.1). Subjects, Asch concluded, use the available information to build up a general picture of the target person and then they go beyond the information given to make new inferences about other characteristics of the person.

Second, Asch wanted to verify whether some – central – traits coloured the big picture more than did other traits and if these had an impact on subjects' inferences. In the series of traits listed above, the item 'warm' happens to be one of these central traits. When it is replaced by 'cold', the impression and the inferences are completely different. Try for yourself, and we bet you will no longer see the fictitious individual as being wise, humorous, popular or imaginative, but she or he will still be strong and serious (see Table 4.1). This reorganization of the impression does not happen when polite and blunt replace warm and cold. In other words, warm and cold are central traits, polite and blunt are not.

Asch's definition of the centrality of traits described the data but did not allow him to predict which traits would be central. In 1960, Wishner was able to diagnose the centrality of the stimulus traits from their high correlations with the response traits – those traits that are inferred.

Rosenberg, Nelson and Vivekanathan (1968) made a new advance. These authors presented their subjects with a long list of pairs of traits (most of them coming from Asch) and asked them to rate the degree of similarity of the traits in each pair. They submitted the resulting matrix to Multi-dimensional Scaling. Clearly, the traits used in the study were organized along two, almost orthogonal, evaluative dimensions. The first dimension concerns intelligence, the second one refers to sociability. As Figure 4.1 reveals, the central traits identified by Asch are extreme on a different dimension than the rest of the stimulus traits. They therefore carry a lot of informative weight. Specifically, all those traits refer to intelligence except warm and cold, which concern sociability. Not surprisingly then, when subjects were later presented with new traits related to sociability, they relied on what they knew about the sociability of that person, that is, if the target was a warm or a cold person.

Some other traits also had a special status for Asch. As a Gestaltist, he defended the idea that there was a direction to perception and impression. This direction is given by the first traits.

> When the subject hears the first term, a broad, uncrystallized but directed impression is born. The next characteristic comes not as a separate item, but is related to the established direction. Quickly the view formed acquires a certain stability, so that later characteristics are fitted – if conditions permit – to the given direction. (Asch, 1946, pp. 271–272)

This primacy effect is important for our purpose because of the inconsistency in the information provided to the experimental subjects. To test the primacy effect, Asch presented to some of his subjects the following list of traits belonging to a fictitious person: 'A. intelligent–industrious–impulsive–critical–stubborn–envious'. Other subjects received the same list but in the reverse order: 'B. envious–stubborn–critical–impulsive–industrious–intelligent'.

Results showed that both persons A and B were evaluated somewhat positively but, more importantly, person A was evaluated more positively than person B. The key idea is that people confronted with list A or B do not, somehow, perceive the same six words equally. The first adjectives in the list set the stage by activating a certain schema, positive or negative, that leads subjects to interpret the following information in a consistent way (Zanna & Hamilton, 1977). Peabody (1967) showed that many words have quasi-synonyms but a different valence. This difference in valence is often found in stereotypes. For example, while ingroup members think that they are parsimonious, outgroup members label them as mean. When we apply Peabody's findings to Asch's list, the subjects 'constructed' these persons: 'A. intelligent–industrious–spontaneous–discriminating–resolute–envious. B. envious–obstinate–faultfinding–reckless–industrious–intelligent.' Notice that two positive adjectives and only one negative trait have no equivalent opposed valences. This imbalance explains why the subjects found both profiles to be somewhat positive.

The briefest conclusion of this line of research is that subjects are both

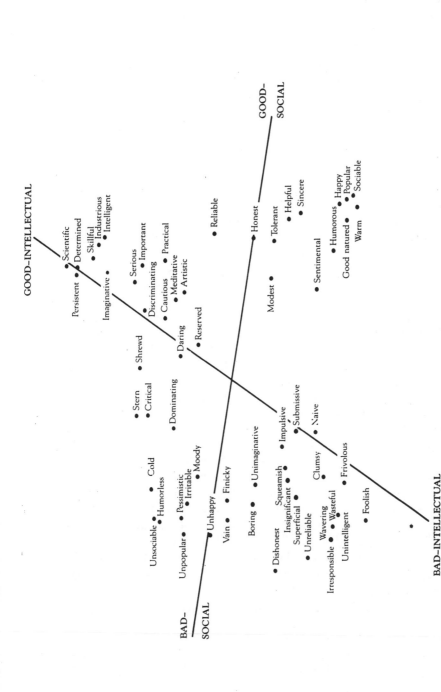

Figure 4.1   *Two-dimensional configuration of 60 traits scaled by Rosenberg, Nelson & Vivekananthan (1968) (Rosenberg & Sedlak, 1972)*

theory- and data-driven when forming an impression of persons. Theory, however, is more important for them than data. They use all the adjectives, at least to some extent, but they organize and interpret them on-line, in light of the adjectives' relations to each other within a larger cognitive structure. In other words, people quickly form a theory about who the target is, and, as they learn more about this person, they integrate the new elements into the established structure.

Anderson (1974, 1981; Anderson & Hubert, 1963) challenged Asch's interpretation by defending a molecular rather than a molar approach. For this author, data dominate theory, and the global impression is a linear function of the combination of each individual element under a weighted average rule:

$$R = (w_0 s_0 + w_1 s_1)/(w_0 + w_1)$$

with R = the final evaluation; w_0 = the weight of the initial opinion; s_0 = scale value of initial opinion; w_1 = weight of the new information; s_1 = scale value of new information.

In this algebraic integration, there are no central traits that guide the general impression. Also, the primacy effect is handled by weighting the traits and is attributed to a decrease in attention, or discounting. Actually, Anderson was not interested in person perception per se but by the combination of valences. He just used personality traits to illustrate his ideas. In some sense, his interest was the reverse of Katz and Braly's who started from an integrated measure, the prejudice, to find the various elements of this global measure. To test his ideas, Anderson confronted each of his subjects with numerous sequences of traits with different valences. It is not surprising that the subjects showed signs of inattention. More importantly, Anderson argued that people do not work with a schema in their heads but take the information as it hits their eyes, clear at the beginning and vague after a while. Supposedly, they are also patient enough to read all the information before coming to an impression.

These findings spurred a hot debate between Asch's supporters and Anderson's. It lasted for years because rules were never set that would allow for a winner to emerge. Each argument was proposed in a non-falsifiable manner. Ostrom (1977) first called for a cease-fire on the ground that the battle was sterile. Then, with Devine, he contrasted this endless duel with an information-processing approach that defines stereotypes as beliefs about social categories.

> No longer is the definition of inconsistency bound to a particular experimental context or to the notion of trait weights and scale values. The definition of inconsistency can be expanded to include behaviors being inconsistent not just with one another, but with prior expectations, previous judgments about that person, or any other component of one's cognitive representation. (Devine & Ostrom, 1988, pp. 240–241)

In other words, this new vision allows psychologists to contrast specific information with theories or categorial judgements based on past experience.

As a good example of the current information-processing approach, we will briefly summarize some of the research conducted by Susan Fiske and her associates on impression formation (for reviews, see Fiske & Neuberg, 1990, and Fiske & Rusher, 1993). The question is no longer whether people obey their schemata *or* the data, but *when* they do one or the other. Fiske posits that perceivers spontaneously start by categorizing targets. If motivated, if the target has relevance for the perceivers' goal, for instance, and if cognitive resources are available, the perceivers will pay attention to the attributes, that is, the specific characteristics of the target. Whenever possible, perceivers will try to confirm the initial category. Otherwise they will resort to a recategorization. If the last two strategies fail, and, again, there is enough motivation and cognitive resources, perceivers will utilize the different bits of individuating information to arrive at a piecemeal integration. They will use this to attribute specific dispositions to the target.

In one study (Erber & Fiske, 1984, expt 1), subjects anticipated working on a creative task with another person who was presented either as highly skilled or as inexperienced and unskilled. Subjects were told the best performance would win a prize but, for half the subjects, the award would be given to the team's work, whereas for the other subjects the award would be given for the best individual input. All the subjects then read different evaluations of their would-be partner. Half of these evaluations were positive and half were negative. In other words, all the subjects had an expectation about their partner's skill, but in only half of the cases were the 'facts' consistent with the expectation. To the extent that the award preoccupied the participants, half of them should not have cared about the skills of their partner; the award depended upon their own performance. In contrast, the other half, whose fate was linked to the partner's skill, were expected to be very attentive to inconsistent information: 'After all, she may not be that inept' or 'Gee, I better be careful; maybe she's good but not that good'. There were several dependent variables: liking for the partner, recall of the information, and attention devoted to the consistent and inconsistent pieces of information (this latter variable is quite innovative for the area). The last variable fully supports the hypothesis. Attention times are significantly longer when the information is inconsistent with the expectation *and* when the subjects are motivated. In the other three conditions they do not differ from one another. It is important to grasp that people have a preference for schema-driven perception, but that they do not necessarily dismiss information inconsistent with their schema. If they are motivated to do so, subjects will attend to the inconsistency.

Inconsistency and person memory

Independent of the renewed research on impression formation, person memory scholars have tackled the issue of inconsistency by testing the implications of different memory models. Let us go back to the American students who go for one year of study in France (Stroebe et. al, 1988). They are told and believe that French persons are open-minded. Indeed, the first individual they meet at their arrival in France glorifies Manhattan and the number of taxis there. He is the taxi driver who takes them to the dorm and he even painted his own taxi yellow. The next person, however, is the cook who disparages American cuisine. The third is surprised that they do not wear boots and string-ties. The fourth sarcastically mimicks their French accent, etc. Obviously, not all French are open-minded. What will the American students think of French people after these encounters?

The person memory perspective has produced two distinct views to deal with the way people handle inconsistent information: *the schema view* and *the network view*. According to the 'schema' view, memory is essentially biased. Schemata are thought to guide information-processing so that information confirming existing expectations is preferentially encoded and retrieved from memory (Rothbart, Evans & Fulero, 1979; Taylor & Crocker, 1981). The reasons for this are numerous: when people have a strong expectation, they selectively pay attention to information that conforms to their hypothesis, they remember it better because it is easier to assimilate into existing representations, they discount the inconsistencies as mere accidents, they insulate them from other facts as exceptions to the rule, they interpret them so as to realign them with the expectation, or they actively forget what displeases them. Moreover, research indicates that people treat consistent information as if it were part of the original information (Johnson & Raye, 1981; Slusher & Anderson, 1987). People's memory may even be affected when the schema is provided after the original information rather than before (Cohen, 1981; Snyder & Uranowitz, 1978). However, there is some evidence that this influence corresponds more to biased guessing than to actual biased retrieval (Stangor, 1988).

Generally speaking, the impact of the schema is strongest when people have well-developed schemata, process information under cognitively demanding situations, or when the delay between the current retrieval episode and the original intake of the information is long. There are empirical investigations aplenty that provide support for the schema view and that make it the orthodox truth (for reviews, see Markus & Zajonc, 1985; Stephan, 1985). Recently, however, a wave of studies contradicted this established common-sense, and 'network' models of person memory were proposed to account for the better memory of inconsistent information. We will sketch one of these models, known as the *associative network model (ANM)* (Hastie, 1980; Hastie & Kumar, 1979; Srull & Wyer, 1989). According to the ANM, each time the American student debarking in France encounters a piece of information about French people, that information is linked by a path to the central node 'French people'. This information may be consistent with the expectation that the French are open-minded (e.g. their taste for movies is international), inconsistent (e.g. everything one does is tallied to the Parisian standard) or irrelevant (e.g. they eat frogs' legs). Every time an inconsistent item of

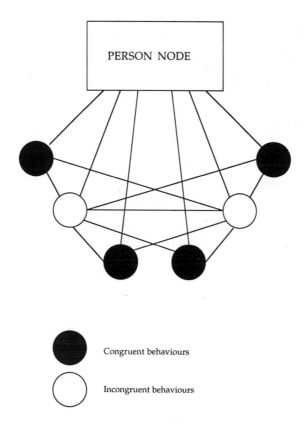

Figure 4.2 *Example of an Associative Network Model*

information is encountered, the student tries to explain its occurrence. To achieve a good state of balance between all pieces of information available about the French, extensive processing is needed to reconcile the inconsistent piece of information with all other inconsistent and consistent items. As a result, inconsistent behaviours are associated with each other as well as with consistent ones. In contrast, consistent items are not linked to one another because there is no difficulty assimilating them into the pool of information. Finally, irrelevant items are linked only to the central node. Therefore, according to the ANM, the between-items associations play a direct role in retrieval of the information (see Figure 4.2.).

The issue of memory for inconsistent information has been at the heart of a huge number of studies, as have relative merits of the schema view and the network view (see Haye, 1989, 1990; Rojahn & Pettigrew, 1992; Stangor & McMillan, 1992). One important aspect of this debate concerns the type of memory measure used by researchers: recall or recognition. Whereas the schema model suggests that information-processing can be measured both ways, the ANM model relies on recall measures.

On the one hand, the schema model makes the very general prediction that people will have a better memory for schema-consistent materials. In addition to this pure memory phenomenon, the schema model also predicts that people's answers tend to be biased by expectancies (Stangor, 1988). On the other hand, several valuable predictions also follow from the ANM model's assumptions concerning the retrieval of the stored information (Srull & Wyer, 1989). First, people are more likely to recall inconsistencies than consistencies because pathways going from or to any given piece of inconsistent information outnumber pathways going from or to any piece of consistent information. Moreover, because irrelevant information is linked only to the node, its recall should be the poorest. A second prediction of interest concerns the pattern of free recall. Assuming that people retrieve materials by following the paths displayed in Figure 4.2, the probability of recalling an incongruent item given that one just recalled a congruent item should be greater than the probability of recalling a congruent item given that one just recalled an incongruent item. A third prediction of the ANM model is that the better memory for inconsistent than for consistent information is helped by the category-size effect. To the extent that the expectation has some basis in reality, inconsistencies are indeed rarer than consistencies. Finally, evaluative inconsistency is more important than descriptive inconsistency (Wyer & Gordon, 1982).

The ANM assumes that people need a substantial amount of cognitive resources in order to encode the inconsistent information and reconcile it with existing consistent materials. As a result, the above-mentioned effects depend upon the extent to which the elaboration of inconsistent information took place. For elaboration, the subject must first acknowledge the inconsistency. It should thus be possible to switch on and off the elaboration work by asking people to form a unified impression of the target person or to simply memorize the information. Indeed, processing goals were shown to have a major impact on people's recall (Hamilton, Katz & Leirer, 1980a, 1980b; Srull, Lichtenstein & Rothbart, 1985).

A second and related issue is that people acknowledge the presence of inconsistency and try to elaborate on it only when it appears reasonable to confront it with other available information. Variability should be less well tolerated for a unique person than for an aggregate of people (Rothbart, Evans & Fulero, 1979; Srull et al., 1985; Wyer & Gordon, 1982). Consequently, more time should be spent examining inconsistent items when a specific individual performs behaviours than when a group of people performs them (Stern, Marrs, Millar & Cole, 1984). In turn, a coherent group of people should behave more consistently than a mere collection of individuals. The same materials may thus lead to better memory for inconsistent items than consistent ones if people think the information concerns a meaningful target (Hastie & Kumar, 1979; Srull, 1981).

Third, despite people's intention to deal with inconsistent information, it may simply be impossible for them to elaborate on it because of a shortage in attentional resources. As a case in point, Stangor and Duan (1991) showed that memory for inconsistent information decreased linearly as the number of tasks people are engaging in increases (Macrae, Hewstone & Griffiths, 1993). In general, superior memory for inconsistent information tends to disappear when people are confronted with more than one target (Stangor & Duan, 1991), with more than one trait per target (Hamilton, Driscoll & Worth, 1989), or when the amount of time available to process the information is reduced (Bargh & Thein, 1985).

Summary

For Asch, information was processed on-line and driven by theory. Anderson, on the other hand, favoured a bottom-up strategy. For him, impression resulted from juxtaposed elements. These conflictual views of impression formation are now outdated. The precedence of theories or schemata over elemental information depends on cognitive and motivational factors present in the situations. In other words, the question is not any longer whether, but when, why and to what extent theories about data or data themselves have the exclusivity and/or priority.

Researchers involved in person memory were convinced that they could solve the same problem by investigating the representations of information in memory. On the basis of an extensive meta-analysis, Stangor and McMillan (1992) conclude that none of the existing memory models, either schematic or network, adequately accounts for all findings. According to these authors, one way of understanding the data is to consider perceivers' motivations as they process the information. Context, they suggest, may lead perceivers to operate under one of two general motivational orientations: a motivation to process carefully and accurately and a motivation to develop or maintain a simple, coherent impression. Whereas in the first case, people are actively involved in processing inconsistent information, in the second case, they are motivated to avoid any inconsistency either by ignoring or by distorting it. Clearly, this distinction between an accuracy mode and an impression-maintenance mode is highly reminiscent of the most recent models of impression formation (Brewer, 1988; Fiske & Neuberg, 1990). Apparently, people are quite flexible in their processing of the information and factors other than memory must be taken into account (Forgas, 1983; Leyens & Fiske, 1994). This distinction also has obvious implications for stereotype research.

Salience as a property of the stimulus

Psychologists have long recognized the importance of salience for stereo-typing. The type-fallacy phenomenon was one of the first explanations advanced to account for stereotypes (Young, 1946). It consists in the following: people who are out of the norm induce particular attention. They represent a challenge to our understanding and we are particularly eager to find an explanation for their peculiarity. The enormous amount of research aimed at establishing a link between physical characteristics and personality provides an example. An abundance of the flesh relative to bone size, or the reverse, the propensity of the ocular globes to jump out of the face or to retreat in it, the amplitude of the forehead, etc. are all salient features that were not difficult to explain 'scientifically' (Gould, 1983). Sex and race are also salient attributes that contribute to stereotyping (Allport, 1954; Campbell, 1958). As we did for the management of inconsistent information, we will sketch the role of salience by examining exemplary research in impression formation and in person memory.

Salience as a 'top of the head' phenomenon

Within the impression formation tradition, Taylor and Fiske (1978) were the first to approach the issue of stereotypes by using salience as a key concept. Remember Tajfel and Wilkes' (1963) pioneering work on accentuation effects presented in the preceding chapter. Taylor, Fiske, Etcoff, and Ruderman (1978) extended this paradigm in order to study the role of social categorization in person perception. Imagine that you observe a group of people as they discuss some topic. One member wears a flamboyant tee-shirt, or has a broken leg, or is the only female, or is the only Black in the group. The solo Black, female, broken-legged, or flamboyantly dressed person are salient. They attract attention and observers readily make special inferences about them without often realizing it.

In one study, Harvard students listened to a discussion between six persons. The discussion had been taped and the faces of the discussants were shown on slides as they spoke. In one condition, all faces were white, in a second, three were white and three black, and finally, in the third condition, only one face was black. As expected, subjects remembered more what the single Black had said probably because they paid more attention to his interventions. Even more interesting is the fact that the students in the solo and three Blacks conditions heard different things. The solo Black spoke more and what he said was of better quality, more persuasive or influential than his counterpart in the three Blacks condition. The evaluative ratings of the single Black were also more extreme but only on items with positive valence.

Taylor et al. also asked their subjects if the different speakers had played a special role during the discussion. The roles that were proposed were: leader, organizer, comedian and deviant. Again as predicted, subjects considered the solo person more fulfilling of a role than the other talkers. In other words, he was identified more by his role than by his individuality. By the way, it is interesting to note the role devoted to Blacks in general and to the solo Black in particular. In this American experiment, Blacks were more often seen as comedians and deviants than Whites. Compared to the three Blacks of the balanced condition, the solo Black was more often assigned the organizational role; it is not as prestigious as group leader, but it is still a silver medal. In a conceptual replication conducted by the same authors, sex rather than race was the distinctive feature. They used the tape and slides technique again. Among the six teachers discussing unionization and children, or simply gossiping, there was either one, three or five males. To increase generalizability of the results, researchers used two different voices for the solo male or female. By a happy accident, one voice sounded much nicer than the other. The results replicated the earlier ones, but the solo status accentuated the direction of the evaluations obtained in the balanced group. In other words, the solo nice voice became even nicer, and the unpleasant one was perceived as even more unpleasant.

In the next extension of this line of research, experimenters varied systematically the number of distinctive category members. Salience was thus manipulated so as to have all possible sex compositions of a six-person group: 6 males, 5/1, 4/2, 3/3, 2/4, 1/5 and 6 females. The procedure was similar to the one above. Male and female subjects were asked, after the discussion, to rate the group as a whole (e.g., 'How well did this group seem to get along?'), to rate each participant on perceived prominence, evaluation dimensions and sex role stereotypes (e.g. sensitive), and to decide whether the participant played any special role in the group. If so, subjects were asked to describe the role in an open-ended format. The sex of the respondents did not make a difference, contrary to the sex of the targets. Interestingly, the importance of the individual characteristics varied inversely with the number of ingroupers. For example, subjects perceived male discussants in general as more confident than females, but the more men there were in the group the less confident they were rated. Contrary to the authors' expectation, however, the stereotyped attributes did not vary as a function of the composition of the subgroups.

The above discussion centred on the impact of increased salience on the impression of a particular target. Taylor et al.'s (1978) paradigm is also ideally suited for studying the impact of social categorization on the way people organize information. The idea is straightforward: if a category influences the encoding or retrieval of information, then perceivers should make fewer between-category than within-category errors. As a matter of fact, Taylor et al. found a higher within-race than between-race error rate. Quite a few studies have replicated this accentuation effect either with race (Hewstone, Hantzi & Johnston, 1991) or with other categories (e.g. Arcuri, 1982; Walker & Antaki, 1986).

All the preceding findings illustrate that the role of salience in impression formation was studied in the footsteps of Tajfel. Still, the work of social cognition researchers greatly contributed in their own right to linking social cognition with studies on stereotyping.

The illusion of correlation

David Hamilton (1979) contributed considerably to a cognitive view of stereotypes. He hypothesized that stereotypes are usually of a correlational nature. A link is claimed between group membership and a given attribute. It is well documented that, in everyday life, people are often quite bad at calculating simple correlations (Nisbett & Ross, 1980; Shweder, 1980). In one such illustration, Chapman and Chapman (1967) found that people overestimated the frequency of some pairs of words presented to them. These overestimated pairs were either unusually long words, or highly associated words (e.g. table–chair). In other words, an illusion of correlation was created on the basis of distinctive or salient stimuli.

Hamilton reasoned that stereotypes may similarly result from a cognitive bias: distinctive features of a distinctive group attract undue attention and induce distorted beliefs about members of social groups. In other words, when people come to know members of a new group, as when they spend their vacation in a new country, they know less members of this new group than of their own group. This makes the new group a minority. People's attention is attracted by rare instances of unusual behaviours. Thus, they tend to overestimate their frequency. Because two waiters of the crowded resort area are rude to them, people decide that all the indigenous people are arrogant.

The experimental test of that hypothesis has become a classic in social psychology. Small groups of four to six New Haven students are told that the study concerns 'how people process and retain information that is presented to them visually' (Hamilton & Gifford, 1976, p. 395). After some expansion on this, the subjects are instructed that they will see a series of slides, each of them showing a sentence about a particular behaviour attributed to a member of either group A or group B. For example: 'John, a member of group A, visited a sick friend in the hospital.' Many more behaviours are performed by members of group A (26) than of group B (13). There are also more positive behaviours than negative ones, but the proportion is equal in the two groups (18/8 and 9/4). The content of the sentences deals with sociability and intelligence. When subjects have gone through all the behaviours linked to membership, one half of the subjects rate the members of groups A and B on a series of attributes related to sociability and intelligence. They then receive a list of the behaviours without indication of the actor's membership. They must remember if it was a member of group A or of group B. The other half of the students must remember membership first, then rate the members on sociability and intelligence. Finally, both groups are told how many behaviours described each of the groups and they have to estimate in both cases the frequency of undesirable behaviours.

As can be seen on Figure 4.3(a), group B is rated more negatively than group A and, conversely, group A is judged more positively than group B. In making attributions of group membership, the most frequent behav-

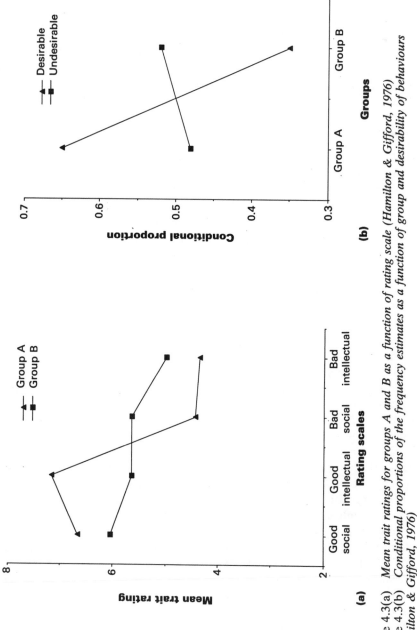

Figure 4.3(a) *Mean trait ratings for groups A and B as a function of rating scale (Hamilton & Gifford, 1976)*
Figure 4.3(b) *Conditional proportions of the frequency estimates as a function of group and desirability of behaviours (Hamilton & Gifford, 1976)*

iours, that is, the positive ones, reflect reality. The minority behaviours, however, are underestimated for group A and overestimated for group B. The results, transformed into conditional probabilities, are represented in Figure 4.3(b) where they are compared to what they should have looked like if all the answers were correct. As you can easily see, there is an illusory correlation between the minority (undesirable) behaviours and the degree of belonging to the minority group B. This is a description of only one of the experiments reported by Hamilton and Gifford (1976). Twenty years later, researchers are still fascinated by the phenomenon. We will devote part of the next chapter to a critical analysis of the relevance of this phenomenon for the study of stereotypes.

Summary

Whether in impression formation or in person memory, research on salient stimuli has pictured most human beings as 'cognitive misers'. For most social cognitivists, heavy reliance on distinctive information is the chief reason for making errors in processing information. This conception has implications for our purpose since many stereotypes are based on distinctive stimuli such as race, sex, language and status. It follows that stereotypes are considered as lazy devices that linger on the surface, rather than at the heart, of the phenomenon.

Spontaneous information-processing

In their classic book *Social Cognition*, Fiske and Taylor (1991) report an anecdote that we like very much. One of their friends was sitting in a mall when he heard shouts. He saw two Black men sprinting up an alley and, behind them, a policeman. Just when the friend realized what was happening, one of the Black men had already gone. However, he had time to tackle the second Black man. This friend, who thought of himself as completely unprejudiced, went through a most embarrassing moment in his life when he realized that the Black man he had immobilized was the owner of the shop that had been burgled just a moment ago. What happened to this friend is that he went along a series of spontaneous, almost automatic, inferences. He drew his conclusions from prior knowledge and built upon the very efficient mechanisms aimed at uncovering meaning from other people's behaviour. What is indeed striking in this automatic processing of information is 'the bedrock trust that people place in the validity of their subjective experience, and especially those forms of information that are the "givens" of conscious experience (i.e. for which people do not feel that much active inferential work was needed or done)' (Bargh, 1989, p. 40).

As in the previous two sections, we give a quick overview of research endeavours in both impression formation and person memory traditions of research, this time concentrating on the issue of automaticity. First, we examine a very interesting line of research launched by James Uleman and his colleagues. These authors tried to show that people are extremely efficient at attributing dispositional meaning to whatever information we collect about a target person. Second, we turn to person memory and look at work on priming. This time, the issue is not so much whether people make inferences upon encountering information but rather how much of their processing is unconsciously affected by prior activation of certain concepts.

Are trait inferences made spontaneously?

Research on impression formation makes extensive use of personality traits. The implicit assumption is that people are extremely skilled at inferring traits. But are people really so quick at making inferences on the basis of observed behaviours? If so, do they preferentially make inferences about the actor of the behaviour or about other aspects of the situation? What kind of attributions do people make? To answer this question, Winter and Uleman (1984) provided subjects with a series of sentences describing a behaviour of a target person (e.g. 'The secretary solves the mystery halfway through the book'). The experimenters instructed the participants that they were to memorize the sentences. A cued-recall task revealed that the sentences were better remembered when the cues were traits linked to the behaviour ('smart') than when cues were semantically related to the actor ('typewriter') or when no cues were given. Therefore, the traits seem to have been generated by the subjects at the time of encoding and stored along with the original information (Tulving & Thomson, 1973). Yet, the explicit request to memorize the materials may not have been sufficient to prevent people from carrying the intention to infer traits. In an attempt to address this important issue, Winter, Uleman and Cunniff (1985) told subjects that the study concerned memory for numbers. The alleged task was to memorize a five-number sequence while reading aloud a distractor sentence. The trick was that the same sentences used in the original study were also used here as distractors. In spite of this manipulation, the trait cues still led to better results than the semantically related cues.

In general, cognitive processes that occur without intention or awareness are called 'automatic' as opposed to 'controlled' processes (Bargh, 1984; Shiffrin, 1988). The evidence presented above suggests that people infer traits automatically. This simple conclusion was soon disputed, however. The first critique concerns the role of intentions. For instance, Bassili and Smith (1986) improved recall performance by asking people to form an impression about the actor rather than to memorize the sentences (see also Uleman & Moskowitz, 1994). It remains to be seen, though, to what extent motivation is a necessary condition for trait inference to take place.

In a second argument against the automaticity of trait inference, critics claimed that automatic processing generally occurs despite existing limitations in cognitive resources. Winter et al. (1985) also addressed this issue in their experiment. They directly varied the cognitive capacity available for inferences by confronting subjects with either easy (single-digit) or difficult (double- or triple-digit) five-number sequences. Whereas digit recall was poorer and more difficult for the difficult sequences, the manipulation of cognitive capacity did not affect the frequency of trait inferences. More recently, however, Uleman, Newman and Winter (1992) showed that the presence of another cognitively demanding task decreases the likelihood of making inferences when confronted with the difficult number sequence. In a related vein, Moskowitz and Uleman (1987) observed a decrease in subjects' performance when they were instructed to pay attention to isolated aspects of the sentences (e.g. the letters). In sum, whereas people readily make trait inferences when they encode new information, a number of results question the automaticity of this process (Newman & Uleman, 1989, 1990). Along with Higgins and Bargh in their superb review of the field, we tend to conclude that

> causal or dispositional inferences are not made in an automatic, uncontrollable fashion. If they were, the particular instructions given to the subjects in the [. . .] studies should not have influenced whether or not a causal inference was encoded with the behavioral stimulus itself. . . . Social judgments are not automatically made during the acquisition of the information but depend on the subjects having the goal of making them [. . .] as well as having sufficient attentional resources available to do so. (1987, p. 378)

Uleman's work on trait inferences showed that attention, intention, consciousness and control are not synonyms (Bargh, 1989). While most authors will agree that an automatic process is 'a fast ($<$ 300 milliseconds), parallel, fairly effortless process that is not limited by short-term memory, is not under direct subject control [. . .] is not itself intended and is difficult to inhibit because it tends to run to completion' (Uleman, 1989, p. 430), this definition does not mean that non-automatic processes are totally controlled, intentional or conscious.

Heuristic as the cued-recall paradigm may be, one still wonders whether spontaneous trait inferences qualify as real dispositional attributions. Are people making person attributions or are they simply labelling behaviours (Claeys, 1990; Newman & Uleman, 1993)? This question has not yet been answered and new paradigms are being developed to uncover the nature of the inferential work people are spontaneously performing when they receive information (Hamilton, 1988; Newman, 1991; Smith & Miller, 1983). Thanks to this line of work, however, we know more about spontaneous inferences. People encode behavioural information about others along with trait information. Impression formation in general and trait inferences in particular thus appears to be one of the most basic activities of person perception. This work also keeps faith with early research on impression formation, which chose to present subjects directly with trait information.

In the previous discussion, we were interested in knowing whether people were inferring traits when confronted with behavioural information. The following section turns to a slightly different question: which factors determine the content of the inferences? More precisely, will previously activated constructs affect the interpretation of newly encountered evidence?

The priming paradigms

For quite some time now, social psychologists have accepted the idea that some concepts have privileged access over others when dealing with new information (for a review, see Bargh, 1984). In the 'New School' approach to perception, Bruner (1957; Bruner, Goodnow & Austin, 1956) was first to suggest the existence of a state of readiness in perceptual processing. For him, perception builds upon the motives, the attitudes and the goals of perceivers. In this sense, people are actively involved in perception. Moreover, perception is explicitly linked to the norms, the social values and the cultural characteristics of perceivers (Tajfel, 1957). In sum, some concepts or categories are more likely than others to play a role in the appraisal of the social world. Whereas many categories are available, some are more accessible than others.

Bruner's thinking led to the idea that some categories may have temporary priority over others. In contrast, Kelly (1955) proposed that people have chronic ways of looking at the world. These 'constructs', as Kelly calls them, help to sort out the useful information in a systematic manner. Whether these categories and concepts are chronically or only temporarily more accessible, person memory researchers have provided much of the knowledge about the mechanisms involved. In contrast to the research reviewed in the previous section, the typical paradigm here takes for granted the inferential work triggered by any given piece of information. What is of central concern, however, is how much of that work may, unknown to perceivers, be influenced by chronically or temporarily accessible concepts.

Higgins, Rholes and Jones (1977) provided the first illustration of the impact of construct accessibility on information-processing. These authors told their subjects that they were involved in a study on colour perception. Surreptitiously, they introduced positive or negative personality traits (e.g. 'adventurous' versus 'reckless'). Subjects then took part in a second, ostensibly unrelated, study on reading comprehension. They were confronted with a series of evaluatively ambiguous behaviours in a vignette and asked to form an impression of the central character. Earlier exposure to the traits influenced subsequent evaluation of trait-relevant information, but not trait-irrelevant information. All memory models more or less build upon the notion that any concept that gets activated becomes more accessible for future use. According to Higgins et al., selected concepts played a role in the interpretation of the vignette because the concepts had momentarily been made more accessible through their use in the first phase of the experiment. In psychological jargon, some traits had been 'primed'.

Srull and Wyer (1979) changed the initial 'priming' paradigm in some interesting and important ways to greatly extend Higgins et al.'s (1977) results. Instead of using traits during the first phase of the experiment, these authors presented their subjects with behavioural information that introduced a different trait dimension: hostility versus kindness. After the priming task, all subjects read a paragraph describing the day of a person named Donald. This paragraph recounts different behaviours which are ambiguous as far as hostility is concerned. For instance, Donald claims his money back from a store clerk immediately after his purchase and he refuses to pay his rent until his apartment is repainted. Participants then have to rate Donald on several scales, some of which deal with hostility. Using more behaviours in the 'priming' part of the experiment, shortening the delay between the priming and impression formation tasks, presenting subjects with scales that are not only evaluatively but also descriptively related to the vignette, and intensifying the ambiguity of the description increased the priming effect. In addition, Srull and Wyer (1980) manipulated the order of presentation of the priming and impression formation tasks. The finding that subjects' ratings were influenced only when the priming task came first supported the idea that priming had its impact at the encoding stage. Interestingly, Srull and Wyer's demonstration of priming effects based on behavioural information agrees with Uleman's contention that people spontaneously infer traits when processing new evidence.

Two arguments led Higgins and his colleagues to assume that priming effects rest upon the automatic activation of contructs and their subsequent role in the interpretation of new information. First, because subjects believe that the priming task and the impression formation task are two distinct experiments, they remain unaware of the link between the particular concepts used in the first task and the vignette presented in the second task. Second, when subjects are asked to recall the particular traits used during the priming task, their performance turns out to be far from perfect, suggesting that activated traits are no longer in conscious memory at the time of judgement. In order to provide a more stringent test of Higgins et al.'s intuitions, Bargh and Pietromonaco (1982) modified the paradigm and eliminated the possibility of consciousness of the trait words by presenting the primes subliminally. Because of the complexity of this classic paradigm, we devote some space to its procedure.

In a first 'vigilance' task, subjects are confronted with a series of flashes displayed on a computer screen and asked to react as quickly as possible by pushing a key. The exact location of the flash on the screen is unknown as it can appear in any of the four quadrants of the screen. The flashes are actually composed of two different elements presented consecutively. A word is displayed during a very short period of time (100 ms) and is then replaced by a mask. Depending on conditions, the proportion of words that are relevant to the critical trait dimension (hostility) is 0 per cent, 20 per cent or 80 per cent. In a second allegedly unrelated task, subjects read a vignette with a series of behaviours ambiguously related to the critical trait dimension and are asked to form an impression of the target person. Subjects then rate the target on a series of scales descriptively or evaluatively relevant to the critical trait dimension. As expected, subjects confronted with specific primes rate the target person accordingly. Importantly, subjects in one control condition were informed that the flashes contained words but remained unable to guess the words when they appeared on the screen. In yet another control condition, a recognition test following each flash failed to reveal any awareness of the prime (Bargh & Pietromonaco, 1982, expt 2). Quite clearly, then, priming effects are found despite the fact that subjects remain completely unaware of their confrontation with the primes.

While the above studies mainly concerned temporary changes in accessibility due to a priming episode, researchers have also turned to the more chronic aspects of construct activation (Kelly, 1955). For example, in order to uncover their subjects' chronically accessible contructs, Higgins, King and Mavin (1982) asked them to list the typical characteristics of two of their male friends, of two of their female friends and, finally, of themselves. A trait was considered to be chronically accessible if subjects used it for themselves and for at least one of their friends or just for three of their friends (see, e.g. Markus, Smith & Moreland, 1985). Subjects were then asked to form an impression of a target person. Experimenters had prepared vignettes that contained moderate behaviours on traits that were accessible for some subjects but not for others. Finally, subjects were asked to recall the original information as precisely as possible and convey their impression of the target immediately after a distracting task and again two weeks later. The immediate as well as the delayed recall and impression data revealed that people disregarded information that was less accessible. These as well as other results provide clear evidence that chronic accessibility plays an important role in person perception (Bargh, Bond, Lombardi & Tota, 1986; Bargh, Lombardi & Higgins, 1988; Stangor, 1988).

In the preceding studies, researchers either prevented people from being aware of the primes (which is essentially what always happens for the chronically accessed constructs) or tried to keep the memory of the primes as poor as possible. One question, then, is the extent to which the awareness of the primes influences the results. (Note that we are excluding here the cases of subjects who suspect a direct link between the primes and the subsequent tasks.) If subjects remain totally unconscious of the priming events, assimilation of the primes appears to be the rule (e.g. Herr, 1986; Lombardi, Higgins & Bargh, 1987). When subjects are conscious of the primes, however, their judgements may reveal contrast effects. This happens when people think that the priming task is completed (Lombardi et al., 1987; Martin, 1986) and when sufficient cognitive resources are available (Martin, Seta & Crelia, 1990). In other words, the production of contrast effects requires two things: people must be aware of the primed constructs and they have to perform additional, cognitively demanding, inferences that involve naïve theories about the judgement (Petty & Wegener, 1993).

Summary

Research in the impression formation tradition only recently investigated the spontaneity of dispositional inferences. Studies on priming, on the other hand, never questioned the evidence of that kind of inferential work but instead examined the conditions under which the activation of concepts influenced the processing of additional information. Besides its practical implications and its methodological ingenuity, this stream of research led to important theoretical developments, namely a clearer understanding of automatic and controlled processes in person perception. This distinction between automaticity and control raises the question concerning whether the expression of stereotypes is unavoidable.

Are stereotypes avoidable?

Although we presented them separately for didactic reasons, inconsistency management, salience and spontaneous inferences are highly connected issues. Few social cognitivists would deny their functional character for information-processing (for a recent illustration, see Macrae, Milne & Bodenhausen, 1994). Still, it is common practice to refer to them in order to illustrate how quickly and how often people fall prey to prejudice. When we spoke of schema-driven processes and of salience as a 'top of the head' phenomenon, one might get the idea that stereotypes continually pop up in people's minds. One has the same impression when looking at research on spontaneous inferences and priming effects. Since it is hard to avoid stereotypes, and if stereotypes are 'automatically' activated, this does not give much hope that people will learn new and unique realities; remember the mishap of Fiske and Taylor's friend.

A series of studies conducted by Devine (1989) makes just that point. Few people dispute the idea that a common stereotype in the US is that Blacks are aggressive. This stereotype is part of cultural knowledge. In an experiment, Devine (1989, expt 1) tested to be sure that both prejudiced and non-prejudiced White American subjects were aware of it. This doesn't mean that everybody endorses the stereotype. When asked to write down all their thoughts about Black Americans, highly prejudiced subjects came up with more derogatory traits than low prejudiced subjects. Although anonymity was guaranteed in this thought-listing task, one can presume that subjects kept some control of what they were writing (Devine, 1989, expt 3). What happens when subjects lose control? To answer this, Devine (1989, expt 2) selected prejudiced and non-prejudiced

White subjects by their responses to the Modern Racism Scale. She then presented all her subjects with one hundred words via a tachistoscope at a speed that prevented recognition of the words. For half the participants, 80 words were related to the social category Black (e.g. nigger, Harlem, jazz, etc.) whereas the other 20 words were unrelated to that category. The proportion was reversed for the other half of the subjects. Finally, subjects formed an impression of a person named Donald – with no indication of ethnicity. The results were straightforward: the number of primes, but not the degree of prejudice, influenced the evaluation of Donald. The more subjects were primed by Black-related words, the more they perceived Donald as aggressive. This was equally true for highly prejudiced and for non-prejudiced subjects.

This series of studies teaches us that people may be involuntary victims of the automatic activation of stereotypes. This happens to the extent that they learn that stereotype – even though they do not endorse it – and to the extent that they are limited in their capacity to inspect the information thoroughly. In order to put the above results into perspective, we would like to examine another study on spontaneous inferences by Gilbert and Hixon (1991). Their experiment was divided into two parts. During the first part, English-speaking Caucasian subjects saw a video of a female experimenter who presented cards with words to complete such as RI-E or S-Y. The experimenter was either Caucasian or Asian. Half the subjects had to complete the task while remembering an eight-digit number. During the second part of the study, the participants heard a tape with a female narrator, ostensibly the – Caucasian or Asian – experimenter, describing a day in her life. Again, half of the subjects were cognitively busy during that task. Thus, some subjects were always, some never, busy, and some others were busy during the first part only or during the second part only. At the end of the experiment, all the subjects had to rate the narrator on a few personality scales. Several of these 11-point scales pertained to attributes usually attributed to Asian persons.

The first series of results concerns the word completion. Several of the selected stimuli words might potentially induce a stereotypically Asian answer, e.g. rice instead of ripe or rise, shy instead of sly or sky. Subjects confronted with the Asian experimenter and who were not cognitively busy provided most stereotypical answers. The second set of results involves the stereotypical responses to the personality scales. As can be seen in Figure 4.4, the subjects who were busy only during the second part stereotyped the most. Only in this condition did a significant difference show up between the judgements made about the Caucasian and Asian experimenters. Actually, most answers ranged near the middle of the scales. The late-busy subjects were the furthest apart from the midpoint.

Gilbert and Hixon interpret their findings as follows: activation of stereotypes is not unconditionally automatic; cognitive busyness can impede it. However, once the stereotype has been activated, its application is facilitated by the lack of cognitive resources. The fact that the never-busy

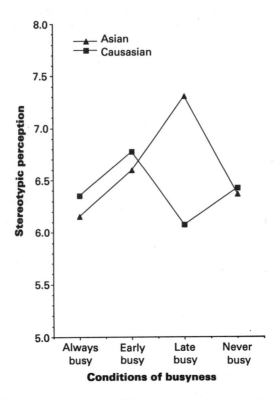

Figure 4.4   *Stereotypic perception of the target as a function of race of the target and condition of busyness (Gilbert & Hixon, 1991)*

subjects did not stereotype at the end may be due to an inhibition or to individuating processing. The authors favour the second solution and present some data that support their preference. How can one reconcile Devine's study and this one? Gilbert and Hixon's explanation bears importance for what we personally conclude about much of the field of person memory in the next chapter. According to them, it is not the same thing to watch a young, female, nice-looking, silent, Asian experimenter, who turns cards, as it is to see the words 'Asian person'. The encounter with the person allows a variety of dimensions to appear ('Dr Gilbert is lucky to have such a gorgeous RA'; 'They seem to have only females in Psychology'); goals of the perceiver enter into play ('Shall I ask her for a date?'; 'She could help me in my Asian culture class'); context effects abound ('Her dark hair matches nicely with the pink cards'; 'This is an easy one: rice, ride, rife, rile, ripe, rive, rite'). Assuredly, it would take a very imaginative person to come up with all these ideas when only reading the words 'Asian person'. If we go back to Fiske and Taylor's anecdote, it is not fatalism that their White friend reacted the way he did. Were the runners wearing numbers on their chests, he could have applauded (or thought: 'Gee, Blacks are definitively better than Whites at racing'). Or if he was finally drained of his daydreams, he might have grumbled about those hectic malls.

More and more work is being done that examines the relative advantages and disadvantages of automatic and controlled processing. For instance, research indicates that highly efficient processing of some pieces of evidence may be a necessary condition for subjects to be able to deal with other important information (Bargh & Thein, 1985). Also, automatic processing does not occur without taking what may be called 'social category applicability' (Banaji, Hardin & Rothman, 1993) into consideration. That is, people match the social categories that are primed and those that are to be judged. In sum, it would simply be wrong to equate automatic processes with the production of invalid knowledge – often stereotypes.

Conclusion

Social cognition brought innovation by abandoning the controversy concerning data versus theories about the data, the confrontation between individuating information and schemata. The quest, in turn, highlighted the factors responsible for the best fit between data and theories about data. This fit is looked upon as the solution to a logical problem, and it is therefore not surprising that the emphasis is on cognitive factors. However, is a logical problem the best metaphor for person perception?

Whether it takes the form of person memory or impression formation, the social cognition approach perceives people as information-processors. Whereas the initial work was characterized by a disregard for the issue of accuracy in person perception, more recent models have focused on what constitutes accurate perception or good memory of oneself and others. Over time, social cognitivists became more interested in biases in person perception and human memory. These biases came to be considered cognitive errors committed because of cognitive limitations of the processors. It follows that researchers in that area are 'naturally' inclined to study the cognitive – and motivational as compensations for cognitive – factors responsible for the emergence or correction of these biases. Indeed, if you believe that you are confronted with a mechanical engine, it wouldn't make any sense to look at the physiology of the engine. What is true of an engine is true of humans.

The presentation of social cognition in this chapter only concerns the reality adequacy level of judgement. There is no question about integrity, culture or theory. Everything functions 'as if' there is a 'good' perception or judgement out there somewhere. This 'as if' condition makes person perception look like an intellectual problem. For this research tradition, stereotypes are certainly not good perceptions, even if they are sometimes inescapable because of limited information-processing. Individuation, or personalization, on the contrary, is the good perception that resists the 'cognitive miser'. We wonder whether this dichotomy between evil and purity is not itself ascribable to cultural rules or some kind of naïve theory. The next chapters will show that the 'cognitive miser' era has expired and that levels of adequacy other than reality are now taken into account. The recognition of these other levels allows a pragmatic, rather than purely intellectual, stance in person perception.

5

Intergroup Phenomena:
A View from the Bridge

We presented the social identity and social cognition approaches in the two previous chapters. At this point, we would like to give a better feel of what these two perspectives tell us about stereotypes and stereotyping and how they complement each other. By doing this, we hope to assess felicitous avenues for investigation, or, more precisely, strategic moves in stereotyping research. Our purpose is not to cheapen one approach and to exalt the other. Instead, we believe that blending parts of each is the best current position.

As an introduction, let us examine the status of salience from the two perspectives. We already saw in the previous chapter that this characteristic is important for social cognition. Salience is obviously linked to distinctiveness, which is one of the main components of stereotypes. The bottom line of socio-cognitivists' argument about the importance of salience is that salient stimuli are excellent for processing information because people are cognitively lazy. Salient, or distinctive, information imposes itself on subjects' attention. Thus, it is easily accessible from memory and is treated with little effort, almost automatically. Stereotypes result from categorizations on the basis of salient features, and they are defects, distortions of reality. To treat one Black person as a Black, because of his or her salience, is an undue generalization caused by laziness or cognitive deficiency. Contrast this view with the following quote from Oakes and Turner:

> The primary function of categorization is not to simplify perceptual input as a rearguard action against limited capacity, but is rather to enrich it through the veridical (selective) representation of real environmental structure in a manner which allows the perceiver to 'go beyond' stimulus information to objects and events with meaning and human relevance. (1990, p. 121)

Remember Taylor et al.'s (1978) study, which we summarized in the preceding chapter. Subjects listened to groups of six members, whose sex composition varied from one female and five males to one male and five females with all the intermediate combinations. The solo position was the one which aroused the most stereotypical answers. According to Oakes and Turner (1986), the task that required subjects to focus on individual characteristics produces these results. Oakes and Turner conducted a replication for which they instructed half of the subjects to attend to the behaviour of a particular male person – the individual orientation – and they instructed the other half to be attentive to all the members of the group – the collective orientation. One half of the subjects heard conversations with one male (or female) versus five females (or males). The other half of subjects received balanced groups composed of three males and three females. In the individual task orientation, the male target was stereotypically described when he was alone or when there was a single woman, that is, in the 1/5 condition when he was either 'most' or 'least' salient. In the collective task orientation, however, the balanced condition – three males versus three females – induced more stereotypes. According to theory, social categorization is most salient in this condition because the ratio between intercategory and intracategory differences is highest. Obviously, subjects in one condition did not err more or less than those in the other condition. They did not err but extracted information relevant for their task or goal within the given context.

As we see it, social cognition focuses on the match between data and theory, between information about an individual and expectations about membership. If the individuating information is not inconsistent and if the group membership is made salient, the theory attracts the data and one male becomes The Male. Social identity proponents set this match into context. They contend that social reality attracts individuating data when data are normatively consistent with the membership at work at any given moment. This membership, in turn, depends on intercategory and intra-category differences (Oakes & Turner, 1990). From this perspective, stereotypes are not erroneous; they reflect reality – a social one. They are used not to simplify the world but to represent it in a meaningful manner.

In the remainder of this chapter, we examine four important intergroup phenomena: outgroup homogeneity, illusory correlations, affect-based judgements and ingroup overexclusion. Whenever appropriate, we contrast views from the social identity and the social cognition approaches.

The outgroup homogeneity effect

When Belgians say that Germans are well dressed and reliable, somewhat law-abiding and serious, not at all lazy or disorganized, it means that they have some kind of representation of Germans as a group. It is likely that they also have different representations for their ingroup – the Belgians – than for outgroups like the Germans. For one thing, people generally perceive outgroups as more homogeneous than ingroups. This is truer for natural groups than for 'artificial' laboratory groups (Mullen & Hu, 1989; Ostrom & Sedikides, 1992). Why would this be so?

Explanations

Cognitive psychologists spent a great deal of time investigating the formation of categories. They came up with several memory models to explain their representations. As we already alluded to in Chapter 4, two of these models especially inspired social cognitivists in their efforts to account for the constitution of groups' representations: the alteration model and the co-existence model.

According to the alteration model, people integrate, on-line, the instances of a group and constantly form an abstract 'idea', or prototype, about that group. Data are accepted within a given category provided that they fit the prototype that guides the perception, that is, the prototype that selects the elements to be attended to and that can erase, for instance, inconsistent attributes. If people function with this model, they should be especially sensible to the central tendency – the mode – of the distribution and less so to its variability. One can imagine, however, that people not only form a single prototype per category but also several sub-prototypes. Besides the 'prototypical' politician, they have politicians as demagogues or as statemen, politicians concerned mainly with status or with power, etc. This variety is itself an indication of variability. It also provides information about covariation between attributes (Anderson & Sedikides, 1991).

According to the co-existence model, people encode only exemplars, and when asked to make a global judgement, they base it on the retrieved exemplars. This computational approach is informative with regard to the central tendency and the dispersion. As for the prototype model, people probably store multiple feature sets, that is, subtypes of the instances (Linville, Salovey & Fisher, 1986). In sharp contrast with the preceding model, however, there is no integration of the information into an abstract form. In other words, people act as if they were bookkeepers: they accumulate the many instances in their mental ledgers.

The controversy ignited by these two conceptions has implications for the explanation of outgroup homogeneity. Not surprisingly, the available research indicates that pure prototypical and exemplar-based models are unrealistic. Park and Hastie (1987), for example, showed that judgements about groups do not differ even when people are led to remember certain relevant traits better than others, that is, when retrieval of some cues is privileged. Moreover, when members of a group expect to compete against another group, they not only recall the outgroup better than the ingroup individuals, but they also form a more homogeneous view of the outgroup than of their ingroup. These different sets of data contradict a radical exemplar-based model and they are only partially supportive of a purely prototypical model. Actually, these results could have been predicted by any soccer or football coach. When you face a competing team, you'd better have a thorough knowledge of this team as a whole and know at the same time all the peculiarities of the individual players.

Judd and Park (1988) also provided evidence that encoding is more important than retrieval in the representation of groups. The retrieval of exemplars does not seem to play much of a role upon subsequent judgements. This suggests that outgroup homogeneity is not due to the number of encountered and remembered exemplars, or at least that this frequency does not have very much of an impact (see also Park and Judd, 1990). Park and Rothbart (1982) offered another interesting and plausible explanation. These authors hypothesized that people memorize different levels of information about the ingroup and the outgroup and that this disparity is responsible for the homogeneity. Specifically, Park and Rothbart were able to show that people remember more subordinate characteristics about an ingrouper than about an outgrouper, whereas they perform equally well for both the superordinate or categorial information. For example, as a Belgian, I may remember incompetent Belgian policemen as Belgian policemen but British hooligans only as British. As interesting as this explanation may be, its significance is seriously limited by the results mentioned in the case of the anticipation of a competition. In this case, recall was generally superior for the outgroup than for the ingroup when competition was introduced.

In conclusion, social cognitivists quite successfully showed an outgroup homogeneity. Still, the memory models fail to explain the phenomenon. A tremendous gap exists between the formation of ad hoc categories when people don't have any prior knowledge about the attributes of these categories and the representations of these social categories which imply pre-existing knowledge.

Social identity theorists adopt a different perspective about the homogeneity effect. First, they do not postulate that outgroup homogeneity exists a priori. Rather they defend the idea that people perceive both ingroups and outgroups as more homogeneous than they actually are because of intergroup categorization. Also, for them a positive social identity does not exist in a social vacuum, but is context-bound. In other words, social identity is linked to social comparison, and this influences which group is considered more homogeneous. To test this, Simon (1992) conducted a series of experiments about the link between a positive social identity and an ingroup homogeneity effect. He reasoned that the outgroup homogeneity effect is generally obtained because people assume that they themselves are part of the majority. If, on the other hand, the ingroup is clearly a minority, its members' self-esteem is threatened and may be restored by ingroup favouritism or ingroup homogeneity. Indeed, for Simon and Brown (1987), perceiving more homogeneity within the ingroup than within the outgroup enhances the perceived 'entitativity' or 'groupness' of the ingroup. Simon and Brown showed that minorities are seen as more homogeneous than majorities, especially ingroup minorities. However, ingroup homogeneity is not restricted to minorities. It also appears for dimensions that define the ingroup. To the extent that I accept the definition of my group as 'spaghetti lovers', I am obliged to assume little variability concerning love for spaghetti. Inversely, if the outgroup is not defined as 'spaghetti lovers', I may well presume that its members show some flexibility concerning love for spaghetti. Still, this demonstration (Simon & Pettigrew, 1990) remains questionable since you could argue that this type of homogeneity simply reflects an acceptance of the group's definition.

The approaches adopted by social cognitivists and by social identity theorists emphasize different aspects of the phenomenon. Social cognition favours information-processing and general memory models. Social identity privileges context-bound motivational factors embodied within cognitive functioning (Lorenzi-Cioldi, 1988, 1993; Monteil, 1991; Simon & Brown, 1987). Also, studies pursued within the social cognition realm are more numerous and their hypotheses are more straightforward.

Outgroup homogeneity and reactions to outliers

If the representation of the ingroup is usually less abstract than the one of the outgroup, then people have probably a more subtle view of the former than of the latter. Linville was especially outspoken in defending the idea that people hold a more complex representation of the ingroup than of the outgroup. She hypothesized that individuals should have more moderate perceptions of outliers who belong to their ingroup than of outliers who belong to the outgroup. In one test of this reasoning, she (1982) first verified that students had a more complex representation of themselves than of elderly people ('in their sixties and seventies'). To other young subjects, Linville presented two vignettes of someone waking up, an elderly person for half the subjects, and a young adult for the other half. One vignette depicted an energetic person in a very positive way, whereas the second one unfavourably described a slow riser. As Linville expected, the judgements for the outgroupers – the elderly persons – were more extreme than for the young targets. One difficulty with these data is that subjects rated the old energetic person significantly more favourably than the young one, but the difference in evaluation was not significant between the old and young zombies (see Figure 5.1(a)). In another series of experiments (Linville & Jones, 1980), the same hypotheses were tested with either a very brilliant or a weak Black or White applicant to a medical school – judges were White students. Exactly the same results were found.

If one follows Linville's reasoning, it means that the French would not have considered their tennis players the best in the world after their 1991 victory in the Davis Cup. This possibility is very hard to imagine. Similarly, in wartime, generals should be more lenient and have more respect for their traitors and defectors than for those of the opposing side. Not only is this not imaginable but Stanley Kubrick could never have shot his fabulous *Paths of Glory*!

Building upon social identity theory, Marques, Yzerbyt and Leyens (1988; Marques & Yzerbyt, 1988; Marques, 1990) defended the idea that reactions to outliers are determined not by cognitive representations of the groups, but by the meanings judges give to the groups. If a positive social identity matters, they hypothesized, those who personify the group at its best should be rated very highly, more so than equivalently brilliant

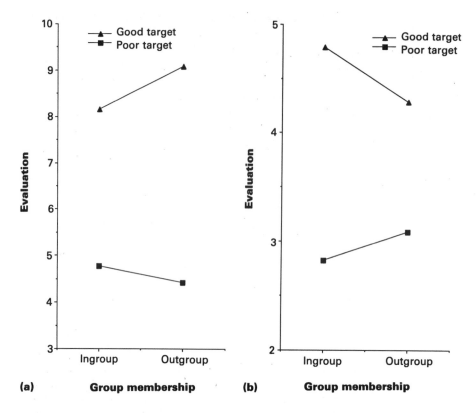

Figure 5.1(a)   *Mean evaluation as a function of group membership and favourability of the person (Linville, 1982)*
Figure 5.1(b)   *Mean evaluation as a function of group membership and skill of the speaker (Marques & Yzerbyt, 1988)*

outgroup members. This hypothesis corresponds to the typical ingroup favouritism phenomenon. On the contrary, those members – the black sheep – who muddy the ingroup should be rejected, a reaction known since early work on deviance. In a series of experiments, Belgian law school students listened to the tape of someone reading a text. The reader was presented as a Law or a Philosophy and Literature student and he performed brilliantly or awkwardly. Depending on the study, one variable was treated as a within-subject and the other as a between-subject. In both cases, the results support the hypotheses (Marques & Yzerbyt, 1988; Figure 5.1(b) reproduces the results of their experiment 1). Interestingly, extreme ratings for ingroup outliers occur only for dimensions relevant to the ingroup (Marques, 1990; Marques et al., 1988).

How can one explain the different results obtained by Linville and Marques? The issue is even more complex because Jussim, Coleman and Lerch (1987) suggested a norm violation hypothesis, which is itself a derivation of Kelley's (1972) augmentation and discounting principles (see also Jackson, Sullivan & Hodge, 1993). These authors indeed found a pattern of results in which ratings conform to those of Linville for the positive outgrouper and to those of Marques and Yzerbyt for the negative ingrouper. First, remember that Linville never found a significant difference for the unfavourable target and therefore her results do not contradict Jussim's. Second, as shown by Marques (1990), the judges' expectations heavily influenced Linville's operationalizations. A brilliant application from a Black to medical school is more unexpected than one from a White. An energetic person is more representative of young people than of older ones. No such differences in expectations are noted for weak applicants or slow risers. It follows then that augmentation factors may be responsible for the data obtained for the positive target in the studies conducted by Jussim and Linville (a hypothesis accepted by Linville & Jones, 1980). These augmenting factors are unlikely to have played a role in Marques and Yzerbyt's studies: Philosophy and Literature students should be as top-notch readers as Law students! We invite you to draw your own conclusions about the French tennis players who won the Davis Cup against the American team.

Thanks to Branscombe, Wann, Noel and Coleman (1993), we now have a way to resolve the debate. These authors recently confirmed Marques et al.'s (1988) intuition that group identification plays a crucial role in the emergence of the black-sheep effect. Branscombe and her colleagues hypothesized that when subjects' social identity is at stake, ingroup extremity will be observed. In contrast, outgroup extremity will emerge when the importance of group membership is low. Students low in identification and students highly identified with their university's basketball team evaluated the author of a sports article. The article described a game between their university (Kansas) and an important rival university (Oklahoma). Information about the author of the article indicated that he supported the Kansas or the Oklahoma team but that he was either loyal or disloyal to his team. Specifically, the loyal author stated his allegiance to his team. In the disloyal condition, the author explained instead that his support very much depended on the success of his team. As can be seen in Figures 5.2(a) and 5.2(b), the data fully confirm Branscombe et al.'s predictions. When identification is high, Marques and Yzerbyt's ingroup extremity effect emerges. In particular, the disloyal ingroup author is evaluated more negatively than a disloyal outgroup author. This finding replicates the black-sheep effect. When identification is low, in contrast, results are in line with Linville's outgroup extremity effect.

Summary

Social cognition sparked numerous innovative studies and raised fascinating questions. However, focusing almost exclusively on information-processing and its presumed representations may have been misleading. In our eyes, this strategy puts the horse before the cart. Instead of explaining

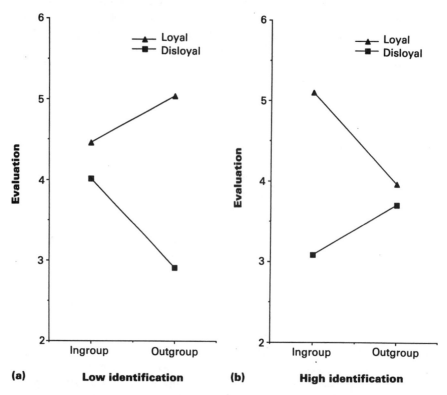

Figures 5.2(a) and (b)　*Mean evaluation as a function of group identification, group membership and loyalty of the author (Branscombe, Wann, Noel & Coleman, 1993)*

homogeneity effects by informational representations, it could be more profitable to search for the factors that lead to particular representations and homogeneity effects, and only then look at the nature of the link between the two. Research inspired by the social identity perspective has also been very heuristic, but it has been less systematic in deriving and testing hypotheses. For this approach, homogeneity effects are not immediate products of informational representations but primarily products of a search for positivity. We believe that, at this time in social psychology, the functions of the phenomena override their plausible representations. We will pursue this line of reasoning in the next section, which is devoted to illusory correlations.

Illusory correlations

In Chapter 4, we summarized the original experiment about illusory correlation to illustrate one approach of social cognition. Remember that subjects overestimate the number of minority behaviours in a minority group and that this overestimation affects the judgement about the minority group. This classic phenomenon has been the subject of many studies (for a review see Hamilton & Sherman, 1989). Precisely because researchers see stereotypes as 'undue' correlations between group membership and specific attributes, they regard the illusory correlation paradigm as an important contribution to the understanding of the development of stereotypes. Here, however, we question this assumption and defend the idea that this paradigm, fascinating as it is, has little in common with the formation of stereotypes. In other words, it is only metaphorically that the illusory correlation paradigm resembles the formation of stereotypes.

Biased encoding due to distinctiveness

The basic phenomenon involves overestimating the number of infrequent behaviours – undesirable behaviours, for instance – performed by a minority. This overestimation is called an illusory correlation because it occurs even though the ratio of infrequent to frequent behaviours within the minority is equivalent to the ratio within the majority. In fact, there is no correlation between type of behaviour and status of the group. Three types of measure are traditionally used to establish the illusory correlation. First, subjects are asked to estimate the frequency of different kinds of behaviours within the majority and the minority. Second, they evaluate the majority and the minority on a series of dimensions. Third, they are given a cued recall test and are asked to remember the group to which each behaviour has been associated.

Illusory correlation supposedly depends on the distinctiveness of the infrequent behaviours within the minority. Because these behaviours are distinctive, or salient, they should attract attention and their encoding should take time. Given this special treatment, the infrequent minority behaviours should be more easily accessible at retrieval. Therefore, their frequency is overestimated and the minority group as a whole is connotated by positive or negative valence of these behaviours. However, a series of new empirical studies raise doubts about the validity of illusory correlation for understanding stereotyping. Some studies question the dependent measures (Haye & Lauvergeon, 1991; McGarty, Haslam, Turner & Oakes, 1993). What Hamilton and his colleagues taught their readers is that 1/2 appears greater than 5/10. In other words, in spite of the fact that the authors of this book know many more Belgians than Portuguese who are not ecologically oriented, they will nevertheless decide that Portuguese, and not Belgians, are non-ecologists because ecology orientation is an infrequent behaviour in both populations and that, in toto, they know less Portuguese than Belgians. To be frank, we are very doubtful that this is the reason of our stereotype about ecology among Portuguese. We also think that French are chauvinists, not because it is an infrequent characteristic among the few French that we know, but because most French we know are chauvinists. (Did you draw the right conclusions about the Davis Cup in the previous section?)

In two recent papers, Smith (1991) and Fiedler (1991b) question the thesis that the bias in the illusory correlation paradigm occurs at encoding rather than at retrieval. Smith conducted a computer simulation of Hamilton's experiments on the basis of Hintzman's exemplar model. This model assumes that every instance that is encountered is encoded and stored, but that the instance may not be retrieved due to being forgotten. By simulating the same dependent variables (evaluation and cued recall) to which human subjects usually respond, Smith's model came close to the classic results and was sensible to variations of the experimental design (i.e. attenuation of the illusion in the presence of a third group: Sherman, Hamilton & Roskos-Ewoldsen, 1989). As Smith argues, the bottom line of this simulation is that illusory correlation may be explained by the numerical difference in the frequent and infrequent behaviours between the two groups. That is, $(Af - Ai) - (Bf - Bi)$, where A stands for the majority and B for the minority, f for frequent and i for infrequent. In other words, assuming that the number of frequent behaviours is constant in the two groups, the illusion will be stronger the less the number of unusual behaviours. If I know only one Portuguese who is rude, I will tend to overestimate the rudeness of Portuguese more than if rudeness is as common as friendliness among Portuguese. On purely intuitive grounds, it is hard to believe that this reasoning explains the formation of stereotypes.

In a brilliant paper, Fiedler (1991b) suggested that illusory correlation is due to a loss of information rather than to the distinctiveness of the infrequent stimuli. He reasons as follows. Given the considerable information subjects are confronted with in the illusory correlation paradigm, it is reasonable to expect that some information gets lost and that the correlation between the exact proportions of behaviours is less than perfect. This leads to regression, that is, to estimates less extreme than the exact proportions. It is easier, however, to detect a difference between positive and negative behaviours in the majority group than in the minority one. As a result, the judgements are more regressive in the latter than in the former group. Regression thus explains that the infrequent behaviours are overestimated in the minority. Regression is even more marked if one assumes that a primacy effect occurs during the presentation of the material. Indeed, the first few observations probably allow the subjects to detect the valence (positive or negative) of the majority group, whereas the valence of the minority may go unnoticed. Similarly, lack of confidence at the time of judgement may lead subjects to adopt a central tendency strategy. Given that the lack of confidence should be more pronounced for small numbers of observation and that, also, the infrequent behaviours of the minority are the furthest away from the centre of the distribution, regression towards the mean may explain illusory correlation. For instance, if on a judgement scale with anchors 0 and 26, $Af = 18$, $Bf = 9$, $Ai = 8$, and $Bi = 4$, it is Bi which is most eccentric and most likely to regress. Two experiments are traditionally evoked to argue that illusory correlation is due to biased encoding. In the first study (Hamilton, Dugan & Trolier, 1985, expt 1), no illusory correlation was obtained when subjects were presented with a summary table of the behaviours instead of a sequential presentation of all items. In the other, unpublished, investigation (Regan & Crawley, 1984), no overestimation of the infrequent behaviours of the minority was noticed when subjects were acquainted only with the behaviours of the minority (and not with those of the majority). Fiedler (1991b) easily accounts for these results. Since the subjects' task is greatly simplified in those two experiments, it is simpler for them to detect the frequent from the infrequent behaviours.

Both Smith's and Fiedler's articles are too rich for us to detail here. Both authors note that their demonstrations do not preclude the influence of biased encoding due to distinctiveness, but this influence is not necessary. Moreover, Fiedler criticizes the operationalization of distinctiveness in the illusory correlation paradigm. Why, he asks, is infrequency more distinctive than frequency? Whichever option you adopt, it is as arbitrary as claiming that men are more distinctive than females. The notion of distinctiveness will take on paramount importance when we consider motivational variables.

The impact of motivation

Although Tajfel was responsible for the cognitive shift in stereotyping research, he was also a very vocal opponent of a social psychology operating in a social vacuum. For him, group membership meant there were values that had to be taken into account. From that perspective, it is interesting to see what happens to illusory correlation when subjects are involved in the groups they have to recall and rate. For example, Spears, van der Pligt and Eiser (1985, 1986) have looked at self-relevance within the illusory correlation paradigm. They presented their subjects with anti- or pro-nuclear power views of a big town and of a small town. While these two towns clearly favoured one side of the controversy in the 1985 study, they were evenly split in their opinions in the 1986 investigation. In the two studies, participants overestimated the importance of their own anti- or pro-nuclear views in the smaller town. That is to say, that no illusion appeared in the 1985 experiment when the small town favoured rather than opposed the side espoused by the subjects. In contrast, Schaller and Maass (1989, expt 1) did not find any illusion when their subjects affiliated to one of the groups, even when such illusion would have led subjects to give a favourable image of themselves.

The interest in illusory correlation for stereotyping stems from the fact that one usually knows less people of the outgroup than of the ingroup, and that positive behaviours are more frequent than negative ones. The paradigm could then explain unfavourable stereotypes towards the minority. Such a picture of stereotyping assumes that people negatively value the outgroup. Unfortunately, the two sets of results summarized above do not shed much light upon the problem of values. Schaller and Maass (1989) suggest that more complex processes are at work when subjects are members of one of the groups and that these processes are differently tapped by the typical measures (estimation of frequencies, cued recall and evaluation). It is unclear, however, how more knowledge can be gathered through the usual paradigm. Spears et al.'s results have generally been interpreted as evidence for distinctiveness. Self-relevant attitudes would be particularly distinctive, and therefore it would not be surprising if they were overestimated when infrequently held by the minority group. We agree with Fiedler that

> interpreting attitude congruence as extra distinctiveness and incongruence as a reduction of distinctiveness (Hamilton & Sherman, 1989) is a less than convincing account. It would be equally plausible to argue for enhanced distinctiveness of inconsistent information (cf. Wyer & Gordon, 1984). (1991b, p. 29)

Individuals versus groups

Sanbonmatsu and his colleagues (Sanbonmatsu, Shavitt, Sherman & Roskos-Ewoldsen, 1987; Sanbonmatsu, Sherman & Hamilton, 1987) found that, when individuals rather than groups are concerned, distinctive targets are associated with the frequent behaviours, not the infrequent ones. Interestingly, these authors suggest that people usually anticipate more coherence from an individual than from a group. Given what precedes, a logical derivation would be that an incoherent target should be particularly distinctive. This target should thus be easy to recall and his or her infrequent behaviours should be overestimated later on. Sanbonmatsu and his colleagues, however, entertain a different hypothesis. They imply that the judges form an on-line impression of the individuals. This on-line processing of information leads to a discounting of inconsistent evidence and to a confirmatory distortion of ambiguous behaviours. As a result, the frequent – consistent – behaviours are overestimated. This on-line process is supposedly more prevalent when the individual target is made salient by calling attention to him or her, for instance.

Pryor (1986) and Schaller and Maass (1989, expt 2) tried to induce on-line impressions by explicitly asking their subjects to form an impression of groups. This time, no illusion materialized in the estimates of behaviour frequency or in the evaluations of the groups. There was simply no difference between the majority and the minority groups! Whether on-line processing is or is not at work in the prior four sets of studies, identical results are not obtained. It is interesting to pause somewhat and to examine the practical implications of memory-based and on-line judgements. Indeed, the typical illusory correlation paradigm displays an overestimation of the 'distinctive' features of the minority only when subjects are encouraged to memorize the material, or, at least, when they are not explicitly induced to form an impression. What they access in memory should tint their subsequent evaluation. However, knowing what people retrieve from their memory is interesting for understanding what people think only to the extent that there is a relationship between the two. Does such a relationship exist?

On-line versus memory-based processing

In a review of the different theoretical positions on the relationship between memory and judgement, Hastie and Park (1986) present five theories that differ on the type of link and on the type of memory at work. The oldest is known as the 'two memories' position, as it was coined by Anderson and Hubert (1963) when they discovered a primacy effect for judgement and a recency effect for recall of person information. They concluded that 'the impression memory is distinct from the verbal memory' (p. 391). Thus, according to this position, memory and judgement are independent. The 'incongruity-biased encoding' theory is the latest one (Hastie, Park & Weber, 1984; Srull & Wyer, 1989). It assumes that judgements influence recall in such a way that there is a negative correlation between the two. More precisely, the judgement is made at encoding. Any subsequent inconsistent information receives extra attention and is therefore better remembered. For the 'biased-encoding model', the judgement made at encoding filters the subsequent input. Here, there is a positive relationship between the judgement and the memory that depends on it. According to the 'biased-retrieval model' (e.g. Snyder & Uranowitz, 1978), the judgement determines a biased search of the information that has been accumulated. The relationship between judgement and memory is thus also positive. The last model, the 'availability' model (Tversky & Kahneman, 1973), supposes that memory directly influences judgement, which has not been formed on-line but is formed on the basis of easily accessible memory. Smith simulated one version of this model with great success.

The traditional explanation of illusory correlation uses a mixture of different memory models. Whereas the 'incongruity-biased encoding' model is invoked for the minority group, one could think that the 'biased-encoding' model is responsible for the majority group. On the other hand, some researchers claim that judgements are not made on-line but are purely memory-based. That is, they would follow the 'availability' model. (It is noteworthy that, with the exception of Smith, no efforts have been made to systematically link the illusory correlation paradigm with memory models.) Hastie and Park (1986) found that the correlation between memory and judgement is high and positive only in the case of memory-based judgements. In the more frequent cases, when the judgement is made on-line, the correlations are weak and thus provide general support for the independence or 'two memories' model. In other words, memory capacities and structures are often poor predictors of impression judgements.

The most important aspect of Hastie and Park's research (1986), in our eyes, is the extreme difficulty in creating conditions that lead only to memory-based judgements (see also Sherman, Zehner, Johnson & Hirt, 1983). There are two lessons to be drawn from this difficulty. First, the terribly complex and volatile person memory models proposed to account for person perception may not be very useful. What would you think of a football-coach who communicates his tactical moves to his players by drawing elaborate scientific designs rather than crude, but efficient, sketches? Second, the illusory correlation paradigm may not be as pertinent for understanding the development of stereotypes as researchers first thought. It is certainly a captivating approach for deciphering errors of covariation, but its reliance on memory misses the fact that most person perception is done on-line, embedded in expectations and values.

Summary

The illusory correlation paradigm is a special case of inconsistency management in the sense that it concentrates on infrequent behaviours performed by minority group members. Its approach was not, however, tied to memory models such as the associative network. Nevertheless, many researchers assumed the illusion was due to biased encoding and differential accessibility, that is, to memory processes. We conclude that, as person memory models may not have much to say about person perception, the contribution of the illusory correlation paradigm to the understanding of stereotyping may not be as crucial as first hoped.

First, the paradigm does not apply when on-line impressions are spurred. It is hard to believe that, in real life, we restrict our impressions to individuals and not to members of groups. Second, when you stereotype, you are always part of an existing group about which you have vigorous impressions. It is unclear how the traditional paradigm can deflect this difficulty. Third, when you arrive for the first time in a foreign country, you probably do not only think in terms of this new country and your own group. Images of other countries probably cross your mind. Thus, by providing anchors and interfering with 'distinctiveness', third groups may seriously attenuate any illusory correlations. Fourth, stereotyping is not a neutral activity, but the typical paradigm is ill-prepared to take values into account.

Of course, all the preceding comments do not mean that values, expectations, impressions, in-group favouritism, etc. cannot be incorporated into an experiment on illusions of correlations (Hamilton & Rose, 1980; McArthur & Friedman, 1980). The most dramatic illustration of this possibility remains, in our eyes, the mesmerizing series of studies by the Chapmans (1967, 1969) on popular diagnoses. These authors repeatedly showed that people were unable to detect correlations – or their absence – when these covariations did not coincide with their own beliefs about correlations in a given domain. For instance, the Chapmans' subjects 'saw' a positive correlation between the intelligence and the size of the head even though the evidence rested upon a completely negative correlation. What the Chapmans' as well as Hamilton and Rose's studies tell us is that it is much more likely that stereotypes provoke illusions of correlations than the reverse.

Affect and cognition

When confronted with members of stereotyped groups, people often feel uncomfortable, anxious, irritated or even disgusted. Indeed, few researchers would deny that stereotypes comprise an important emotional component of social perception. As we saw in Chapter 1, prejudice plays a major role in many theories of stereotypes. Not surprisingly, the measurement of stereotypes and intergroup attitudes similarly stresses evaluative aspects. However, the traditional perspective emphasized only the global and negative emotional experience called prejudice. Things have changed dramatically in recent years. Quite a few social cognitive models now take affect into account (for reviews, see Fiedler & Forgas, 1988; Fiske & Pavelchak, 1986; Forgas & Moylan, 1991; Higgins & Sorrentino, 1990; Schwarz, 1990; Sorrentino & Higgins, 1986). The renewed interest in the motivational aspects of social information-processing allows us to reconsider the impact of affect in the maintenance or change of stereotypes (Hamilton, Stroessner & Mackie, 1993).

Affective foundations of cognition

We can summarize current views on affect and stereotyping by saying that affect – including both mood and emotion – plays two distinct roles in the construction of social judgement (Forgas, 1992). First, affect leads people to use either simplified, heuristic processing or more substantive processing. Theorists put forth a similar distinction between a top-down and a bottom-up strategy in person perception (Brewer, 1988; Fiske & Neuberg, 1990) and in persuasion (Chaiken, 1980, 1987; Petty & Cacioppo, 1981, 1986). As far as affect is concerned, it appears that positive mood is concomitant with cognitive and motivation deficits (but see Hamilton et al., 1993). As a result, perceivers tend to rely on suboptimal processing strategies. Second, the impact of affect at the more extreme automatic and at the more extreme controlled end of the continuum is different. Whereas irrelevant affect may directly impact on judgements when people adopt a simplified processing style, type of affect plays a more important role when people adopt careful, analytic processing strategies.

Heuristic versus systematic processing

As we will examine in greater detail in Chapter 6, recent thinking about impression formation suggests the existence of a continuum of processing strategies ranging from simple heuristics, where categorial information dominates, to effortful consideration of individuating information (Brewer, 1988; Fiske & Neuberg, 1990). The lack of cognitive resources and/or motivation increases people's reliance on simplified processing. Stereotypic responses are typical examples of strategies based on heuristic processing. Within this perspective, Bodenhausen (1993) argued that some but not all types of emotional responses may diminish the motivation as well as the capacity of perceivers. Specifically, happiness often leads to impaired judgements: people only examine relevant information superficially. In contrast, sadness facilitates systematic thinking. Bodenhausen and Kramer (1990b) directly assessed the impact of happiness and sadness on stereotyping. After subjects' mood had been manipulated, they were confronted with one of two ambiguous cases of alleged student misconduct, either a case of cheating or a physical attack on a fellow student. For each case, subjects read that the offender was or was not identified as a member of a group stereotypically related to the offence (a student athlete for the cheating and a Hispanic for the attack) and made a series of judgements including an evaluation of guilt. Whereas sad mood or the control neutral mood subjects did not differentiate between the stereotyped and non-stereotyped student, happy subjects rated the stereotyped student significantly more guilty (see also Bodenhausen & Kramer, 1990a). More generally, Bodenhausen (1993) suggested that extremes of arousal lead to a greater reliance on stereotypic judgements. As a case in point, Bodenhausen and Kramer (1990b) found that angry subjects displayed the same pattern of results as the happy subjects. In the same vein, Kim and Baron (1988) demonstrated that aroused subjects were more likely than non-aroused subjects to show a stereotypic pattern of responses in the illusory correlation paradigm. Finally, Bodenhausen (1990) used the time-of-day variations of mental efficiency to establish that people rely more on stereotypes at lower portions of their circadian cycle. As a set, these studies illustrate the role of arousal and affect in the adoption of a particular type of processing strategy.

These findings are clearly related to current research efforts showing that mood may constitute a useful indicator of the level at which information must be processed. Schwarz (1990) suggests that positive affective states may inform individuals that their environment is currently a safe place. As a result, there is little need to apply careful or effortful processing strategies. In contrast, negative mood states may inform the individual that something is amiss in the environment. This leads to heightened information-processing. Isen (1984, 1987) challenges Schwarz's cognitive-motivational explanation of mood effects on information-processing. According to Isen, positive mood subjects are motivated to maintain their positive state and thus avoid difficult and extensive thinking about an issue, while negative mood people are motivated to distract themselves from the negative state by engaging in systematic processing. The relative merit of each explanation is not yet known but it is clear that affective states have an impact on problem-solving, judgements and attitude change. In an illustrative study on persuasion, Bless, Bohner, Schwarz and Strack (1990) provided evidence that negative mood people are more sensitive to the quality of argumentation in a persuasive communication. In other words, cheerful people are more compliant with persuasive messages (for similar findings, see Mackie & Worth, 1989, 1991).

Affect-priming versus affect-as-information approaches

In one of the earliest attempts to combine affect and person memory models, Bower (1981) suggested that affect may be directly linked to other cognitions within an associative network and that 'activation of an emotion node also spreads activation throughout the memory structures to which it is connected' (p. 135). According to this affect-priming model, affect is expected to help the mood-congruent interpretation of ambiguous information, facilitate the learning of mood-congruent materials, and improve the recall of mood-consistent information or materials encountered in a matching mood (Bower, 1991; Isen, 1987). The initial ambition of the associative network model of affect was to account for all above-mentioned phenomena (but see Blaney, 1986). It now appears that the predictions of the model may well be restricted to those situations in which perceivers engage in substantial processing of the relevant information (Clark & Isen, 1982; for a review, see Singer & Salovey, 1988).

In a remarkable essay, Norbert Schwarz (1990) argued that affective states may serve informative functions. People may form evaluative judgements on the basis of their feelings (Strack, 1992). The trick of the matter is that individuals may rely on affect that hardly corresponds to their reactions to the object of judgement. In a well-known illustration of this phenomenon, Schwarz and Clore (1983) found that respondents reported being more satisfied with their life when they were interviewed on sunny rather than rainy days. In order to check the status of the transient affective states, the interviewers pretended to call from out of town and asked some of the respondents about the local weather. Subjects who were questioned about the bad weather reported being as happy and satisfied as subjects called on sunny days. This finding reveals the impact of the misattribution of the irrelevant affective state on people's answers. It also contradicts an explanation of the initial difference between the two groups that was framed in terms of selective mood-congruent recall of life events. According to Schwarz, these results indicate that 'the information provided by one's feelings is only used in making evaluative judgments if it is relevant to the judgment at hand, and if its informational value is not discredited' (1990, p. 542). Because it constitutes an efficient low-cost strategy, people may consult their feelings when confronted with a lack or with an overabundance of relevant information. It is worth noting that, consistent with the work on the processual impact of mood states, only bad weather subjects appear to have searched for relevant explanations of their affective state. The mention of the weather had no impact on subjects questioned during the good weather (Schwarz, 1990). This finding again stresses the dual role of affect (Schwarz & Bless, 1991; Schwarz & Clore, 1988). In the next section, we turn to models that integrate these two aspects within a single framework.

On stage twice

Fiedler (1990, 1991a) proposed a dual-force model that nicely combines the possible impact of affect at the processing level and at the substantial level. According to this author, bad mood leads people to stick to the facts and to provide judgements that are logically constrained; they are realistic information-processors. In contrast, positive mood people tend to engage in active transformation, revision or elaboration of information; they typically go beyond the information given. People in a negative mood are thus less prone to constructive biases than people in a good mood. As a result, Fiedler argues, mood influences will be more likely to play a role in productive tasks than in reproductive tasks.

In a suggestive illustration, Fiedler, Asbeck and Nickel (1991) presented their subjects with an ambivalent description of a target named David. After subjects had read the vignette, they first saw an affectively pleasant or unpleasant film. They then rated the applicability of 17 adjective attributes, 12 of which were all extremely negative or all extremely positive. Finally, Fiedler et al. asked their subjects to evaluate the extent to which David would engage in each of 16 behaviours, 8 of which related to the negative and 8 of which related to the positive adjectives presented in the earlier questionnaire. Because negative adjectives have been shown to trigger more constructive effects (Reeder & Brewer, 1979; Reeder, Messick & Van Avermaet, 1977; see also Yzerbyt & Leyens, 1991), positive mood but not negative mood subjects were expected to rate the negative but not the positive behaviours as more applicable. They did. This finding suggests not only that mood can influence judgement, but also that affect combines with the nature of the information encountered. This is particularly important with regard to the perpetuation of stereotypic beliefs.

On the basis of an ambitious research programme, Forgas (1992) presented a multi-process view of affect integrating the selection of a processing strategy on the one hand and the influence of the content on the other. First, a direct-access strategy assumes that pre-existing judgements are available and that the target is sufficiently familiar to the subject. In that case, affect may have little if no influence on social judgement. Second, people may adopt a heuristic processing mode when cognitive resources are scarce or motivation is low. Presumably, positive affective states are more likely to lead perceivers to adopt simplified processing strategies. Third, when people are confronted with novel and otherwise atypical information and both motivation and cognitive capacity are present, people will use a systematic mode of processing. Finally, Forgas contemplates the added possibility for a motivated processing strategy. This means that a particular judgemental outcome is preferred. Negative feelings and high personal relevance are most likely to induce such a processing strategy. In sum, the mood state of perceiver, among other things, influences the selection of a particular processing strategy. In turn, the processing strategy constrains the impact of the affective state on social judgement.

Summary

Recent years have witnessed a blossoming of models integrating affect in information-processing and showing that 'hot' and 'cold' cognitions blend together. These efforts must still be coordinated but, given the frequency with which they surface, this will probably be the task of the coming years. Most of these models come from so-called social cognitivists and not from social identity theorists (but see Hogg, 1992; Smith, 1993). This observation is somewhat surprising since social identity insisted from its inception on motivational factors that were, at that time, neglected by social cognition. These two fields are bridging.

The ingroup overexclusion

On 18 May 1302, as the sun rose over Bruges, all visitors in the city were asked to repeat the words 'Schild en Vriend' (the Flemish words for shield and friend). If they didn't use the proper accent, they were supposed to be French spies and were met with a 'goedendag', an impressive weapon which forced you to bow a 'good morning' for the last time in your life. The question is: how many Flemish died during the 'Matins of Bruges' because their pronunciation was inappropriate?

One of the major contributions of social cognition is certainly its concern for the relations between the features of stimuli and the processes they spark. According to social cognitivists, if people are information-processors, what they process should undoubtedly impact upon how they process. For SIT, another element has to be added. How people process information is not only influenced by which information they process, but also by what they process information for. In other words, the goals or values behind the processing are also of utmost importance. For SIT, this nuance is unquestionably consequential. We illustrate this triple interest – what, how, for what – by examining a phenomenon that we coin the '*ingroup overexclusion*'. By this expression, we refer to the caution with which people are judged to be members of the same group as the judges. Actually, this is an old problem in social psychology.

Responding to the stories of Jews who were caught or denounced during the Second World War, several social psychologists asked themselves whether Jewish faces were more accurately recognizable than non-Jewish faces, and whether antisemitic persons were better at this task than non-prejudiced people. The answer to the first question is moderately positive, but it is the second question which is of interest. The typical paradigm for researching this question is as follows. US university students are selected on the basis of their feelings about Jews, and they have to classify pictures of faces as being Jewish or non-Jewish. The pictures are taken at random from yearbooks after ascertaining the ethnicity of the persons in the photos. Half of them are Jews. There were of course differences in the setting of the various studies as well as in the procedure used to calculate accuracy. These differences are, however, less interesting than the convergence in the results. The majority of the experiments indicated that, indeed, Jewish faces were better recognized by antisemitic judges than by others (Allport & Kramer, 1946; Dorfman, Keeve & Saslow, 1971; Himmelfarb, 1966, expt 1; Lindzey & Rogolsky, 1950; Pulos & Spilka, 1961; Quanty, Keats & Harkins, 1975, expts 1 and 2; for a null difference between the two groups, see Carter, 1948; Elliott & Wittenberg, 1955; Himmelfarb, 1966; Scodel & Austrin, 1956; Secord & Saumer, 1960). Another finding appeared in almost all the studies: antisemitic persons classified more people as Jews than did non-prejudiced judges. At the time, this result was essentially considered an obstacle for the precise explanation of the accuracy data.

Is the potentially greater accuracy of the antisemitic subjects due to a vigilance against Jews, to an increased alertness for threatening outgroup members? If so, it means that antisemitic judges are particularly attentive to the slightest clue of Jewishness. Or is the greater accuracy simply an artifact consisting of setting a low criterion of acceptance for Jews? This explanation is suggested by the different distributions of pictures into categories by the prejudiced and non-prejudiced individuals. Researchers, thus, focused their attention on the fact that antisemites either were particularly expert at detecting Jewishness, or were particularly prone to put an ambiguous face in the Jewish category. However, the same observation could mean that the antisemitic judges were reluctant to accept an ambiguous face in their ingroup. In other words, because their social identity is put at stake by the possibility of a misidentification of the outgroup as an ingroup member, people may need a lot of information before taking the risk to say: 'Yes, this is one of us.' Compared to the post-Second World War explanation, this one stresses the ingroup rather than the outgroup (see the idea of sentry matrix in Bruner, Goodnow & Austin, 1956; Tajfel, 1969; see also the optimal distinctiveness theory in Brewer, 1991).

To test this explanation, Leyens and Yzerbyt (1992) took advantage of the long history of conflict in Belgium between two linguistic groups: the French-speaking Walloons and the Dutch-speaking Flemish. The subjects, French-speaking students from Louvain-la-Neuve, were given diagnostic personality traits one at a time of either a French-speaking person or a

Dutch-speaking person. For each linguistic group, these pretested traits were equally negative or positive, with the negative traits being as polarized as the positive ones. Participants had to decide whether or not a given target was a member of the ingroup.

The results strongly supported the hypotheses. First, more errors occurred classifying ingroup than outgroup members. Second, subjects showed an ingroup bias in that they more frequently rejected the 'bad' outgroup member, that is, the target with the negative Flemish personality traits, and they more often accepted the 'good' ingroup member, the Walloon with positive traits. Third, in order to make their decision, subjects requested less information about the negative outgrouper. This may all appear trivial. What is more interesting and clearly in line with the hypothesis is that subjects needed the most information about a positive member of the ingroup. In other words, and somewhat paradoxically, the participants to the experiment were most cautious when encountering a friendly person with the appropriate characteristics – or stereotypes – for the Walloon ingroup. Figure 5.3(a) shows the weight of each individual piece of information. It is worth noting that the results cannot be explained by the differential complexity of the stereotypes for the ingroup and the outgroup (Linville, Fisher & Salovey, 1989). People did not need more positively consistent information about their ingroup because this information was more complex or less redundant than in the outgroup. Indeed, it was verified that the different sets of stereotypical traits were equally complex in terms of the latent dimensions.

Now the question arises: is this effect simply due to the characteristics of the information? For instance, the items of information were stereotypical of Walloons and of Flemish. Given the question asked to French-speaking subjects ('Is the target a Walloon?'), the information for the 'good ingroup member' was thus positive and confirming, whereas this information was negative and disconfirming for the 'bad outgroup member'. Further, would we obtain the same results if we required our Walloon subjects to decide whether the targets were Flemish (rather than Walloon)? We believe we would, but the criticism is not altogether convincing because someone could argue that the subjects process the question as if they were asked to decide about ingroup membership. Indeed, in the given context, not to be Flemish is to be Walloon. This question is important because negative information carries more weight than positive information (e.g. Peeters & Czapinski, 1990), and because disconfirming information is more compelling than confirming information when decisions are important or when specific goals are aroused (Lewicka, 1988). Thus, Leyens and Yzerbyt's (1992) results could be explained simply by looking at the characteristics of the stimuli (see Yzerbyt & Leyens, 1991).

Actually, we believe that the effect is not due to the features of the stimulus information per se. The features interact with the context, the targets and the judges in this case. As we saw in the section on outgroup homogeneity, an excellent Belgian is superior in the eyes of a Belgian to an

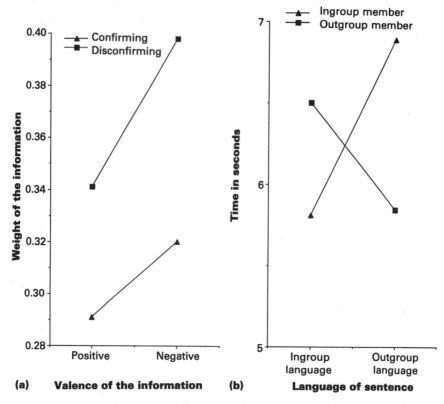

Figure 5.3(a) *Weight of the information as a function of valence and confirmatory status of the information (Leyens & Yzerbyt, 1992)*
Figure 5.3(b) *Reaction time as a function of language of the sentence and group membership of the target (Yzerbyt, Leyens & Bellour, 1994)*

excellent Swiss, or Swede, or whatever. In the same manner, what is very consistent for you may be less so for me, not because we are different as individuals, but because we belong to two categories whose goals diverge. To examine this question, we performed a laboratory experiment similar to the linguistic anecdote reported at the beginning of this section (Yzerbyt, Leyens & Bellour, 1994). The material was not 'Schild en Vriend' but it came close to that. The judges were Flemish or Walloon students who heard easy and difficult, French and Dutch, sentences that were enunciated by Walloon or Flemish targets. Half of these judges had to say whether the target was Flemish and the other half whether the target was Walloon. Besides the judgement, time of decision was also recorded. Here is a summary of the results.

As anticipated, the phrasing of the question did not make much of a difference. In the Belgian context, to be a Walloon is not to be Flemish and vice versa. For the type of judgement, the linguistic origin of the sentences did not make a difference when the target was an outgroup member. It did matter, however, when the sentences were pronounced by an ingroup member. The Walloon judges, for instance, made more mistakes for Dutch than French sentences when sentences were read by Walloon targets. Obviously, this effect was more pronounced for the short sentences, which were more difficult for the listeners. In view of these findings, the strategy used in Bruges by the Flemish against the spies of the Duke of Burgundy may have been the most efficient and least dangerous one for the Flemish people. The time taken for the decision is a conceptual equivalent to the amount of information needed in Leyens and Yzerbyt's study (see Figure 5.3(b)). The time was shorter when the sentence was read in the speaker's mother-tongue but, more importantly and as expected, it was longest when the speaker was an ingroup member who read a sentence in the outgroup language. These results indicate that ingroup overexclusion is not limited to the positive and confirming information. How information is processed does not depend solely on what is processed. It also depends on the stakes of the judgement. The lesson from the present research with respect to the earlier studies on recognition of Jewish faces is that antisemitic judges in the American studies were probably less concerned with Jews than with 'not clear-cut' Americans. The danger for the ingroup does not arise from those who are clearly outgroupers but from those who may threaten it from within.

From a pragmatic point of view – think of the 'Matins of Bruges' – the ingroup overexclusion phenomenon is very interesting. It illustrates that people make judgements in ways that protect their social identity, that respect their social integrity. The more danger there is for social integrity, the more pronounced ingroup overexclusion should be. It is, therefore, not surprising that extremist (political, religious or delinquent) groups are often very selective in their admissions and force their potential adherents to go through rigorous initiations. To be accepted in an extreme right-wing party in Belgium, for instance, candidates had to prove that their great-parents were of White European origin. Would our German friends accept the idea that the current political doctrine requiring 'German blood' in order to easily obtain the German nationality reflects the same phenomenon? The 'black-sheep' effect that we summarized in a previous section also illustrates a strategy for identity maintenance and integrity protection.

Here is another study that, in our opinion, can easily be interpreted along the lines of the ingroup overexclusion effect. Pettigrew, Allport and Barnett (1958) worked in South Africa with five samples of subjects: Afrikaners, English-speaking Europeans, Coloured people (Mulattoes), Indians and (Black) Africans. They exposed each subject to a two-second stereoscopic presentation of two racial photographs, with all possible combinations. Subjects had to identify the race of the person they saw. We will restrict our summary to the data obtained from the Whites and Indians. These persons are less prone to consider social mobility in terms of their race, and, therefore, their misidentifications in the judgements of races are less susceptible to be due to social mobility strategies. When shown two European faces, 100 per cent of Afrikaners and 93 per cent of English-speaking Whites see a European. When presented with two Indian faces, 87.5 per cent of Indians see an Indian. Also, Whites and Indians are equally accurate for other races. The results are quite different when the faces are racially mixed. In these cases, 40 per cent of Afrikaners and 37 per cent of English-speaking Whites see a European while 63 per cent of Indians see someone of their race. In other words, members of the White minority less easily see someone of their race than do the Indians when the stimuli are ambiguous. This is not the case when the stimuli are clearly recognizable. If we consider only the mixture of European-Indian faces, the percentages of recognition of subject's race are 54, 46 and 74 for the Afrikaners, the English-speaking Whites and the Indians, respectively.

Americans from Mexican, Cuban and Puerto Rican origins are minorities whose social identity is often threatened in the United States. One should therefore expect a more pronounced ingroup overexclusion among these Americans than among Anglo-Americans. This observation is exactly what Huddy and Virtanen (1993) found. Cubans, Mexicans and Puerto Ricans were more likely than Anglos to rate members of their own subgroup as different from other subgroups of Latinos. Even more striking, each subgroup of Latinos regarded the generic term 'Hispanic' as more applicable to members of its own than other subgroups. This exclusion of other Latino subgroups was correlated to ingroup bias and did not seem to be mediated by familiarity with the different subgroups. This finding again indicates that motivation, and not merely cognition, is important for the processing of information.

Summary

People do not approach social objects as they do so-called non-social objects (Rothbart & Taylor, 1992). The causes and reasons why I interact with exotic people are much more varied than those why I lie on a beach in the Seychelles. I may value the island as well as the indigenous people, but only the latter can value, or devalue, me, see me as a tourist to be exploited or as a potential friend. When processing information about people, I take into account rules, values, beliefs and functions. In this section, we provided evidence that what a person processes interacts with the reasons or goals of processing. When people process information about ingroup members, they do it differently than when they process information about outgroup members. The type of information is only partly responsible for this state of affairs. The relevance of the information for the ingroup is most important. In everyday life, people often confound information features and relevance. That people seem particularly cautious when processing information about ingroup membership suggests that they are very sensitive to the integrity of their group. To the extent that a chain is as strong as its weakest link, this strategy is very efficient for the ingroup. If there is, however, an antagonism with a given outgroup, the efficiency for the ingroup will be equal to the nuisance for the outgroup.

Conclusions

Building upon the presentations of social identity work and social cognition, this chapter has critically reviewed selected intergroup phenomena. We started with salience as an underlying theme and examined outgroup homogeneity, illusory correlation, affect and ingroup overexclusion. For each phenomenon, we adopted a view that bridged the social cognition and the social identity perspectives on the problems and interpretations of the data. We hope we were convincing in reflecting the complementarity between both perspectives and interpretations.

What are the lessons of this review for the different levels of adequacy? Assuredly, social cognition is more faithful to the level of reality than is social identity. For many social cognitivists, people rely too heavily upon salient stimuli and therefore are not good at detecting covariations. People also blend unknown individuals into the same mould because of memory deficiencies. In sum, people do not respect the intricacies of reality. For social identity, on the other hand, there is no single reality. There are realities that change with the context of judgement and the interplay of values. These realities impose upon people certain perceptions, such as the homogeneity of what is grouped together. These perceptions are inherent to people's cognitive functioning and should thus not be regarded as errors or misjudgements. Whereas both approaches have much to say about the reality level, they are silent about the cultural level, at least for the phenomena examined in this chapter. This chapter has portrayed people who had cognitive and mnesic capacities, albeit not necessarily as much as one could wish. They also had values and affects, but they behaved as if they were not social actors or agents with specific roles. On the contrary, their roles were interchangeable except for the fact that, sometimes, they belonged to one group rather than to another.

The social part of the integrity level was illustrated by the ingroup overexclusion, and, to a lesser extent, by the 'black-sheep' effect. People are driven to make desirable conclusions about their ingroup and they process information accordingly. This caution about the ingroup also reveals pragmatic concerns. Information features do not exist in a vacuum. They are part of social actions and they are processed not merely to achieve an intellectually satisfying judgement, but mostly to allow people to interact efficiently. Finally, the theory level will be more present in subsequent chapters. The only time the theory level was alluded to was when we referred to the Chapmans' studies on illusory correlations. Contrary to classical studies on stereotypes and illusory correlations, these studies showed that the illusions were actually due to the theories – the stereotypes? – held by subjects.

6

Confirmation of Categorial Information

Imagine that you attend a party, and that you spend your evening going from one group to another because you are a very sociable person. Later on, a close friend asks you about your impression of the party. Besides a summary of the drinks and the food, you'll probably tell her about the different guests. For instance, you may remember that there was a very bright and friendly European, an Italian who smoked a lot and whose jokes were very funny, partly because of his accent. His wife, on the contrary seemed conceited and wore expensive jewels. You may go on and tell her about the characteristics of the new dean of student affairs, of a car designer, etc. Another possible strategy is to blab about the yuppies (the car designer, the Italian jewellery, etc.), the intellectuals (a dean, a writer, etc.), the gluttons, etc. In fact, when you describe the party, you organize the information around the people who were present. Either you depict the most salient persons one after the other, or you assort them into different subgroups according to their social roles. Assuredly, there are other possible criteria: those who wore something blue, those who ate salmon rather than steak tartare, those who were born east of Massachusetts, etc.

People do not necessarily organize their information around persons (Pryor, Simpson, Mitchell, Ostrom & Lydon, 1982). It is easy to imagine that a fashion designer, a cook or a bigot could use another mental map than a psychologist. Ostrom, Pryor and Simpson (1981), however, have shown that people have a predilection for functioning as psychologists, for taking people as the core of the information. If people live in a world where their naïve theories centre on the notion of personality, it is hardly surprising that people, and their personalities, serve as organizing principles. Remember Asch's studies on impression formation that we presented in Chapter 4. His work illustrates that people can easily integrate different pieces of information, form a category and activate a schema (Asch & Zukier, 1984). This is what the fictitious party-goer did when he recounted the meeting with the arrogant woman concealed behind her expensive but not especially elegant jewels.

What happens when a category (e.g. the yuppies, the politicians) is given, or when several features are integrated and that additional information is provided? What happens when an impression is about to be reached but people are still looking for more information? In this chapter, we review how psychologists solved this problem raised by Asch and Anderson by outlining models that account for the integration of categorial and individuating information. All these models have in common the assumption that categories attract attributes, that expectations invite data. Cognitive resources and motivational palliatives traditionally provided safeguards against this unidirectional scheme. Besides these important factors, we propose to add the goals of the perceivers that contribute to the personal and social integrity of these perceivers. We also examine the status of hypothesis confirmation and suggest that useful information is not to be confused with diagnostic information. Finally, since person perception is a social action, it must take place within a given culture with specific rules about when a target is deemed judgeable. These rules partially determine whether perceivers feel entitled to judge.

Implications of the categorization process

Categories serve several important purposes. When receiving information about a person, people's most natural tendency is to slot this person into one of their categorial pigeon-holes: 'He's a businessman', 'She's a typical woman'. There are many reasons for this first reaction, which are supported by empirical evidence. In our view, the most important one is that categorization gives meaning to the world. If I want to convey a precise impression about a man, it doesn't make much sense to tell the audience that he doesn't read much, is always busy, and wouldn't buy a pig in a poke. Does this mean that he is a hectic person, stupidly suspicious? Or that he is more clever than bright? Or that he is a self-made man? Maybe he is a good politician? All these questions are answered when the information is encapsulated under the label: 'businessman'. The same demonstration applies to the stereotype of the typical woman. (We will let readers try their hand at this by themselves.) Categorization thus gives meaning to the environment and facilitates communication between individuals sharing the same system of categories.

Obviously, categorization also simplifies things. The name of the category summarizes all the features contained in that category. Categorization also helps to integrate new information with older information. Once people have a certain number of categories for classifying animals, for instance, a view of an unknown creature will not revolutionize their perception of the world. Giving meaning to things, making known the unfamiliar, relating things together, simplifying the array of surrounding stimuli, should all have an effect upon behaviour. It should make the environment more predictable. Often, psychologists especially emphasize the simplifying function of categorization. The preceding list should make it clear, however, that it is only one of many functions and probably not the most important. 'Categorizing is not only a way of managing a vast amount of data, it is also a manner of extrapolating from a little information' (Leyens, 1983, p. 35).

The match between data and theories about data

Categories activate schematic knowledge. In other words, they are expectations that are resistant to change. People use inferences to fill gaps within the structure. They interpret ambiguous information to fit the schema. Moreover, people initiate behaviours that result in the confirmation of the schema. Likewise, inconsistent evidence is reconciled, distorted or ignored. There are times, however, when clashes occur between the evidence, what we call data, and the schemata, what we call theories about data. If people are completely bonded to their schemata, either they cannot interact anymore or they live in a status quo world. One knows, though, that people are capable of validly interacting in a changing world. What do they do then with their schemata? General models have been proposed to account for the global process of person perception. The key commonality of these models is their stress on people's ability to perform well when having to make a judgement. In other words, people are capable of questioning the validity of early commitments.

In reaction to more local models aimed at explaining particular content problems, Kruglanski formulated a general model of lay epistemology (Kruglanski, 1989; Kruglanski & Ajzen, 1983). His ambition is to propose a model that spans all knowledge processes. This does not mean that contents are no longer relevant. Kruglanski himself warns that people must pay attention to contents in order not to confuse them with processes, but this does not imply that specific processes need to account for particular contents. According to Kruglanski's model, when a person says that Europeans are cultivated or that chickadees are birds, that person goes through two stages: the generation of a hypothesis and its validation. These two stages alternate until they come to a freeze: the hypothesis is accepted and expressed. Hypothesis generation depends on two general factors, capacity and motivation, and the validation process follows the rules of deductive logic. In other words, a hypothesis comes first and is then put to test by means of an 'if–then' argument. Up to now, Kruglanski has not provided details about this latter part of the model, the validation process. His empirical efforts mainly concern the illustration of motivational variables. Kruglanski distinguishes three types of needs (the names vary depending on the publications): the need for non-specific structure (sometimes called the need for closure), the fear of invalidity (which Kruglanski & Klar, 1987, presented as deriving from a more general need for ambiguity), and the need for specific structures (sometimes called the need for specific conclusions).

Brewer (1988) proposed another model of impression formation. Her dual-process model basically distinguishes automatic processing of non-relevant stimuli from conscious processing of relevant stimuli. Moreover, motivation determines the amount of processing the perceiver will engage in. Brewer singled out four different stages. First, in the identification stage, the perceiver decides that a stimulus is indeed present in the environment. If the stimulus is deemed relevant, the perceiver enters a different – more conscious – mode of processing. In this respect, physically perceptible and culturally meaningful dimensions are used so frequently that they are processed automatically in the initial identification of any target person (Brewer et al., 1981; Brewer & Lui, 1989). At this level, the perceiver checks for self-involvement. If not motivated, the perceiver enters the categorization stage by searching for an appropriate category. In some cases, an insufficient match between the category and the stimulus forces the perceiver to go to the individuation stage. One way of individuating is to differentiate the members of a category into subtypes (Weber & Crocker, 1983). Whenever the stimulus is self-involving, personalization takes place. Clearly, this stage involves the explicit processing of data-driven information.

Fiske and Neuberg's (1990; see also Dépret & Fiske, 1993) continuum of impression formation is another model that focuses directly on stereotypes. Fiske postulates that the first reaction to new information about someone is an initial categorization. This stage is followed by an assessment of the relevance of this new information. If there is no relevance, the process freezes, to use Kruglanski's terminology. If, however, the information appears relevant or interesting, then the perceiver pays more attention to this new information. People also focus attention towards additional information and examine the match between the initial categorization and the incoming data. If the match is fair enough, the perceiver confirms the initial categorization. If not, he or she moves on to recategorization: 'maybe he's not a businessman but a used-car dealer'; 'She's definitively not a typical woman but she reminds me of my mother'; or 'She's me when I was her age.' These three examples correspond to three kinds of re-categorization according to Fiske. Corrections to the initial categorization can be brought about by invoking a subtyping of the general category (used-car dealer), a particular exemplar (my mother) and often a significant other (Andersen et al., 1990) that lowers even more the level of abstractness of the category, or a self-schema. Of course, people may also access a completely new category.

> Note that the recategorization process is neither purely category-based nor entirely devoid of the initial category influence. That is, the initial categorization surely affects the selection of a new category, exemplar or self-reference. But this process is also attribute-oriented to the extent that the new category is determined largely by the particular attributes of the target. (Fiske & Neuberg, 1990, p. 7)

If, recategorization fails because no particular category is directly available, and if motivation and cognitive resources are sufficient, then unfreezing occurs and the subject integrates individuating information. That is, the subject considers all the information as attributes to be pieced together. This examination may or may not reactivate a category – it is a continuum model – and the process ends when the match is judged satisfactory or when motivation and cognitive capabilities are depleted.

Important features differentiate Brewer's and Fiske's models. Some are essentially technical, concerning the processes involved. For instance, while Fiske proposes that both motivational involvement and ease of categorization, depending on information match, are decision rules that apply at each stage, Brewer's model posits different rules of inference following each stage. Another difference concerns the consequences of involvement. For Brewer, self-involvement causes the processing to be person-based and data-driven. This implies that motivated perceivers disregard stereotypes. As Fiske (1988) points out, this seems unrealistic. Probably because they are very involved, many South Africans (or Walloons or Bosnians, etc.) do use stereotypes to explain others' behaviours. The role devoted to attentional processes also differs, as it is more central in Fiske's perspective. Other differences concern theoretical distinctions. Brewer argues that 'the majority of the time, perception of social objects does not differ from nonsocial perception in either structure or process' (1988, p. 4). In contrast, Fiske states that 'people are not things' and establishes a fundamental distinction between the two domains of perception. She argues, for example, that the perception of social objects implicates the self because the target is more similar to the perceiver than any object could be (for this debate, see Fiske & Taylor, 1991).

Despite these distinctions, the two models share important similarities. First, Fiske's and Brewer's models propose that perceivers can form impressions both in stereotypic, category-oriented ways and in individuated, attribute-oriented ways. People use both schemata and data. In other words, both approaches integrate a holistic configural model with an algebraic, elemental model of impression formation. Moreover, as Fiske (1988) indicates, both models assume that the more category-oriented processes dominate the more attribute-oriented processes. Finally, certain kinds of information, such as social roles, professions, biographical information, etc., are prone to be used to organize the categories. It is possible then, as a consequence, to draw a line between 'strong' and 'weak' categories.

This last question leads us to consider the nature of the distinction between category and attributes. 'The feature that a perceiver uses to organize and understand the remaining features defines the category label; the other features are defined [. . .] as attributes' (Fiske & Neuberg, 1990, p. 9). Of course, some features will be privileged: race, religion, sex, nationality, profession. It is only a privilege, though, not an obligation or a necessity. According to Schul and Burnstein's analysis, it is quite realistic to expect the subject to reconsider, at each stage of the inference process, the category–attribute hierarchy: 'At any given point, the observer may choose to consider particular attributes of the object. One or more of these attributes become a category, a salient identity of the object, while the remaining become subattributes of that identity or are dropped from working memory' (1988, p. 148). Imagine that you hear about an American who is sophisticated, knows geography and wears stylish clothes.

If you have a negative category for Americans but are not completely stubborn, your category may be shaky and you may be tempted to judge that American as a person rather than as a member of a group. Assume further that you are additionally informed that this person has one of the most famous voices in the world and holds an honorary degree from the Université de Louvain. You may now classify her – Barbara Hendricks – as a star. In consequence, it is quite reasonable that an output judgement may be more 'categorial' at the end of the process than at some point along the process. In other words, it is possible that a first individualized judgement becomes increasingly categorized or stereotypic.

In sum, according to the available models, theories about data attract data. Schematic knowledge dominates and stereotypes are privileged. The power of categorial information will be weakened provided that several conditions are fulfilled. First, the data cannot be moulded into the current categories. Second, people have sufficient cognitive resources to process the information. Third, people are motivated enough to find a match between data and their theories about data. Although the second condition is not considered in all the models, it is presupposed by the first condition; before catalysing their motivational energies, perceivers must first notice that the data rebel against a theory. In the next section, we concentrate on the influence of motivational factors upon the match between data and theories about data. Although the notion of motivation encompasses a large variety of goals, we mainly discuss it as a substitute for cognitive resources.

The accuracy goal

Given that there is no one-to-one correspondence in person perception between a social object and a category, and given that the structure of a category is somewhat arbitrary (i.e. it is not a reflection of objective reality), there can't be one absolute true perception. In their daily life, however, people have to function as if there was a true or correct perception, thus they spend energy in trying to be accurate. We define accuracy here as the correspondence between a judgement and a commonly agreed upon criterion that is supposed to represent objective reality (Funder, 1987; Kenny & Albright, 1987; Kruglanski, 1990). Specific goals or situations may prompt the need for accuracy. Indeed, impression formation does not occur in a social vacuum. For instance, superiors, experts or loved ones may stimulate persons not only to give a judgement but also to deliver one that is as correct as possible. A person's profession could require that he or she be accurate and consequences may be costly if they are not. The following sections summarize relevant research about these motivational variables (Fiske, 1992, 1993; Hilton & Darley, 1991; Stangor & McMillan, 1992).

Need for closure and fear of invalidity

According to Kruglanski, if an individual has the capacity to generate a hypothesis, the amount of time and effort spent in this activity depends on the *need for closure*. To put it another way: does one really have to express a hypothesis? Imagine a father takes a walk with his young daughter. She chatters all the time and her babbling is sprinkled with questions. Sometimes the father does not answer the questions because he knows they are not real questions but part of the babble. Other times, he shrugs his shoulders because he feels unable to answer or because he simply doesn't want to drain himself. Suddenly, his daughter points to a creature on a stump and asks: 'Dad, what kind of animal is that?' He may simply respond: 'It's a bird' because he didn't look carefully at what she was pointing at, or because he is not particularly knowledgeable about birds but wants to give her the impression he knows everything by responding quickly, or because he does not want to encumber her vocabulary by teaching her too many new words. 'I know very well it's a bird, but what kind of bird?', his daughter insists. Shall he reply 'A great tit' or 'It's a kind of tit'? He'll probably respond with the first thing that comes to mind. What's important is that he gives an answer – he has a need for closure.

There is a second need according to Kruglanski. It relates to the tolerance for ambiguity and often takes the form of a *fear of invalidity*. If he were sensitive to such a need, the father would tell his daughter that 'It's a kind of tit, but let me look more carefully to see whether it is a great tit or a blue tit . . . Ah, it's undoubtedly a great tit; I've seen the black cap.' There are many reasons why he may comply with this need. He may want to appear scholarly, he does not want to tell lies to his daughter, or he might love birds and would not want to mislabel two birds as different as a blue tit and a great tit. Whereas the need for closure tends to freeze the epistemic process, the fear of invalidity tends to unfreeze it. As we said earlier, Kruglanski conceives of these needs and their freezing/unfreezing consequences as part of any epistemic search. That means that these needs will apply to primacy effects as well as to stereotypical judgements. The following study conducted by Kruglanski and Freund (1983) illustrates the two needs at work.

Subjects had to predict the future success of a person as president of a company on the basis of his past performances. For half the subjects, the information concerning the past jobs of the candidate started with successful performances and ended up with less positive information. The other subjects first learned about the candidate's inattentiveness to subordinates, inefficiency, disorganization and lack of persuasiveness, and then they heard about behaviours that implied courtesy, leadership, sensitivity, interest in the employees' welfare, etc. Need for closure was operationalized by manipulations of time pressure, and fear of invalidity by induction of evaluation apprehension. In one condition, subjects were told that their prediction, to be revealed and explained to other subjects, was a measure of their own ability to judge people, and that they would have an unlimited time to complete their task. In a second condition, subjects were also made apprehensive about being evaluated and were further warned that they would only have at their disposal three minutes to make a decision. The third quarter of subjects was instructed that the selection method being tested was in a pilot stage, that its validity was yet unknown, and that their predictions would not be publicly compared. Also, their time was unlimited. Finally, the remaining subjects were not made apprehensive but time pressure was applied. The dependent variable was the primacy effect (see Figure 6.1). As expected, the two main effects for time pressure and for evaluation apprehension were significant. Subjects under high time pressure evidenced a greater primacy effect than those under a low time pressure. Moreover, subjects who thought they would be publicly evaluated were less influenced by the items of information presented early than were the other subjects. Figure 6.1 also shows an interaction that qualifies the main effects; actually, when subjects have no need for closure but they do have fear of invalidity, the primacy effect is least pronounced. In other words, freezing the epistemic process occurs latest for these subjects.

In another study using the same independent variables, stereotyping was the dependent variable. Freezing of the epistemic process, Kruglanski and Freund (1983) reasoned, could lead people to judge an individual in terms of his or her ethnic identity rather than in terms of specific information. This is exactly what occurred. In the experiment, Tel Aviv students had to judge a dissertation. Those who were under pressure to give an answer but had no fear of evaluation were especially likely to take into account the ethnic origin of the writer and to rate the dissertation on this basis.

Accountability

Accountability refers to persons' needs to justify their judgements to some other people. It is another variable that motivates people to process information in an especially complex way. With this factor in mind, Tetlock (1983a) questioned the classical definition of the social perceiver as a 'cognitive miser'. Indeed, this metaphor highlights important facts but also obscures other equally consequential phenomena. For instance, there is the possibility that people use different processing rules when the stakes are high as opposed to low. 'The appropriate question may not be "What kind of machine is the human information processor?" but, rather, "What kinds of machines do people become when confronted with particular types of tasks in particular types of decision environments?"' (Tetlock & Kim, 1987, p. 707).

Because Tetlock thinks too little attention is devoted to the communicative functions of social cognition (see Hilton, 1990, for a related view), he investigates the impact of accountability on judgemental processes. Accountability demands put subjects in a self-critical mental set in which

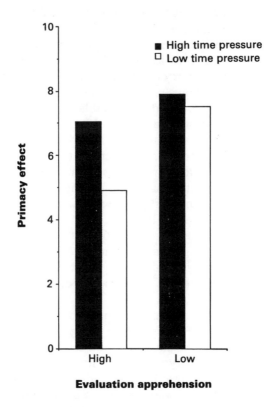

Figure 6.1   *Estimated likelihood of success as a function of time
pressure and evaluation apprehension (Kruglanski & Freund, 1983)*

they actively try to anticipate the objections or counter-arguments that
might be raised against their positions. If people anticipate having to justify
their positions or judgements, they should pay close attention to the
available evidence, they should avoid judgements based on insufficient
information, and they should try to integrate inconsistent data. Tetlock
(1983a) calls this tendency 'preemptive self-criticism'. Thus, Tetlock
hypothesizes that accountability leads to a reduction of diverse judgemental biases by the mediation of an increased complexity of thought. A series
of empirical studies indicates that accountability does have a de-biasing
effect. For instance, Tetlock (1983b, 1985) showed that accountability both
improved the recall of evidence and eliminated primacy effects in a legal
decision-making task. In another study, Tetlock (1983a) illustrated that
subjects who were expected to justify policy positions to an audience with
unknown views were much more likely to think about those policy issues in
integratively complex ways than were unaccountable subjects.
    More in line with our present concerns, Tetlock and Kim (1987)
investigated the impact of accountability on how people process infor-

mation in a personality-prediction task. Their subjects read the actual responses of three persons to the first 16 items of a personality inventory. They then wrote a personality sketch of each person and predicted their responses to another set of 16 items. Subjects also rated their confidence in their own judgements. In the no-accountability condition, subjects were assured before reading the target's responses that their impressions would stay completely confidential. In two accountability conditions, subjects learned that they would be interviewed by a researcher interested in exploring the types of information that people use to form impressions of others. Some of the subjects received this accountability instruction before reading the responses while the other subjects received the same instruction only after reading the targets' responses and after expressing their impressions. As expected, pre-exposure accountability led subjects to form more complex impressions of the targets, to make more accurate predictions concerning the next 16 responses and to report more appropriate confidence ratings about their predictions. These effects did not occur among post-exposure accountability subjects. This pattern of results indicates that accountability is effective in de-biasing social judgement and that the increased complexity of thought may explain this effect. It is here that cognition and motivation converge in Tetlock's perspective.

Accuracy goal or self-presentational strategies?

Clearly, fear of invalidity coupled with a need for closure, as well as demands for accountability, correspond to the goal of accuracy. However, was Kruglanski really testing some kind of accuracy goal rather than self-presentational strategies? As a matter of fact, in the experiments that we summarized, the only unfrozen subjects were those who were apprehensive about evaluation and had enough time to make their decision. Could these subjects have thought that it is bad to judge someone on first impressions or to favour members of a prestigious group? Kruglanski and Freund (1983, expt 3) provide one answer to this alternative interpretation. In a new experiment, they obtained the same pattern of results as before, with the same independent variables, in two probability tasks where self-presentation was of no relevance for the subjects.

The same interpretation of the effect of accountability in terms of impression management also fails to explain the difference between pre-exposure and post-exposure subjects in Tetlock and Kim's (1987) experiment. If impression management mediates the impact of accountability, the same results should obtain among post-exposure subjects. However, accountability has an impact only on the initial impression formation process, presumably because of the cognitive processes underlying the judgemental biases. Subjects who are warned that they will be held accountable have an opportunity to control their analysis of the social information; such self-consciousness should disrupt automatic processing. Conversely, subjects who are told about accountability after the information-processing only have access to the products of an automatic process. So, they cannot correct the inferences that they already drew. Nisbett and Wilson (1977) already established that people have access to the products of their cognitive processes, but not to the processes themselves.

Interdependence and outcome-dependency

In the context of her continuum model of impression formation, Fiske and her colleagues studied another set of motivational factors. You will remember that the willingness to examine information inconsistent with a general category depends upon the conjunction of cognitive resources and motivational variables. The motivational aspect is typically presented in a situation of interdependence, where the perceiver's fate depends upon the actions of the target of perception. To the extent that impression formation regulates interactions, it is vital that encoding of information takes into account the interactive consequences of the judgements. Collaborating with someone, or competing against someone, should make people more attentive to difficulties in the anticipated interaction. For example, in the typical paradigm created to verify Fiske's continuum model, subjects are provided with a label and discrete information about another person whom they expect to meet. The information is either consistent with the category-label, inconsistent or neutral. At this point, two other variables – motivation and attention – are either manipulated and/or measured.

Imagine a subject who comes to a psychological office to participate in a patient reintegration programme co-sponsored by a hospital and the psychology department. He expects to meet a patient and to interact with him. Supposedly, psychologists believe this interaction may have therapeutic effects and prepares the patient to confront more threatening situations like job or college interviews. The subject is told that the interaction consists in designing creative games with a variety of colourful wind-up toys. Moreover, a prize for the most creative games goes either to the team or to the best contributor. A situation of interdependence is created when the award goes to the team rather than to the best contributor. The patient allocated to the subject happens to be a schizophrenic. Reports obtained from himself or from the clinical staff describe him as either outgoing, determined and adaptable, or as nervous, indeterminate, and edgy. Pretests found that the first of these profiles was inconsistent with people's expectations of schizophrenia, whereas the second is perfectly consistent with that expectation. In this particular scenario (Neuberg & Fiske, 1987, expt 1), the experimenter conceals a stopwatch in his pocket and records the time spent by the subject reading the information concerning the patient. Finally, the subject rates his partner's likeability.

When the information is consistent with expectations and the motivation is low, subjects do not pay much attention to individuating information ('He's schizophrenic allright'). The reaction is quite different in the other three conditions. When the experimenter induced outcome-dependency between the subject and the patient, subjects are attentive to any kind of information because their prize may be in jeopardy. When the profile doesn't correspond to the typical schizophrenic, attention is drawn to the bizarre information even though the financial fate of the two interactors is not interdependent ('Gosh, I didn't know there were schizophrenics like this one'). Judgements of likeability also vary as a function of the consistency of the information and of the outcome-dependency. When the schizophrenic is atypical, he is judged not as a schizophrenic, but as a sociable and adaptable, therefore likeable, person. The same is true, albeit to a lesser extent, when the information is consistent but the subject knows he must interact in order to win the prize.

Other studies by Fiske and her associates demonstrated that such piecemeal judgements take place because inconsistencies and motivation prompt attentional processes. Outcome-dependency is just one possible operationalization of motivation. Rusher and Fiske (1990) also manipulated interdependence via individual competition. People closely attend to the characteristics of a rival, especially if this rival is unusual, i.e. has a profile inconsistent with what they expect. These experiments on outcome-dependency vividly illustrate the power of social interactions upon the formation of impressions: 'thinking is for doing' (Fiske, 1993).

The self as a motivating agent

Judges sometimes motivate themselves to be accurate. They may, for instance, encounter situations that cue certain especially relevant aspects of their self-concept. As a result, they will 'read' the situation as one that requires special attention and accurate perception of other actors in order to be true to their self-concept. In other words, the integrity of the self induces people to process information in given ways, to use specific strategies.

Fiske and Hendy (1992) created an experimental situation that triggers the accuracy goal from either low or high self-monitoring subjects. On the assumption that low self-monitoring individuals generally look inwards for cues to behaviour, they induced their (high and low self-monitoring) subjects to believe that they had the kind of personality that individualizes or categorizes other people. Only low self-monitoring participants were sensible to that manipulation, and among these, those who believed that they were individualizers spent more time scrutinizing information inconsistent with their expectation. In another study, Fiske and Hendy led their subjects to believe that the appropriate way to behave in a situation was to categorize or to individualize others. As expected, only the high self-monitoring subjects were influenced by the manipulation since they usually tend to look at situational cues for guides to their behaviour. In other words, internalized norms ('You are the kind of person who . . . ') or external ones ('This is a situation which requires that . . . ') motivate the judges to be as accurate as possible when forming an impression about other people. They do it because these norms speak to who the subjects are. That is to say, the self induces people to adopt certain strategies of information-processing because these strategies correspond to what these people deem important for them. It is a question of process, not of content.

The integrity of self

If interest drifts towards contents, one must confess that preference for desirable answers was not investigated in much detail – maybe because nobody doubts its existence. Are Europeans cultivated or are they snobbish? Depending on who I am, I may answer differently because I prefer one conclusion to the other. Beyond mere preference, my answers may also differ because it matters terribly for my personal or social identity. For Kruglanski, this need for a specific conclusion leads either to freezing or to unfreezing. Kunda (1990) is one of the few researchers who devoted special attention to this variable. She does not deny the possibility that directional goals lead to more or less lengthy processing under different circumstances, but she also defends the idea that different goals will induce the consideration of different beliefs and rules.

For example, if students are led to believe that extroversion helps in academic success, they more easily retrieve extroverted autobiographical episodes than those who link introversion with success. They also rate themselves as more extroverted. Thus, the desired conclusion is reached. There are constraints to it, however, and people take them into account. If, for instance, the students are in fact introverts, they do not present themselves as extroverts. They simply accentuate the extroversion component of their personality (Sanitioso, Kunda & Fong, 1990). What is interesting in Kunda's perspective is that she does not consider people prey to their own desires, even though they want to fulfil their wishes. 'People motivated to arrive at a particular conclusion attempt to be rational and to construct a justification of their desired conclusion that would persuade a dispassionate observer. They draw the desired conclusion only if they can muster up the evidence necessary to support it' (Kunda, 1990, pp. 482–483). For instance, people tend to perceive information consistent with their preferences as more valid than information that is inconsistent with their preferences. This tendency is not merely a matter of taste; it is based on rational strategies. For example, Pyszczynski and Greenberg (1987) argued that people evoke more alternative hypotheses, search more extensively for mitigating facts, and process evidence more carefully when they stumble on information that is injurious for the self than when this information is favourable to the self. Ditto and Lopez (1992) also provided several tests along that line. In one experiment, they led subjects to anticipate an interaction with a dislikeable partner. Before evaluating the partner's intelligence, subjects needed less information when the information depicted the partner as unintelligent than when it depicted the partner as intelligent. No such difference was observed when no preference for a specific partner was induced. In another study, subjects were induced to believe that they did or did not have a health problem. This belief was manipulated through a saliva test that the subjects had to administer to themselves. Subjects who thought they had a health problem took more time per test, tried more tests, and considered the tests less accurate than those who were not threatened by a health problem.

People not only strive to reach social judgements that preserve their personal identity, but they also do it to keep their social identity intact. Remember the experiments on the detection of Jewish faces among prejudiced subjects and the studies on the ingroup overexclusion (see Chapter 5). In these studies, specific strategies were also calibrated to guarantee the integrity of the ingroup. In the experiments on ingroup overexclusion, mobilization of cognitive resources did not always prevent errors, nor did desirable conclusions necessarily lead to inaccuracy. Error is thus not the fate of directional goals, whether these are or are not coupled with an explicit accuracy goal.

Summary

Theories about data attract data but this link is moderated by an accuracy goal. However, nothing guarantees that a motivation to be accurate really brings about accuracy. Moreover, an individuated impression and a categorial one are not synonyms of, respectively, accuracy and error. In the example of the great tit, when the father contented himself by saying 'It's a bird' or 'It's a kind of sparrow', he may have been more accurate than if he had looked carefully whether it was a great tit or a blue tit and decided it was 'A great tit!' (it was in fact a blue tit). Remember also Barbara Hendricks: is she not a star?

People are not always nor mostly driven by an accuracy goal. Often, people are more motivated just 'to get along' with someone than 'to get to know' this person (Snyder, 1992). This distinction is completely in accordance with the pragmatic concern that we defend throughout this book. It also corresponds with what Hilton and Darley (1991) call assessment and action sets. The assessment set coincides with the goal to be accurate and the action set conforms more or less to the goal of being efficient. Being efficient often implies the perceiver has directional goals such as preserving integrity of the self as an individual or as an ingroup member. Directional goals may not only bias the selection and construction of beliefs about the self, they may also bias the selection of inferential rules. Kunda (1990) suggests that the simultaneous presence of directional and accuracy goals increases rather than reduces the biases. Because people desire a given conclusion, and because they want want to be correct in their reasoning, they go to great lengths to show that they are right.

In the preceding paragraphs, we regarded subjects as perceivers who weighted social information in order to achieve an adequate judgement. Rarely could they themselves select the information or formulate the questions needed to reach a conclusion. We will now evaluate this aspect of the judgement construction.

The confirmation of hypotheses

Clearly, one of the main processes in impression formation is a confirmation of the hypothesis embodied in an initial category. This observation is most obvious in Fiske's formulation of her continuum model, but it is pervasive in other approaches as well. Here, we will not try to survey the research about hypothesis confirmation. This would be a whole enterprise in itself and it has been done well elsewhere (e.g. Jussim, 1991). Our ambition is simply to outline different perspectives that researchers have adopted about the phenomenon of hypothesis confirmation and to relate these perspectives to issues of accuracy and functionality in social interactions. First, we must review a few but important reference points.

Social psychology has witnessed successive waves of interest in the rationality of people, each of which has been forgotten about by the time the next rolls along. Over time, humans have been considered essentially emotional, rationalizing, rational but handicapped, rational but lazy, somewhat clumsy statisticians, mindless and many other sometimes contradictory descriptions. The itinerary of the research on hypothesis confirmation is particularly revealing in this respect. In an impressive series of experiments, Snyder and his colleagues (e.g. Snyder, 1984; Snyder & Gangestad, 1981) defended the idea that, in interviews, people work to confirm their hypothesis. In the typical paradigm, subjects are instructed to verify if the person to be interviewed is introverted or extroverted. Before the interview, they have to select a given number of questions among a prepared list containing items typical of extroversion, introversion, or that are irrelevant. In line with the idea of a confirmatory bias or strategy, Snyder's experiments consistently revealed that individuals expecting to verify extroversion (introversion) selected significantly more extroverted (introverted) than introverted (extroverted) or irrelevant questions (but see Semin & Strack, 1980).

Looking for diagnostic information

According to Trope and Bassok (1982, 1983), hypothesis confirmation is not the most intelligent strategy. People conform to it, however, not because they lack intelligence, but because they are forced to by Snyder's paradigm. Snyder's questions, they argue, are not ordinary but biased ones. In other words, his questions relevant to extroversion or introversion are worded as if the interviewer already knew the interviewee's personality (e.g. 'What do you usually do to warm up a party?' or 'What don't you like in parties?'). According to Trope and Bassok (1982), these biased or leading questions are non-diagnostic because it is difficult for interviewees to answer positively or negatively, irrespective of their personality. Interviewees thus comply with what is suggested by the questions rather than answering according to their own personality.

To test this, Trope and his associates conducted a series of experiments revealing the intelligence rather than the stubbornness of people. As expected, their subjects showed a clear preference for diagnostic questions, that is, questions that can be answered by 'Yes' or 'No' and that distinguish between the alternative hypotheses – introversion and extroversion, for instance (see also Skov & Sherman, 1986). Subjects display this preference regardless of the fact that the formulation of the question matches the hypothesis to be tested (e.g. for extroversion: 'Are you sociable?') or matches the alternative hypothesis (e.g., for extroversion: 'Are you shy?'). Only when people can hardly see an alternative hypothesis, or when the hypothesis is extreme, do they prefer diagnostic questions whose formulation matches the hypothesis. Kruglanski reached about the same conclusions as Trope. His reasoning is as follows: if people have only one hypothesis in mind, they tend to confirm it more – to freeze the epistemic search more rapidly – than if they simultaneously entertain two hypotheses. Moreover, they freeze the epistemic search more quickly if they are under pressure for closure than under fear of invalidity. To test this reasoning, Kruglanski and Mayseless (1988) asked some subjects to determine whether a target was an architect, others whether the target was a painter, and still others whether he was an architect or a painter. Subjects requested more diagnostic questions in the case with two hypotheses rather than one, and when the fear of invalidity was high rather than low.

These results seemed convincing enough to be quoted by Higgins and Bargh in their *Annual Review of Psychology* paper: 'people select diagnostic over nondiagnostic questions [. . .] but will display a preference for hypothesis matching questions when the hypothesis under consideration is the only accessible alternative and is believed to be true' (1987, pp. 401–402). An additional claim by Higgins and Bargh will retain our attention: 'When given an opportunity to formulate their own questions [. . .], people almost never spontaneously construct leading questions. Nor apparently is there a special preference for hypothesis matching questions' (p. 400). Higgins and Bargh here refer to a study conducted by Trope, Bassok and Alon (1984) where subjects formulated rather than selected their questions before an interview (which never took place). We can easily imagine the scenario: the subjects are invited to write down, at their own pace, the type of questions they would like to ask if they had to verify if the personality profile of someone does or does not correspond to an extrovert or an introvert. The situation is conducive to being as rational as possible, enabling subjects to come up with the most informative questions. In the study, subjects spontaneously formulated a lot of diagnostic questions, the most popular ones being bi-directional, that is, simultaneously diagnostic of extroversion and introversion ('Are you shy or outgoing?'). Almost no biased questions were asked in these circumstances. Replicated twice by us, this finding is thus very reliable (Leyens, 1989).

Looking for useful information

Trope et al. (1984) did not tailor their material to surmise the interviewee's personality. They established an ideal situation where the behaviours of the subjects would not interfere with their rationality. However, the results are quite different when going from a paper and pencil situation to real behaviour, that is, when people really have to interview someone and ask questions as the interview proceeds. In the real interview, people do not have ample time beforehand to formulate questions. It is hard for them not to react to the preceding answer. In two studies, Leyens (1989) found that, in a real interview, subjects do ask questions biased towards their hypothesis, i.e. questions whose formulation matches the hypothesis under consideration but are not diagnostic. These biased, or leading, questions are not the most numerous ones but they are far from being infrequent. As Leyens (1990; Leyens & Maric, 1990) suggested, asking leading questions after having generated a hypothesis about the client's personality has several effects. If the hypothesis is correct, the interviewer shows that she or he is in control of the situation and empathizes with the interviewee's personality. Moreover, the use of biased questions may contribute to the fluency of the interview (Leyens, 1989). If the hypothesis is incorrect, it remains possible for the interviewee to correct the expectation and the answer to a biased question may be particularly diagnostic for the interviewer. The sentence 'I don't like parties' in response to the question 'What do you do to warm up parties?' is much stronger and more informative than the same sentence given after the question 'Do you often go to parties?'

Trope's et al.'s subjects provided evidence that people can test a hypothesis without falling prey to a confirmatory strategy. However, our own perspective is that motivations play a crucial role in determining people's preferred strategies in this situation. The interviewer's main or only goal may not be mere accuracy. Snyder (1992) defends the same idea. He distinguishes between the functions of 'getting to know' and 'getting along' in behavioural confirmation. In one of their experiments, Leyens, Dardenne and Fiske (1994) asked their subjects to rate different types of interview questions (diagnostic or biased, matching or not matching the hypothesis) along several dimensions: the information the questions were supposed to provide, the empathy they were conveying from the part of the interviewer towards the interviewee, and the extent to which they allowed the interviewee to present himself or herself as a unique individual. In complete disagreement with a rationalist perspective, subjects believed that questions inviting a 'No' or 'Yes' answer were not particularly interesting in an interview. They considered that bias towards the hypothesis was both very informative and very empathic. To recognize the interviewee as a unique individual, however, they gave their preference to questions biased against the hypothesis. In another experiment, Dardenne and Leyens (in press) verified that biased questions were favoured by socially competent persons in sensitive situations. Compared to low self-monitors, high self-monitoring people resorted to more biased questions when interviewing a higher-ranked person than when interviewing a peer.

Neuberg (1989) showed that broad, supportive and encouraging questions can disconfirm a negative expectation. This author found that, when given the goal to be accurate, interviewers challenged a negative – and false – expectation by asking questions that were not diagnostic in Trope et al.'s sense. Interviewers in this condition used encouraging questions as well as questions giving the interviewees ample opportunity to present themselves in a favourable manner. This strategy, in turn, improved the performance of the interviewee, as determined by external judges, and this performance led to a final positive impression of the applicant.

Summary

Let us recapitulate our main points. We do not claim that biased questions are intrinsically better than diagnostic questions. We defend the idea, however, that diagnostic questions are not necessarily better and more intelligent than biased questions. It is true that biased questions may erroneously produce behavioural confirmation that leads to detrimental consequences (Fazio, Effrein & Falender, 1981; Snyder & Swann, 1978). In contrast, however, they may uncover lots of information and even strong disconfirming evidence. At the same time, biased questions may also ease the interaction. Person perception is an action whose outcomes have to be gauged.

Feeling entitled to judge

Whether in the context of impression formation or hypothesis testing, a unanimous feature of current perspectives on social inference is that perceivers start by using their a priori knowledge in the form of categories and general expectancies. When motivation is present, people reconsider this initial commitment in light of the available raw data. Cognitive resources are also very important for finding the best match between data and theories about data. This approach gives the picture that impression formation and hypothesis testing within the framework of person perception are basically identical to some kind of intellectual problem-solving task. There is a correct answer. Motivation as well as special attention help the perceiver bypass the obstacles on the way to a judgement. In the preceding section, however, we saw that the road people took to test a hypothesis and form an impression is not necessarily the straight one imagined by strict rational thinkers. People may be 'motivated tacticians' as suggested by Fiske and Taylor (1991), and more sensitive to the functionality of their social interactions than to some extrinsic and antiseptic 'Truth'.

To wind up this chapter, we would like to present a paradox. If people's first reaction is to accept a categorical label, how come they sometimes resist? Why are people not ready to consider an artist, for instance, like any other artist, that is, like a stereotypical artist, when they have no individuating information? In contrast, will people categorize the artist, when provided with non-diagnostic, or at least completely ambiguous, information concerning the person? Why is an artist who loves shrimps and Stravinsky, reads astronomy books, lives in the countryside with two dogs, Floyd and Gordon, and two cats, Phil and Zim, more like a stereotypical artist? None of the models that we have reviewed so far envisages such a situation or contains the sufficient ingredients to account for it. This situation, however, is not fictitious and was illustrated in an ingenious experiment conducted by Darley and Gross (1983).

In this study, subjects observed a video of a child, Hannah, in her neighbourhood and school that clearly depicted either a high or a low socio-economic background. Whereas by itself, this information was not sufficient to produce a biased judgement of Hannah's abilities, additional ambiguous information about her performance on an intelligence test triggered evaluations consistent with initial expectations. Not only was there a difference in the judgement of intelligence but also the fictitious test was viewed as more difficult and the performance of the child superior for the condition with the privileged girl as compared to that with the poor Hannah. Darley and Gross argue that category information activates stereotypes, but subjects do not consider stereotypes a valid basis for making judgements when the targets of the judgements are individuals. However, additional target information allows subjects to confirm the initial hypothesis.

The illusion of being informed

The fact that participants in Darley and Gross' study did not rate Hannah's abilities differently when knowing only her poor or privileged background is not an isolated phenomenon. An identical finding was obtained by Quattrone and Jones (1980) when they asked their subjects to evaluate a specific student from a given university. Other subjects, however, were quite willing to evaluate the student body of that university. People are often aware that judgements based on categories constitute undue generalizations. Whereas it is probably not a problem for people to infer that Tom, an ice-hockey player, likes to play hockey, it may trouble people to state that Tom has an aggressive personality. Enjoying the game of hockey in that particular case is not a generalization but having aggressive dispositions may be an overgeneralization. Moreover, the overgeneralization concerns a negative content. Negative overgeneralizations have not always been considered undesirable. When Katz and Braly (1935) initiated their work on stereotypes among White Americans, they obtained stronger public than private – negative – stereotypes for Blacks. This finding is quite relevant for the theory of social judgeability (Leyens, Yzerbyt & Schadron, 1992; Schadron & Yzerbyt, 1991).

When trying to find the best match between individuating data and their theories about data, people are influenced by cognitive and motivational factors as well as by their interaction goals and their personal and social integrities. Furthermore, they are also affected by social rules about the appropriateness of the judgement. Remember that, for us, social perception is essentially an action that takes place in a given context, with specific rules. In other words, people are also sensitive to *theories about judgements* that evolve from their culture. This is exactly what Darley and Gross said when they claimed that categorial information may not be a valid basis for judgement. In our culture, at this time, one tends not to judge an individual on the grounds of her or his category membership alone. According to Darley and Gross, the ambiguous performance by Hannah on the intelligence test allows subjects the opportunity to experience and confirm the stereotype that was activated by the categorial information but that was blocked by the social rule.

If people resist applying their stereotype because they feel they have no valid basis for their judgement, it follows that they would hesitate less if they thought they had relevant individuating information (Schadron, 1991; Yzerbyt, 1990). We believe that this conviction in having adequate information and not hypothesis confirmation is the sufficient factor to release the judgement. Stated otherwise, people develop a sense of 'judgeability'. Once they feel informed, they feel entitled to judge, and they do so. The quandary with this reasoning is that it necessitates giving to subjects the impression that they are informed and at the same time preventing them from using that information in a confirmatory way. Squarely put, this means that subjects should not receive any information at all but they should still have the illusion that they have in fact acquired some. Here is how we bypassed this quandary.

In one study (Yzerbyt, Schadron, Leyens & Rocher, 1994, expt 1), subjects were called into the laboratory to perform a series of tasks as part of a research programme on the influence of daily activities on social judgement processes and impression formation. The experiment consisted of three parts. Subjects first received minimal category information about some person. They heard the beginning of a taped interview where the information was limited to the target person's name and profession. Whereas one half of the subjects received category information diagnostic of extroversion (the target was a comedian), the remaining participants learned that the interviewee was an introvert (i.e. an archivist). Second, subjects performed a vigilance task which was presented as the formal equivalent of the pressure of daily activities; they were asked to 'shadow' a text during a dichotic listening task. In no way was the material related to

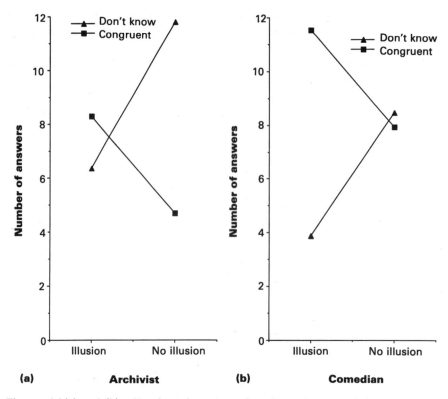

Figures 6.2(a) and (b)   *Number of answers selected as a function of the category membership of the target, the illusion of individuating information, and type of response (Yzerbyt, Schadron, Leyens & Rocher, 1994)*

introversion or extroversion. Upon completion of the vigilance task, half of the participants proceeded immediately to the third part of the experiment. The other persons learned that, unknown to them, they had been given information about the target during the vigilance task, in the non-listening ear. In the final part, all subjects conveyed their impression of the person by filling out a series of questionnaires. The results followed the predictions. Subjects rated the target as more introverted (or extroverted) when they believed they had received the individuating information than when they received only categorial information. One set of results is particularly interesting and reflects the confidence subjects feel in their ability to give a judgement. One questionnaire contained items related to introversion and extroversion and each of the items could be answered 'True', 'False', or 'Don't know'. When subjects are in a social judgeability condition, the number of 'Don't know' answers decreases drastically and it is replaced by answers congruent with the stereotype – introverted or extroverted – that was activated by the profession. These results are represented in Figures 6.2(a) and 6.2(b).

Because people have the illusion of being informed, they are willing to make a judgement. Because the only information they have is categorial, their judgment corresponds to a stereotype. Debriefings revealed, however, that subjects in this experiment did not at all believe that they had stereotyped the target. On the contrary, it was difficult to convince them that they did not get individuating information. In another study (Yzerbyt, Schadron, Leyens & Rocher, 1994, expt 2), some subjects were told after the dichotic listening task that they had received information about comedians (that is, about the profession in general and not about the particular target). As expected, these subjects held back their judgement. This finding clarifies that the operationalization of informational illusion is not due to a privileged accessibility of the category nor to demand characteristics. The threat of demand characteristics was also discarded in an experiment using a bogus pipe-line procedure (Yzerbyt, Leyens, Corneille & Geeraerts, 1994). After the induction or not of the illusion of being informed, subjects answered the questionnaires in two different conditions. In one condition, subjects were successfully led to believe that the computer was able to detect their possible lies (the bogus pipe-line condition). The procedure was standard in the other condition. The illusion of being informed provoked more stereotypical judgements, regardless of the bogus pipe-line procedure.

Other experiments (Schadron, Yzerbyt, Leyens & Rocher, in press), with different professions and interfering tasks, have reproduced the same results. Also, people feel especially confident when they are 'in a position' to judge, that is, when they are induced to believe that they deserved a special status (Caetano, 1993). This latter condition corresponds to an often encountered situation. People commonly confound their status in a particular domain with knowledge in another domain. One observation is especially noteworthy in Yzerbyt, Schadron, Leyens and Rocher's study (1994). Some subjects who were led to believe that they had received information about a category of persons rather than about a specific individual misunderstood the instructions. They reported that they received information about the target rather than about the profession in general. In other words, it is easy – but not inevitable – to replace the category with the particular. What this research indicates is that, besides data and theories about data, people also pay attention to their theories about judgements when answering the question: 'When is it OK to judge?'

Conclusions

This chapter has illustrated the role of three levels of adequacy in social judgement: the reality, integrity and cultural levels. Theories attract data. Different models of impression formation take for granted that the first response to a judgement is a categorial one because it is easy and comprehensive. Moreover, individuating information is considerably mouldable, but not endlessly so. Judges take into account individuating information to the extent that they have sufficient cognitive resources, such as attention, and are motivated because, for instance, their task or their future outcomes require them to be as accurate as possible. Examination of individuating information alters the initial categorial hypothesis. These models assume that there is a correct judgement corresponding to some kind of objective reality. What people need to find the solution is ability and/or its motivational substitute. In that view, person perception is equivalent to an intellectual task and the level of adequacy corresponds to reality.

Motivation may enter into the impression process through another door than cognition. People often select information and strategies to achieve desired conclusions. More often than not, this selection is quite rational. People may also struggle to keep their self-concept intact, or to preserve the integrity of their social identity. Depending on the conditions, this leads to quick or slow, erroneous or errorless judgements. In fact, categorization is not a synonym of error and individualized judgement is not akin to accuracy. Researchers have often debated whether people give precedence to biased or diagnostic information when they have to verify a given hypothesis. It seems to us that another, very potent, factor to take into account is the utility of the information for the social interaction. This second stream of research fits in with the integrity level of adequacy.

If person perception is an action more than an intellectual task, social utility is certainly of utmost importance. This utility, however, is constrained by the rules of the culture within which the action of person perception takes place. One such rule seems to be that an individual should not be judged only on the basis of categorial information, that is, stereotypes. This means that people judge only to the extent that they deem the target judgeable, or that they feel entitled to judge. This point corresponds to the cultural level of adequacy and it is elaborated in the next chapter.

7

Dilution of Stereotypes

Cedant arma togae.

De Officiis, Cicero

Cicero's statement can be translated as follows: noble information about individuated behaviours should take the place of more crude evidence like stereotypes to the same extent that gowns have to replace weapons. This liberal translation reflects the logic of many impression formation models. As we saw in Chapter 6, overgeneralizations such as stereotypes regretfully took precedence over more precise, individuated information. The present chapter tells the story of another regret that mirrors the previous one. People seem to give credence to 'non-informative' individuated behaviours when they should rely on stereotypes instead. For example, an engineer, Robert, who is 45 years old, married and has two children, is judged less mathematically oriented than a typical engineer (Denhaerinck et al., 1989). Many authors consider this judgement faulty because name, age, marital status and number of children have nothing to do with the characteristics of engineers. These features are non-informative, or not relevant. In other words, whereas people sometimes have been accused of not sufficiently taking into account individuating information, here they are accused of relying on worthless data. This phenomenon has been coined *the dilution effect* by Nisbett et al. (1981). Before reviewing their explanation of this phenomenon as well as other more traditional explanations, we will present our own account of this phenomenon. Finally, we will re-evaluate research on the dilution effect from that latter perspective.

The social judgeability explanation of the dilution effect

For the social judgeability approach, there is nothing strange in the above example of the engineer who is married and has two children. We saw in the previous chapter that people entertain theories about judgements, one of them being that one should not stereotype a given individual. Numerous studies have shown that people reluctantly apply typical features of a group to a particular member of this group, whereas they do not hesitate to attribute these characteristics to the members as a whole (Quattrone & Jones, 1980). It may be that people have learned to distrust overgeneralizations, that it is not socially desirable to generalize, or both.

What do you learn when you hear that Robert is a middle-aged engineer with a wife and two children? Or when you are told that Thomas bursts into tears? Every piece of evidence contains a specific content, *the information itself*. The examples provide some content about Robert and about Thomas. In addition, another feature of the evidence, which may be called the *meta-information*, signals that information is conveyed and that this information concerns specific individuals. Admittedly, very little is said about these individual targets, who, you will agree, must have many other characteristics. Still, you are more informed about the target than you were a few moments before. Think about the experiments presented at the end of the last chapter in which subjects were ready to make a judgement about a specific target even when they did not have any information about that target. Subjects thought they were informed, but, in those studies, there was only an illusion of information. Still, if the meta-information indicates that a specific target is under scrutiny, and if the information is empty, completely irrelevant as far as the judgement is concerned, we predict that subjects will not feel they are entitled to judge. As a result, they will refuse to judge or they will give an omnibus response. Sometimes this ends up as a middle-point answer on the response scale.

It is easy to understand how the above reasoning applies to the dilution effect. We conjecture that dilution takes place, that is, subjects' judgements do not reveal the impact of stereotypes, when meta-information makes individuation salient and no special information is provided. In other words, dilution occurs when people have to judge specific individuals but don't feel they are entitled to do it. This happens when only categorial information is available and when it is clear that the individuating information is worthless for the judgement. In contrast, subjects will give a judgement, or will not provide an omnibus response, if they believe that they received some relevant information about the target. Stated otherwise, people stereotype to the extent that they believe the individuating information is relevant. In this case, ratings will reflect stereotypes because the only 'real' information for the judgement at hand is categorial. Importantly, our explanation for the dilution effect implies that stereotypes are not diluted but avoided. For social judgeability, the lesser use or expression of stereotypes as a consequence of receiving individuating information does not necessarily mean that judges have less stereotypes, or that their stereotypes are erased.

According to the above reasoning, providing non-diagnostic individuating information can lead either to polarization or to dilution. Nisbett and his collaborators (1981) recognized the possibility of both patterns existing. For these authors, the addition of non-relevant and non-diagnostic individuating information to a stereotype could lead to polarization. Through a process of confirmation, people find diagnosticity in otherwise non-diagnostic information (Darley & Gross, 1983; Duncan, 1976; Sagar & Schofield, 1980). Chapter 6 developed this line of research at length. Again, we want to state very clearly that, although polarization may indeed result from confirmation, we think that polarization may also be a consequence of meta-informational factors. As will be shown immediately, a traditional approach needs two mechanisms to account for the data: confirmation for polarization and limited cognitive capacity for dilution. More parsimoniously, the social judgeability explanation allows us to account for the results either when people rely only on the stereotypes or when they rely only on the individuating information. First, let's examine the attempts at explaining the dilution effect.

A far cry from the Bayesian ideal

A social cognition perspective often defines stereotypes as general beliefs about the distribution of characteristics in groups of people (McCauley & Stitt, 1978; McCauley, Stitt & Segal, 1980). In this line of reasoning, stereotypes can be considered as base-rates: membership of a group provides perceivers with a priori probabilities concerning the occurrence of certain characteristics. At the origin of this conception lies a classic series of experiments by Kahneman and Tversky (1973), who revealed that people are not good at relying on base-rates.

Neglect of base-rates

Kahneman and Tversky (1973) presented their subjects with slips of paper taken at random from a bag containing 70 (30) vignettes describing engineers and 30 (70) describing lawyers. Some of the vignettes contained (1) only the name of someone, (2) the name and some irrelevant information, or (3) the name and information tying them to engineering or law. The subjects had to estimate the probability that the target person described in the vignette was an engineer or a lawyer. Except when no information other than the name was provided, subjects neglected the base-rates. In other words, the fact that there were 70 or 30 descriptions of engineers (or lawyers) in the bag had almost no impact on subjects' answers. To make things concrete, one vignette read as follows: 'Dick is a 30 year old man. He is married with no children. A man of high ability and high motivation, he promises to be quite successful in his field. He is well respected by his colleagues' (1973, p. 242). Unless the subject supposes that family status, talent and motivation are unevenly distributed among engineers and lawyers, this individuating information tells nothing about the profession of the target. In line with Bayesian logic, subjects should thus neglect it altogether, rely on the base-rates and answer 70 or 30 per cent depending on the experimental conditions. Quite a different picture emerges from the observed data. As far as the above vignette is concerned, for instance, subjects said Dick had 50 per cent chance of being an engineer (or a lawyer).

According to Kahneman and Tversky (1973), people have limited cognitive capacity. As a result, they are not good at using Bayesian statistical rules and rely instead on fallible judgemental heuristics that do not sufficiently take into account prior probabilities. After the publication of Kahneman and Tversky's work, social psychologists quickly perceived the connections with their own concerns. At that time, findings in attribution research generally supported Kelley's (1967) covariation model. Intriguingly, perceivers apparently neglected consensus information (McArthur, 1972). Consensus information concerns the way other people behave. In order to appreciate fully the meaning of a particular behaviour, it would seem quite reasonable to examine what others do in similar circumstances to the one being judged. However, people are often unwilling to take that sort of evidence into consideration. According to Nisbett (for a general overview, see Nisbett & Ross, 1980), people's neglect of the base-rates is highly reminiscent of, and could probably explain, the underutilization of consensus information (but see Wells & Harvey, 1977; and Borgida, 1978, for a reply).

Here is one concrete example to illustrate the above reasoning. Suppose you read the procedure of a classic experiment on helping behaviour (Darley & Latané, 1968). According to the synopsis, 15 New York University students are told that the study concerns a discussion of personal problems. Six persons, one of whom is a confederate of the experimenter, take part in the same experimental session. Upon the subjects' arrival at the lab, they are directed to individual rooms. To make the discussion less embarrassing, the experimenter asks subjects to debate with the other participants over an intercom system. Thanks to a mechanical switching device, each participant talks in turn for about two minutes. The confederate speaks first. He mentions some problems getting adjusted to New York as well as a proneness to seizures, particularly when studying hard and taking exams. After the five other participants have discussed their respective problems, the confederate then goes on to the second round of the discussion. After a few comments, he begins a feigned seizure. Two minutes after the confederate took his turn, the microphone is simply switched off. The dependent measure is the time it takes subjects to help the confederate. Finally, the synopsis gives information about the debriefing portion of the experiment.

How do you think you would behave if you were a subject of this helping experiment? What do you think the real subjects did? Nisbett and Borgida (1975) asked their subjects the same question. The original data collected by Darley and Latané (1968) are surprising, to say the least. The 15 participants behaved as follows: 0 helped as soon as the confederate began stuttering, 0 when he asked for help, 1 when he stammered that he had a seizure coming on, 3 by the end of the speech, 5 within four minutes after the end of the speech, and 6 never helped. Nisbett and Borgida (1975, expt 2) set up several experimental conditions. In the no-consensus condition, subjects received non-diagnostic information about two 'randomly chosen' participants by means of clips of interviews. Information provided in the interviews concerned place of birth, parental occupation, major, grade point average (GPA), career plans and hobbies. Subjects were asked to indicate how they thought each of the targets had behaved during the helping experiment. The consensus condition was a variant of the first one. Before seeing the video-clips of the two 'randomly chosen' participants, subjects read Darley and Latané's data in tabular form. In a third condition, other subjects also saw clips of interviews with two non-helping participants. These latter subjects were asked about the behaviours of the other 13 participants in the experiment.

The results are particularly striking. The no-consensus subjects are particularly optimistic and believe that almost everybody helped and did it quickly. Subjects who were informed about the original data (the consensus condition) remembered them well but, when they predicted the behaviour of the two targets, they reproduced the guessing data. Despite statistical evidence, they expected that help would be provided and very quickly. This is not at all the reaction of the subjects in the last condition, who generalized the behaviour of the two targets who didn't help to the entire sample. In other words, these findings mean that people are ready to go from the particular to the general but not from the general to the particular. This experiment is thus an excellent example where the neglect for consensus also applies to base-rates (see also Pietromonaco & Nisbett, 1982). If stereotypes are similar to prior probabilities, subjects should use Bayesian logic to make proper judgements. However, if Kahneman and Tversky are right, people are unable to apply the sophisticated Bayesian computational rules and end up giving too much weight to individuating information and not enough to stereotypes.

Stereotypes as base-rates

Ann Locksley deserves credit for being the first social psychologist explicitly to build upon a base-rate definition of stereotypes and for showing that perceivers sometimes disregard category membership information. Indeed, for Locksley (with Borgida, Brekke and Hepburn):

> Social stereotypes may be viewed as popular beliefs about distributions of characteristics within social groups. Thus, social stereotypes have the logical status of prior probabilities for social judgments about particular members of stereotyped social groups. To the extent that this view of social stereotypes is valid, one would expect stereotypic beliefs to behave like any distributional belief in the context of prediction or judgment tasks. Perhaps the most striking implication of this line of reasoning is that social stereotypes may not exert as pervasive or as powerful an effect on social judgments as has been traditionally assumed. Social stereotypes may affect judgments of individuals about whom little else is known besides their social category. But as soon as individuating, subjectively diagnostic characteristics of a person are known, stereotypes may have minimal, if any, impact on judgments of that person. (1980, p. 830)

In an experiment in 1980, Locksley et al. (expt 2) first asked their subjects to rate the assertiveness of males and females in general, and then to rate the assertiveness of six targets. Two of these targets were identified only by their (masculine or feminine) name, two were identified by their name and diagnostic (assertive or passive behaviours) information, and finally two were identified by their name and non-diagnostic information (behaviours unrelated to assertiveness or passivity). The effect of sex was overridden by the diagnostic information but not by the non-diagnostic information. In a subsequent study, Locksley, Hepburn and Ortiz (1982, expt 1) asked their subjects to give their stereotypes about diurnal and nocturnal people. Afterwards, the same subjects were randomly assigned to one of six conditions and asked to rate eight targets on a series of traits typically associated with diurnal and nocturnal persons. All eight targets were either diurnal or nocturnal and they were described by their social category alone, or with diagnostic or non-diagnostic information. In this experiment, any kind of individuating information was capable of alleviating the effect of categorization.

Later on, we will add more details and our own interpretation to these experiments. For the moment, it is sufficient to say that Locksley et al. adopted Kahneman and Tversky's explanation for why subjects underutilized base-rates.

The representativeness heuristic and its variations

Kahneman and Tversky (1973) defended the idea that people's reliance upon a representativeness heuristic accounts for their neglect of the base-rates. When having to judge whether a given target is, say, an engineer, people look at the common features between the prototypical instance of an engineer and the particular target person being rated. Whenever experimenters provide additional non-diagnostic information about a target, it decreases the similarity between this target and the prototypical engineer (Tversky, 1977).

This reasoning was slightly modified in subsequent research. Instead of the prototype of a category, researchers focused upon the prototype evoked by a given behaviour (e.g. Nisbett et al., 1981). When people make a judgement about a target person, they supposedly initiate the process by figuring out an ideal instance of the behaviour suggested by the experimenter's question. For instance, if asked to rate the cruelty of someone's behaviour, a subject would activate the representation of the prototypical cruel person (e.g. tall male, short haircut, blue eyes, no lips, and who loves to shout and to put down people). What happens, though, when people have both category and individuating information about a target person? Membership of a category (e.g. cruel persons) is expected to cue the behaviour cruelty. That means there is great similarity between the target and the behaviour. The presence of additional non-diagnostic information (e.g. age, colour of hair, artistic tastes), however, is supposed to reduce the ratio of common features between the target and the prototype, thus rendering the target less similar to or less representative of the prototype. In other words, the prediction of the behaviour is estimated by looking at the degree to which the individuating information is similar to, representative of, the essential features of the behaviour being predicted. The non-diagnostic information seems to dilute the effects of the diagnostic one. The expression 'dilution effect' thus comes from an explanation of the phenomenon itself.

The representativeness heuristic still constitutes the major point of reference in the dilution literature (Sherman & Corty, 1984). Moreover, several subhypotheses have been deduced from the similarity or representativeness heuristics. Normally, subjects should be sensitive to the size of the correlation between the individuating information and the behaviour to be predicted. When the correlation is high, perceivers should neglect background information, but when the correlation is low, base-rates should have a decisive impact on final judgements. Suppose that people know that ownership of guns is positively correlated with votes for extreme right-wing parties. They may predict that Mr Untel, who owns many guns, votes for an extreme right party. Suppose also that people discover that Mr Untel has only moderate fascist attitudes, another usual predictor of votes for right-wing parties. They should hesitate and become less extreme in their predictions. In contrast, knowing that Mr Untel spends a moderate amount of time in front of his TV should not effect people's predictions concerning Mr Untel's vote at the future elections because TV watching is uncorrelated to preferences for right-wing parties. However, according to Zukier (1982), reliance on the representativeness heuristic would lead subjects to disregard the nature of the correlation between the individuating information and the behaviour to be predicted. Instead subjects would rely on the shared features between the individuating information and this behaviour. Because both characteristics are similarly moderate – moderate fascist attitudes and moderate amount of TV watching – they should dilute the prediction of an extreme behaviour such as voting for a far right-wing party. This is exactly what Zukier found.

Causal relevance

To be sure, people analyse the available data and try to use them according to some reasonably well-founded rule of judgement. Zukier (1982) showed that people are sensitive to moderate features when predicting an extreme outcome, but that they disregard the correlation between the features and the outcome. Ajzen (1977), on the other hand, defended the idea that people make use of base-rates to the extent that these are believed to be causally linked, or correlated, to the judgement under concern. In two experiments (Ajzen, 1977, expts 1 and 2), subjects were asked to predict the success of a student in an exam. They were provided with information, which did or did not relate to success in the exam, either implicitly or by experimental construction. For example, subjects were informed about the number of hours spent in studying for the exam as well as about the distance from the student's home to the campus. The first information had an implicit causal link with success whereas the second did not. Depending on the experimental conditions, the subjects were told about the real correlation between the information and success. Ajzen found that people's predictions were strongly influenced by base-rate information but only to the extent that these base-rates had causal implications for the judgement. When the base-rates did not have causal implications, they were largely neglected in favour of individuating information.

Causal relevance thus seems to be a critical aspect of the information. It leads the perceiver to neglect the individuating information and focus instead on the base-rate information. For Ajzen, subjects in Kahneman and Tversky's (1973) experiment neglected base-rate information for a very good reason: 'the proportion of engineers and lawyers in the original sample did not cause any member of the sample to become an engineer or a lawyer, nor did it provide information about any other factor that might be viewed as having a causal effect on a person's professional choice' (1977, p. 304). Moreover, most of the time, people have good reasons for relying on implicit causal links. Would you personally place more importance on the distance to campus than on the number of hours spent studying in order to predict success in the exams? Of course not. People have intuitive causal theories of events and they act upon them. In other words, people often make judgements based on their theories about judging. It is therefore not surprising that dilution is, to a large extent, influenced by the interpretation of the relative status of category and individuating information with respect to social rules of judgement.

Typical or atypical targets?

Let us take this reasoning concerning theories about judgements one step further by examining Zukier and Jennings' (1984) work. Put quite simply, Zukier and Jennings ask the following: About whom do you think you are more informed? Julie, who has two friends, or Gregory, who has a German shepherd and a Belgian shepherd? Gregory, of course, because anybody can have two friends but not many people have two dogs from a special breed. According to Zukier and Jennings, Julie is typical and Gregory is atypical.

In one experiment, subjects were to act as jurors in the trial of a man accused of murder. Subjects in the baseline condition read evidence indicating guilt. They were asked not only to estimate the likelihood that the defendant was guilty, but also to sentence him. In two other conditions, subjects received additional non-diagnostic information, i.e. information that had no implication whatsoever for the defendant's guilt. In the typical condition, the defendant was described as average in dimensions unrelated to guilt (e.g. average in height). He was extreme on the same dimensions in the atypical condition (e.g. extremely tall). Non-diagnostic information effected predictions as a function of its degree of typicality. Compared to those in the baseline condition, subjects diluted their judgements in the typical condition but not in the atypical one. In another study, subjects had to estimate the GPA of two students. The diagnostic information in the control condition led them to believe that one of the students had a high GPA whereas the other target student had a low GPA. In a second, typical, condition, subjects also learned that the two students were average on dimensions unrelated to GPA (e.g. enjoy swimming). Finally, the additional information given in a third, atypical, condition described the students as being extreme on dimensions unrelated to the GPA (e.g. wear size 14 shoes). Results indicate that a student having skiffs around his feet was judged to have more extreme grades than the swimmer. Judgements were diluted when additional information depicted an 'average, typical' person, but no dilution was observed in the atypical condition (see also Zukier, 1982, about dispersion, a concept related to typicality).

Clearly, the finding that the type of non-diagnostic information has such a powerful impact on the judgement is an indicator that something other than a simple computation of common and non-common features with a prototype is taking place in people's minds. According to Zukier and Jennings, 'people consider not only the diagnostic properties associated with a category, but also a broader network of implicit interrelations, not necessarily derivable from the general category itself' (1984, p. 195). Different as this explanation may appear at first sight, it broadly builds upon the similarity heuristic and largely remains in line with the traditional interpretation of the dilution effect. Bar-Hillel (1980), for instance, argues that perceivers rely to a greater degree on information that appears to be relevant for the judgement at hand. Individuating information often dominates people's ratings because it is usually more relevant than base-rate information. In particular, specificity effects the relevance of the information. Similarly, Ginossar and Trope (1980) insist upon the diagnosticity of the information rather than upon its specificity (Lyon & Slovic, 1976). As a result of people's sensitivity to the relative diagnosticity, individuating data often dominate judgements because they appear to be more diagnostic than background information (but see Hinsz, Tindale, Nagao, Davis & Robertson, 1988).

Under the present perspective, however, Zukier and Jennings' (1984) data indicate that we rely on larger theories about judgements. To be sure, content aspects of the information strongly influence the judgemental steps taken by the perceiver. As will be illustrated, however, content may also influence the selection of judgemental rules.

Modes of approach and conversational rules

Other researchers have indicated that there are limits to the neglect of base-rates and tried to specify in which conditions people are susceptible to that bias. Zukier (1986), for instance, hypothesized that the bias may be more present when people adopt a narrative rather than a paradigmatic mode of approach to the problem. Whereas the latter corresponds to a cold, rigorous, scientific approach, the former is closer to a clinical orientation, where the judge immerses him- or herself in the richness of every detail. To test this, Zukier and Pepitone (1984) presented the engineer–lawyer task to half of their subjects as a study to examine 'how much people will use scientific thinking when making decisions on the basis of a few pieces of information. [. . .] Make your judgment as if you were a scientist analysing data. Do not simply indicate whether you believe that the person described is an engineer' (p. 353). To the remaining subjects Zukier and Pepitone said:

> This study examines an individual's general sensitivity and intuitive understanding of another person and in particular of professional interests, on the basis of only a few cues about the person. . . . Try to understand the individual's personality, professional inclinations and interests as best you can. Call on your general knowledge, sensitivity and empathy. (p. 353)

In that particular study, the 'correct' response corresponded to a base-rate of 30. The means obtained are 31 and 42 in the scientific and clinical orientations, respectively. In other words, Zukier and Pepitone grasped part of what is going on in the base-rate fallacy. In the same vein as the paradigmatic and narrative modes, Ginossar and Trope (1987) distinguished algorithmic and heuristic approaches.

Schwarz, Strack, Hilton and Naderer (1991) also questioned the representativeness, or similarity, heuristic by taking into account Grice's (1975) cooperative principle of social discourse. According to this cooperative principle, speakers should respect four maxims when communicating information to someone.

> There is a maxim of quality that enjoins speakers not to say anything they believe to be false or lack adequate evidence for and a maxim of relation that enjoins speakers to make their contribution relevant to the aims of the ongoing conversation. In addition, a maxim of quantity requires speakers to make their contribution as informative as is required but not more informative than is required, and a maxim of manner holds that the contribution should be clear rather than obscure, ambiguous, or wordy. (Schwarz et al., 1991, pp. 68–69)

On the basis of Grice's principle, Schwarz and his colleagues note that Kahneman and Tversky (1973) formulated their instructions for the engineer–lawyer problem in a way that emphasized individuating information. Indeed, Kahneman and Tversky's subjects were told that 'a panel of psychologists have interviewed and administered personality tests' to engineers and lawyers, that their task would be to assign a probability 'on the basis of this information' accumulated by psychologists, and that 'the same task has been performed by a panel of experts who were highly accurate'. In line with Zukier's narrative mode, we may assume that subjects believed that, like psychological experts, they were to use all the individuating information provided by Kahneman and Tversky. To test this hypothesis, Schwarz et al. presented the study as a psychology problem or as a statistics problem. Moreover, the individuating information was written by a psychologist (for the psychology problem) or a non-specified

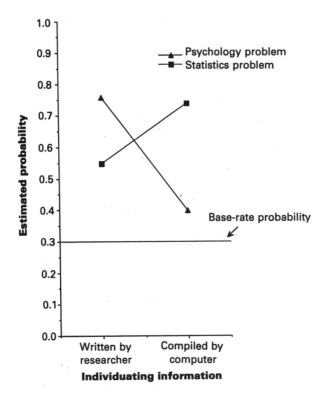

Figure 7.1 *Estimated probability of target's being an engineer as a function of conversational context (Schwarz, Strack, Hilton & Naderer, 1991)*

researcher (for the statistics problem), or it was selected at random by a computer (for both problems). Whereas the human person is supposed to comply with Grice's principle, this is not the case for the computer. The results are presented in Figure 7.1. As expected, the base-rate (i.e. 30) is less adhered to when the information provided by a human being concerns a psychological problem rather than a statistical problem. The opposite occurs when a computer selects the information at random. This suggests that the consistency between the task framing (statistics versus psychology) and the presentation mode (human being versus computer) may be very important.

Besides the formulation of the instructions, there is another feature of Kahneman and Tversky's study that is relevant to Grice's cooperative principle. There are many targets with different types of individuating information. Remember the engineer (or lawyer) Dick whom Kahneman and Tversky present using non-diagnostic information. Gigerenzer (1991) showed that when the vignette about Dick is presented alone, or first in the series, rather than in a series of vignettes varying in the type of available information, people tend to respect the base-rates. In our view (not necessarily Gigerenzer's), this means that base-rates are considered informative when Dick is presented alone or first. On the other hand, when Dick is lost in a series of vignettes, judges place importance on the differences between the various descriptions; they try to give meaning to these differences by attributing informative weight to what is said about Dick (see also Ginossar & Trope, 1980, 1987; Schwarz et al., 1991; Wells & Harvey, 1977).

Accountability

Up to now, we have seen that people neglect base-rates only under certain circumstances. First, when they believe there is no causal link between these base-rates and the individuating information (e.g. a good student who loves soccer). Second, when they encounter an uninformative, typical, piece of evidence (e.g. a student who prefers partying to studying). Third, when they are in some way encouraged to favour individuating information over categorial information (e.g. this is a psychological test). Four, when the variety of individuating information induces them to think that they should take this variety into account (e.g. given that I have to judge all these different individuals, it means I should not answer the same thing for all of them). All these conditions indicate that people try to make sense of what they are asked to do and verify whether they have something to say about the person they have to judge. We suggest that people build theories about judgements and apply social rules to these judgements. Is the target judgeable or not? In other words, we want to show how the cultural level of adequacy is relevant for the dilution effect.

Before we do this, let us step back for a moment. If people really try to make sense of every bit of information they are provided with, accountable subjects should react to the presence of non-diagnostic information more than non-accountable subjects. Because accountable subjects will process the information more thoroughly, they will 'dilute' the diagnostic information more. This should not be the case when only diagnostic information is available. Tetlock and Boettger (1989) tested this set of hypotheses. In their study, all subjects first received diagnostic information concerning the GPA of a student or concerning the probability that a psychotherapy patient could be a child abuser. In a control condition, subjects did not receive other pieces of information. In the dilution condition, they received non-diagnostic information for the judgements concerned. In the augmented-information condition, they received additional diagnostic information that was consistent with the first diagnostic information. In the contradictory-information condition, the additional diagnostic information was inconsistent with the first diagnostic information. The manipulation of accountability was the same as in Tetlock and Kim's (1987) study, and it took place prior to receiving any information (see Chapter 6). After reading the evidence, the subjects had to estimate the GPA of the target or the likelihood that he was a child abuser. They were also asked to report their thoughts about the target and to assess their confidence in their prediction. The pattern of results is in line with the authors' predictions. Most importantly, accountable subjects in the dilution condition 'diluted' the diagnostic information more than their unaccountable counterparts. Predictions of the accountable were significantly less extreme and they were less confident in their judgements. The results in the other conditions indicate that the underlying mechanism responsible for this effect is the tendency for accountable subjects to process evidence in more complex ways than unaccountable subjects. First, accountability did not lead to more moderate predictions when only diagnostic evidence was available as in the control conditions. Second, the thoughts reported by the subjects reveal that accountable subjects formed more complex impressions of the evidence. Third, accountability led subjects to express more extreme predictions in the 'augmented-information' and to express more moderate judgements in the contradictory-information conditions.

Thus, the presence of extra information was necessary to induce a difference between accountable and unaccountable subjects. This difference was always due to accountable subjects, who moved in the direction expected by the type of information and who used more complex thoughts. Of course, as Tetlock and Boettger (1989) acknowledge, these results do not absolutely demonstrate the mediational role of complexity of thought, but they are consistent with this hypothesis. Two important implications of these findings are worth mentioning. First, the difference between accountable and unaccountable subjects is related to their (lack of) consciousness of their own cognitive processes (Nisbett & Wilson, 1977). Social perceivers are aware of the outcome of their perception, but they are often unknowing of its determinants. Therefore, it is difficult for them to 'adequately' monitor their perception. The second implication of Tetlock and Boettger's findings is that the same information can lead to very different judgements depending on the cognitive set of the subjects.

Reinterpretation of Locksley et al.'s results

We are now in a position to offer another explanation of Locksley et al.'s results. Remember, first, that non-diagnostic individuating information did not override the categorical information in Locksley et al.'s 1980 study, but it did in the 1982 study. The authors explain the difference between the two sets of results by saying that the non-diagnostic information of the 1980 study was unindividuating as well. An example of the 1980 non-diagnostic information is as follows: 'Yesterday Tom went to get his hair cut. He had an early appointment because he had classes that day. Since the place where he gets his hair cut is near the campus, he had no trouble getting to class on time' (1980, p. 827). In that particular case, subjects had to evaluate Tom's assertiveness. According to the authors, this non-diagnostic information 'was so common that it could not permit subjective discrimination of a given target from any other target' (Locksley et al.,

1982, p. 38). In 1982, the target was presented as a diurnal or nocturnal person. Here is an example of individuating information, low in diagnosticity, but which consisted of more discriminative information, more clearly conveying an individuated impression of a particular target: 'Gene W. has an IQ of 118 and does fairly well in his college classes. His mother works as a nurse and his father is a lawyer in the town where Gene grew up. Gene has a couple of friends in college, one of whom went to the same high school as he did' (1982, p. 38). In our opinion, this comment refers to a very important distinction. Evidence about the target combines two independent dimensions. Of course, one crucial aspect of the evidence is its usefulness for the judgement at hand: its diagnosticity. Still, information can lead or not lead to the individuation of the target. For instance, it probably makes a difference whether I say 'She is feminine' or 'It is a female'. This distinction between information and meta-information, though, did not concern Locksley and her colleagues. It is, however, totally in line with our approach.

Remember also that, in both studies, subjects were first requested to provide the experimenter with their stereotypes. In other words, all subjects were first asked to judge an abstract category. In the 1980 experiment, subjects went on to rate the assertiveness of six targets, two of them identified by their name (male or female) only, two by their name and the descriptions of assertive or passive behaviours that they had performed, and two by their name and non-diagnostic information. Because all six targets were presented in one section of the questionnaire, subjects may have been aware of the differential information available for each of the three kinds of targets. When targets were presented along with instances of assertive or passive behaviours, subjects obviously were provided with useful information. This was completely different for the two remaining kinds of target. When only the name was provided, the only clever answer was to respond along the base-line like one had done at the beginning of the experiment. When completely non-diagnostic information was furnished, it should appear particularly irrelevant, especially given that some other pieces of information were diagnostic. Again the only astute answer was to go back to the stereotype that had been elicited at the start of the study. In other words, people were led to differentiate between diagnostic and non-diagnostic information. As a result, subjects reproduced the global estimates when the only thing they knew about a particular person was the name or the name and trivial information. In the 1982 study, experimenters confronted subjects with quite a different situation. All the targets within a given condition were described by the same kind of information: categorial, categorial and individuating non-diagnostic, or categorial and individuating diagnostic. In this design, subjects were clearly prevented from making comparisons between the kinds of information given to them. What could be the impact of such a manipulation? In our opinion, using eight targets with different descriptions leads subjects to avoid using their stereotypes because the focus is on specific individuals. What differs in the information presented to the subjects is not the kind of information but the individual targets. In fact, the design stresses the contrast between the mere knowledge of category membership (the first question that was asked) and the knowledge of individuating information, be it diagnostic or not. The informativeness of the evidence is not questioned, the diagnosticity of the information does not matter, and, as a result, the so-called dilution effect ensues for any kind of individuating information.

This reasoning also applies to the results obtained by Nisbett et al. (1981). They showed that subjects predicted that individuated targets tolerated less electric shocks when they were majoring in engineering, or attended less movies when majoring in English. Again, the procedure rendered the individuating information uninformative and typical. In the 'dilution condition' of the first and main experiment, subjects saw four videotapes. In each of them, a student in biology, engineering, music or English answered the same series of questions such as: 'What is your name?', 'What is your year in school?', Where are you from originally?', 'What is your religious background?', etc. One of the questions concerned the field of studies. It was related to the dependent variables which were tolerance to electric shocks and attendance to movies. Such a series of questions certainly individualizes the target, but it makes clear that the information is mostly irrelevant. What does the fact that Tom was born in Detroit and Georges in Houtsiplou, tell me about shocks or movies? You're responsible for the shocks you take, not for the place you are born. Neither Catholicism nor Anglicanism forbid watching movies, do they? The videotaped interviews just show that the targets were taken at random, that they are average people.

This reinterpretation of classical studies does not challenge the view of stereotypes as base-rates. It does challenge, however, the idea that people dilute their stereotypes because the individuating information reduces the ratio of common features with a prototype. We propose that people receive cues from the context indicating whether they are judging an individual or a category, and whether they have enough or insufficient information to do it according to social rules. Moreover, the same information in a different context does not carry identical weight. As everyone knows, the expression 'I love you' has many different meanings according to its context (see also Krosnick, Li & Lehman, 1990).

Summary

From the above discussion, it seems particularly important to pay attention to the subjectively experienced contexts, the methodological details of the studies, and the kind of individuating and categorial information provided to the subjects. In particular, the roles given to the subjects, whether the study is a within- or a between-subjects design, and the order of presentation of the information and questions may greatly matter. We hypothesize that non-diagnostic information leads to less polarized stereo-typical judgements because subjects individuate targets. Locksley and her colleagues (1982) emphasized the importance of individuation. They suggested that the absence of dilution in the case of non-diagnostic information in their 1980 study was probably due to the fact that this information was not individuating enough. Locksley et al. neglected, however, the context created by their experimental design. Indeed, the context in which the individuating information occurs may make salient the absence of content, or it can favour the reliance on general beliefs. Our interpretation of the so-called dilution effect is in complete accordance with research on the cooperation maxims in conversation. To the extent that I believe that you are providing me with true, clear, relevant and sufficient information, I will try to use it well. I will take into account that you first asked me for a stereotypical judgement. I will also take advantage of the fact that you vary the kind of information or the targets you want me to evaluate. From our point of view, this reinterpretation of the dilution effect clearly indicates that person perception is not essentially an intellec-tual task, but an action taking place in a social context.

Pseudo-information: dilution and polarization

Even according to the representativeness heuristic, not all non-diagnostic information should have a diluting effect. Some information does not point out non-common features with the prototypical category member; it is simply irrelevant. Hilton and Fein (1989) distinguished irrelevant infor-mation from pseudo-relevant information. The latter type is diagnostic across a wide variety of judgement tasks but not for the one which actually matters. For instance, learning that Tom drinks coffee at breakfast is irrelevant for deciding that he is macho. On the other hand, the fact that he is intelligent is pseudo-relevant. Intelligence is often predictive but there are probably as many machos who are not intelligent as there are non-machos who are stupid. Here are two other examples of, respectively, irrelevant and pseudo-relevant information: 'Bob found 20 cents in a pay phone in the student union when he went to make a phone call', and 'Bill and two friends rented two classic Fellini movies to watch on a VCR over the weekend' (1989, p. 203). According to Hilton and Fein, pseudo-relevant information should dilute stereotypes contrary to irrelevant information because the features it suggests are typically important. Their presence therefore should reduce the representativeness of the target.

In Hilton and Fein's first experiment, students were asked to rate the assertiveness of twenty-four targets. Half of them were presented targets with a female name and the remaining ones targets with a male name. For a third of the targets, the individuating information was irrelevant, for another third, it was pseudo-relevant, and for the rest it was relevant (the results for this latter category are not reported). It is thus a completely within-subjects design. When the information was irrelevant, both men and women were evaluated as more assertive than the mid-point of the scale and men were judged somewhat more assertive than females. Interestingly, the difference between the sexes disappears when the information is pseudo-relevant. The authors concluded that this dilution effect was due to the pseudo-relevance of information, in accordance with their hypothesis about the similarity or representativeness heuristic. Their results, however, also show a strong main effect: the targets are considered much more assertive when the information is pseudo-relevant than irrelevant. Why is this so?

Except for a few details, studies 2 and 3 are identical. We will therefore only sketch study 2. This second study concerned college majors and competitiveness. After reading the general instructions, which looked like those of the previous experiment, one half of the subjects had to think about the typical pre-med major and to rate this student on a scale ranging from very non-competitive to very competitive. When this was done, they read a vignette about Bill H., a pre-med major, described by either irrelevant or pseudo-relevant information and they rated him on the competitiveness scale. The other subjects did the same for a typical social work major. Except for the repeated judgement, the other variables were treated in a between-subjects design. There was a dilution effect for the pseudo-relevant information, but not for the irrelevant information.

Hilton and Fein interpret their results according to the similarity heuristic but they have problems with the polarization observed in their first study. Obviously, Hilton and Fein also have difficulties accounting for Darley and Gross' (1983) results that were summarized in the previous chapter. Remember Hannah, the little girl portrayed in the experiment. Subjects rated her more stereotypically after her ambiguous performance during an intelligence test than after diagnostic information concerning her social background. Assuming that Hannah's ambiguous performance corresponds to pseudo-relevant information, Darley and Gross obtained a polarization in the judgements rather than a dilution. In addition, we showed in Chapter 6 that people who have the illusion of being informed feel entitled to judge. They deem the target judgeable and, because they have no real information other than that which is categorial, they end up with stereotypic judgements. Obviously, the illusion of being informed has connections with pseudo-relevant information. Hilton and Fein state that this kind of information provides no real data for the case at hand. How do we reconcile the judgeability approach with Hilton and Fein's data and interpretation? Let us apply the lessons from previous experiments that we summarized above.

Ways of presenting the information are of great importance. To say 'He's a rich lawyer' or 'he's rich; he's a lawyer' does not convey the same meaning of 'rich' and 'lawyer'. You will probably more often infer that lawyers are rich in the second than in the first case. We alluded to this fact earlier (Ginossar & Trope, 1987; Zukier & Pepitone, 1984). In accordance with Grice's conversational rules, Krosnick et al. (1990), for instance, illustrated that the recency effect for base-rates or individuating information results from subjects' inferences that they are expected to rely most on the piece of information presented last (see also Schwarz et al., 1991; Schwarz & Bless, 1992). In other words, depending on the rhetorical structure of the information, this information can dilute and diminish the expression of stereotypes or contrastingly, it can also lead to more confident and polarized judgements. When pseudo-relevant information is provided all at once with the category membership of the target, the pattern of meta-information emphasizes that some content has been delivered and that, as a consequence, the target person is judgeable. This should not be the case when the evidence is clearly irrelevant, when a real individual is at stake but no 'real' content is provided. This contrast of impressions – that almost no information is provided for some targets and that quite a bit is given for others – should be especially significant in a within-subject design. In those conditions, like in the first study by Hilton and Fein, we expect more polarized judgements with pseudo-relevant than with irrelevant information. In fact, this is what Hilton and Fein obtained. When, however, pseudo-relevant information is provided after a categorial judgement, subjects switch from perceiving a stereotypical member or a category to a real individual about whom little is known. Dilution occurs. When the evidence following the categorial judgement is irrelevant, the focus is again on the content and it is clear that no meaningful content has been added. The judgement should thus remain stereotypical. These conditions concur with the second and third experiments by Hilton and Fein. The expectations comply with their data.

Yzerbyt, Leyens and Schadron (1994) conducted two experiments to test these a posteriori explanations. In one of the studies, subjects had to rate the ambition of economic majors. In a stereotype condition, participants were simply asked to indicate the impression of the other university students about the ambition of a student majoring in economics. Figure 7.2 shows that the stereotype is quite ambitious, which was expected on the basis of pretests. The typicality condition replicates the pseudo-relevant condition in Hilton and Fein's experiment 2. Subjects first rated the 'typical student in economics'. They then read four pieces of individualized information that were pretested as pseudo-relevant and rated the target again. The results show a dilution like the one observed by Hilton and Fein. In a third condition (permission/pseudo-relevant) that replicated the pseudo-relevant condition in the third experiment conducted by Hilton and Fein, subjects received information about 'Thierry, a 21-year-old student majoring in economics'. Before they conveyed their impression, it was stressed that subjects had received very little evidence to do the job and that, consequently, information about the major might provide the best cue to perform well in the rating task. Subjects then went on to read the four pieces of pseudo-relevant information and rated the target a second time. Again, the results indicate a dilution effect and therefore replicate

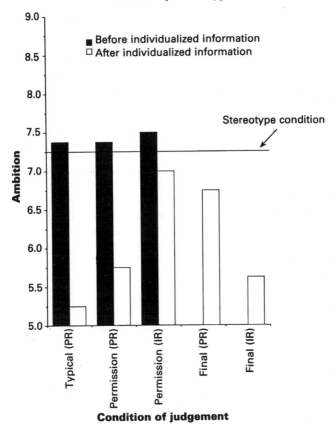

Figure 7.2 *Estimated ambition of the target person as a function of time and condition of judgement (Adapted from Yzerbyt, Leyens & Schadron, 1994)*

Hilton and Fein's findings. In a fourth (permission/irrelevant) condition, everything went as in the third one except that the information given after the categorial judgement was irrelevant. As expected, and as found by Hilton and Fein, there is no change in the judgement. It remained stereotypical. The fifth and sixth conditions conceptually replicate the Darley and Gross study and our 'illusion of being informed' experiments reported in the preceding chapter. They also correspond to Hilton and Fein's first study. This time, pseudo-relevant or irrelevant information was given with the categorial information. As hypothesized, and in accordance with Hilton and Fein's findings, judgements were more polarized in the pseudo-relevant condition than in the irrelevant one.

All these results conform to our theory's hypotheses. People stereotype to the extent that they are encouraged to do so or when they believe they have enough information about the judgement target and this information is in fact categorial. Pseudo-diagnostic information in an appropriate rhetorical structure facilitates this false belief in sufficient information.

Stated otherwise, pseudo-diagnostic, or pseudo-relevant, information is not enough in itself to induce subjects to feel they are entitled to make a judgement. When the context, the rhetorical structure or the kind of information make salient the individuality of the target, people refrain from judging if the only basis for this judgement is categorial. Hence, the dilution of stereotypes is a refusal to use only categorial information to take a position about a given individual. In sum, the social judgeability theory approach can account better than any other explanation of the various findings in the dilution literature. It is more comprehensive and more parsimonious than the representativeness heuristics that have to absorb all kinds of specificities, at best, or exceptions, at worst. The social judgeability theory is also more in tune with what person perception is. Social perception is a social inter-action with rules, more than it is an intellectual task that uses sophisticated computations.

Conclusions

People try to make sense of the information and of the tasks they are presented with. To perform this adequately, they need cognitive resources and the help of motivation. People also can resort to social norms or rules. One of these rules is that you should be cautious in judging an individual simply on the basis of categorial information unless you possess the necessary information about the individual. The problem is, therefore, determining when a person feels entitled to judge, to express his or her impression. This explanation is more parsimonious than one that relies on a computation between common and non-common features with a proto-type. We showed that the experiments about the dilution phenomenon, or the base-rate fallacy, actually vary the relative impact of information and meta-information. To the extent that the meta-information – 'you are judging an individual' – is more powerful than the information – 'here is what this individual is' – dilution occurs or the base-rate is not respected. This happens when people have to form an impression about someone for whom they don't have relevant information whereas they are informed about other people. This also occurs when people are implicitly asked to switch from a stereotype to an individualized judgement based on almost no information. It can also occur when subjects are warned that they will have to defend their position.

In contrast, the structure of the situation may cause the impression of having information to obliterate the meta-information that one is judging an individual because people rely on previous experiences where that kind of information was predictive. We also argue that receiving categorial and pseudo-relevant information together could create the impression of being in a judgeability condition. Also, to the extent that you know some peculiarities about someone, you feel you know him or her better than if only trivialities are available. Finally, situations will vary in their ability to induce cautiousness about judging an individual on the basis of categorial information. Not surprisingly, when asked to take a clinical orientation and concentrate on the richness of a single case, people adopt another strategy than when required to judge 'in cold blood'. Similarly, when they express a stereotype and then receive information that is clearly irrelevant, people stick to the stereotype rather than give the impression that they are a weathercock.

Thus, in this chapter we claim that people rely on theories about judgements. These theories about which judgement is adequate are constrained by the ambient culture and its social rules. In that sense, this chapter has illustrated the culture level of adequacy of social judgements.

8

Overattribution Bias as Naïve Theory

In this chapter, we turn to a quite different literature: the attribution literature and, more specifically, the overattribution bias, also dubbed fundamental error or correspondence bias. Researchers have rarely linked attribution and stereotyping (but see Deschamps, 1973–1974; Hewstone, 1989). This is hardly surprising. Person perception is concerned with three kinds of information: information about categories to which the actors belong, information about behaviours performed by individuals, and information about the situations in which these behaviours are enacted. Impression formation consists in the integration – or trade-off – of the first two kinds of information. Given the categorial type of information taken into account in this tradition, the link between impression formation and stereotyping is obvious. This is much less the case with attribution theory, which deals with the last two types of information: individual behaviours and situations. In our view, it is the judgement, in terms of personal dispositions or of situational demands, that makes the connection with stereotyping. Resorting to an individual attribute to judge a person's behaviour does not mean that the person has been placed into an 'individual' framework. Often, the perceiver assigns a social category to this person (Dubois, 1987). If Miss Prude remains silent at a party, it is because she is an introvert. If Mr Wayne endorses the present Cuban regime, he must belong to the old-fashioned Marxist-Stalinist movement. In other words, the personal disposition that is attributed to someone often categorizes that person into a given group. Moreover, people attribute personal dispositions to groups. Depending on the positivity of the behaviours, these attributions may differ for ingroups and outgroups. This also applies to stereotyping. With this chapter, we will make clear that stereotypes, like causal attributions, are social explanations (Heider, 1958; Hilton, 1990). The following quotation from William Boyd's *Stars and Bars* illustrates this idea:

> He was (he categorized himself with no trace of self-pity) a shy man. Not chronically – he didn't stammer or spit or flinch or sweat in the manner of the worst afflicted – no, he was shy in the way most of his country-men were shy. His flaw was a congenital one: latent, deep, ever present. It was like having a birth-mark or a dormant illness; an ethnic trait, a racial configuration. (1985, p. 16)

Henderson Dores, Boyd's hero, is an Englishman who comes to America to get cured.

Attribution models

For a long time, Heider vacillated between becoming a painter or a psychologist. This may explain why he has always been an avid admirer of cartoons, which provide a mass of information in a few drawings. If so much information transpires in so little space, this must mean that people are especially tuned to extract the slightest intentions portrayed in those drawings. Heider was also impressed by Michotte's (1946) work in Louvain. Michotte looked at how people perceive the movements of animated geometric figures. Depending on the pattern and speed of these movements, people perceive that one figure is pushing, throwing or carrying another figure. In other words, people see causality where objectively there is none. Heider himself, with Simmel (1944), published a study in which subjects, presented with (almost) erratic movements of geometric figures, told stories about the emotions, intentions and actions of these geometric figures to account for their motions. This led Heider to next study causal attributions and naïve psychology.

Other researchers followed up on Heider's ideas, mainly Kelley (1967) and Jones and Davis (1965). They proposed models of reasoning that they supposed people used when making causal attributions. However, research on their models rapidly accumulated and consistently showed that people were not following their postulates. They then had two alternatives: either the models did not correspond to what laypersons did in everyday life, or these laypersons were victims of errors or, at least, of systematic biases. They concluded that people erred in making attributions. In other words, the descriptive models had become prescriptive! As a result, the 1970s witnessed a flowering of studies unveiling all kinds of biases and errors of inference (Beauvois, 1984). Nisbett and Ross (1980) forcefully presented this research in their classic book *Human Inference: Strategies and Shortcomings of Social Judgment*. Social psychologists held, at that time, that human beings were intellectually handicapped. Researchers joyfully unmasked people's deficiencies. Today, it seems that the tide has reversed . . . but let's not go too quickly.

At the time psychologists proposed their descriptive models, they emphasized the important distinction between causes located inside or outside of the actor. If the cause is internal to the personality of the actor, people think it is stable. They are better able to predict the actor's future behaviour and to anticipate their own actions. On the other hand, if they attribute the behaviour to circumstances or haphazardness, they feel less in control of what may happen in the future. Investigating the deviations between the descriptive models and what people really do, researchers frequently found that people overestimate dispositional causes and under-estimate situational factors in the explanation of behaviours. This mis-attribution received several labels. Since it was 'discovered' within Jones and Davis' correspondent inferences theory, and since it constituted an overattribution to an actor of a disposition correspondent to an imposed behaviour, researchers first called this misattribution a correspondence bias or an overattribution bias. Because this bias was not restricted to a particular paradigm but seemed extremely pervasive in much of social reasoning, Ross (1977) called it a fundamental error.

In a landmark paper on the differences between actors and observers, Jones and Nisbett (1972) speculated that the overattribution bias should be more prevalent among observers than among actors. This difference in the attributions between actors and observers has relevance for stereotypes. Indeed, people are often in the position of observers when applying stereotypes. Nisbett and Jones reasoned that the amount of available information as well as its treatment leads actors to consider situational factors more than observers do. A simple but convincing demonstration of the difference is the fact that people use an 'it depends' solution more often when they have to answer a personality questionnaire for themselves than for close friends (but see McGill, 1989).

The ultimate attribution error

Take two groups in conflict and you will always be able to find an uneven sharing of personal and situational attributions. 'We are hard-working and they are lazy. They have more culture because they had more money than we and because they oppressed us.' 'We were heroes and they were cowards. We are in bad economic shape because of our former Premier. They are better off than we because we sacrificed ourselves for them.' This sort of reasoning seems endless. It happens when you take a Flemish and a Walloon, a British and a French, a Black and a White, a native and an immigrant, etc. Pettigrew coined the expression *ultimate attribution error* to refer to this phenomenon. He meant a 'systematic patterning of intergroup misattributions shaped in part by prejudice' (Pettigrew, 1979, p. 464).

> Across-group perceptions are more likely than within-group perceptions, especially for prejudiced individuals, to include the following: (1) For acts perceived as negative (antisocial or undesirable), behavior will be attributed to personal, dispositional causes. Often these internal causes will be seen as innate characteristics, and role requirements will be overlooked. (2) For acts perceived as positive (prosocial or desirable), behavior will be attributed to any one or a combination of the following: A. to the exceptional, even exaggerated, special case individual who is contrasted with his/her group; B. to luck or special advantage and often seen as unfair; C. to high motivation and effort; and D. to manipulable situational context. (Pettigrew, 1979, p. 469)

These differences would be especially strong not only for prejudiced individuals, but also for people aware of each other's group membership, and for those members whose groups have a long history of conflict.

When Pettigrew proposed these hypotheses, he reported only three published studies on the topic. A decade later, Hewstone (1990) reviewed the available – and not abundant – literature. Research sustained most of

Pettigrew's intuitions, but with important nuances. First, people attribute a positive behaviour to internal factors for their ingroupers more often than they do for outgroupers. Similarly, they attribute a negative behaviour to external factors for ingroupers more often than for outgroupers. Second, this kind of ethnocentric attribution is not universal. Hewstone and Ward (1985), for instance, failed to find it among Chinese subjects living either in Malaysia or in Singapore. Third, people tend to make more personal attributions for a positive than for a negative act accomplished by ingroupers. It is much less the case for behaviours performed by outgroupers. Fourth, group attributions are limited to certain attributional dimensions. For instance, people rarely rate the ease or difficulty of a task in order to discriminate between groups.

Importantly, some psychologists have argued that the classical taxonomy between internal and external attributions is due to people's naïve theories. For instance, spontaneous attributions by laypersons do not always coincide with this taxonomy (Hewstone, Gale & Purkhardt, 1990; Sousa & Leyens, 1987; Vala, Leyens & Monteiro, 1989). Moreover, explicit ideologies may interfere with this taxonomy and upset Pettigrew's hypothesis. Vala, Monteiro and Leyens (1988) found that very radical Portuguese subjects attributed an aggressive act committed by a policeman to internal causes and the same act committed by a delinquent to external causes. However, very conservative Portuguese subjects more equally distributed both types of attributions for the two actors. In fact, these patterns of attributions reflect the subjects' ideologies (Ibáñez, 1994; Moscovici, 1982). In other words, the 'ultimate attribution error' is such only to the extent that it corresponds to subjects' explanatory system of the world.

We now turn to the overattribution bias at the individual level. We aim to show that the same principles are at work and can enlighten the stereotyping process.

The overattribution bias paradigm

Let us be clear: we assume that the reader knows the basics about attribution models (Beauvois, 1984; Hewstone, 1989; Leyens, 1983) and it is not our intention to review all their new developments here, such as the very numerous studies dealing with Kelley's cube (Fosterling, 1989; Hilton, 1990; Hilton & Slugoski, 1986; Jaspars, 1983; Lipe, 1991; Medcof, 1990). For the rest of this chapter, we will concentrate on the over-attribution bias (OAB), a phenomenon first noticed by Jones and Harris (1967). The rich literature will give us the opportunity to treat stereotyping as a reliance on theory.

When Jones and Harris (1967) started to run their first subjects, they had a very clear idea of the results they would find. They based their predictions on the correspondent inference theory (Jones & Davis, 1965) that had, in some ways, already been tested by Jones, Davis and Gergen (1961). In the experiment by Jones et al., the researchers wanted to show that behaviour appropriate to role expectations has little informational value for highlighting individual characteristics. In contrast, behaviour that departs from role expectations takes on special significance for appraising a person's characteristics (Jones & Thibaut, 1958). Experimenters gave subjects a tape-recorded interview between a psychologist and a student. According to the instructions on the tape, the student had to convince the interviewer that he was ideally suited for a particular job: submariner or astronaut. Short presentations of the job requirements made clear the importance of other-directedness for the submariner and of inner-directedness for the astronaut. By current standards, the pairing of inner-directedness and the job of astronaut may appear somewhat surprising. Still, as the movie *The Right Stuff* nicely illustrates, technical constraints in those days required astronauts to be of the introvert type. During the interview, half the students in each condition – astronaut and submariner – did not present themselves as expected. There were four conditions. The target clearly displayed in-role behaviour when presenting himself as an extrovert for the submariner job or as an introvert for the astronaut job, or the target clearly displayed out-of-role behaviour for the two jobs. After listening to the interview, experimental subjects had to rate the candidate on extroverted and introverted items. In line with Jones et al.'s (1961) hypotheses, subjects' statements concerning the student were more extreme and more confident when the behaviour was out-of-role. This study concludes that 'individual characteristics are obscured when a person is exposed to strong and demanding stimulus forces' (Jones et al., 1961, p. 309).

In Jones and Harris' (1967, expt 1) experiment, the targets were not left 'free' to behave in accordance or not with expectations. Their task was to write an essay in favour of or against Castro (with the understanding that the anti-Castro stand was clearly the popular one). Half of the targets were free to select the side – pro- or anti- – of the issue, and the other half were forced. After reading one of the dissertations, subjects had to decide about the true position of the essay's writer on the issue. Given the results obtained by Jones et al. (1961), subjects should rely on the content of the text when the author's choice is unconstrained. In contrast, subjects should depend on ambient norms when the author is forced. This latter hypothesis means that if the author's behaviour is essentially the consequence of the experimenter's pressures, subjects can hardly infer anything else than what they know a priori about people like the target. Thus, judgements should rely on category-based expectations.

Here is how we present Jones and Harris' experiment to our students and their reactions. 'Imagine that you are an American student in the early sixties. Everyone there is viscerally anti-Communist. The Cuban regime is like a bomb deposited at your doorway. As part of a psychology experiment, you read an essay and you realize that its author has chosen to

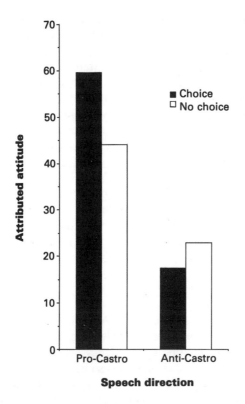

Figure 8.1 *Means of attributed attitude scores as a function of speech direction and choice (Jones & Harris, 1967)*

write it in favour of Castro. What is the author's opinion about Castro?' Almost without exception, students claim that the author is in favour of Castro. 'Yes, presumably, he is one of those rare eccentrics who is both American and Communist. What if another author decided to write against Castro?' Again, the reaction is unanimous. 'He is of course against Fidel Castro, as are all the other students except the previous one. Now, imagine that the author was not free to elect the stance of the essay. He was actually forced by the experimenter who shows you a text written against Castro and warns you about the injunction. What is the true belief of the writer?' In this case, students hesitate and we sometimes have to remind them of the political climate in the USA in the 1960s. 'OK, the author is evidently against Castro like everyone else at that time in the States and the injunction probably has no effect since he would at any rate have selected to write against Castro. What, now, if he was forced to write in favour of Castro? What would you predict about the author's real political attitude?' Like Jones and Harris, our students expect the author to be against Castro.

As the reader knows, this pattern was not obtained. When the essay's writer was forced, a significant difference emerged between the anti- and pro-Castro conditions (see Figure 8.1). It takes some time to convince our Belgian students that the original subjects answered that the forced author was pro-Castro and that this unexpected result is not due to some cultural peculiarity or experimental artifact. For instance, we go over the fact that the experiment was replicated a number of times (Jones, 1990), with an essay of lesser quality (Schneider & Miller, 1975), with subjects having been warned that the arguments presented in the essay were suggested by the experimenter, where the targets read a dissertation written by someone else rather than prepared by the experimenter (Miller, 1976), and with subjects having themselves been previously forced to write a counter-attitudinal essay (Snyder & Jones, 1974). How to explain this over-attribution bias given that it was not predicted by the correspondent inference theory, that it was not expected on the basis of Jones et al.'s (1961) findings, and that external observers such as our students have difficulties accepting its genuineness?

Anchoring and adjustment

A long time ago, Heider predicted the OAB when he wrote that, although 'changes in the environment are almost always caused by acts of persons in combination with other factors, the tendency exists to ascribe the changes entirely to persons' (1944, p. 361). This is so because 'the behavior engulfs the field' (Heider, 1958), because the actors and their actions are especially salient and form a figure against the circumstantial background. To Jones (1979) and other researchers, invoking salience is merely substituting one description for another. Why should salience of behaviour, Jones asked, lead to person attribution rather than to situation attribution? We agree with this objection. After all, our students as well as Jones and Harris expected the latter effect. Moreover, the writer emerges merely through what she or he has written. This is a far cry from a salience manipulation.

In his Distinguished Scientific Contribution Award address, Jones did not downplay the role of salience, but changed the content of what is salient. For him, the behaviour itself is not at the foreground, but the link – the causal unit – between this behaviour and the actor. 'What is more reasonable, after all, than the brute, palpable fact that there can be no action without an actor? The notion that situations can cause an action is abstract and derivative, almost metaphorical in its implications' (1979, p. 114). According to Jones, the actor–act unit is most readily available. Following Tversky and Kahneman's (1974) heuristic, this unit – the author wrote a dissertation in favour of Castro – serves as an anchor – the author is pro-Castro – and this anchor must be subsequently adjusted as a function of situational factors – yes, but wasn't she forced to write in favour of Castro? Often, however, the adjustment is insufficient and therefore people overestimate the weight of the dispositional variables. This in-sufficiency has not yet been accounted for. In the following sections, we will review the different factors which were responsible for anchoring and insufficient adjustment. For Jones, 'any one of [these factors] might be sufficient to create the effect' (1990, p. 147). In other words, the anchoring-adjustment is still the privileged explanation even though it only substitutes one bias to account for another.

Anchoring the judgement

The quality of the essay

To the extent that the OAB depends on an initial anchor, the quality of the essay should have an impact upon the attribution process. Readers, for instance, may entertain the hypothesis that the persuasiveness of an essay is diagnostic of the real attitude of its writer. Using the issue of the legalization of marijuana, Jones, Worchel, Goethals and Grumet (1971) altered the intrinsic strength of the arguments to produce strong and weak essays. Specifically, strong essays used four good arguments whereas weak essays contained two strong and two weak arguments. The familiar Jones and Harris' results come out when the strong essay is presented. With the weak essay, the pattern reverses in the no-choice conditions: the opposite side is taken as the author's true position. This reaction seems normal because only a convinced person can masterfully defend a position and only coercion can explain the lack of any well-articulated ideas (see also Miller, Ashton & Mishal, 1990). In a related vein, Schneider and Miller (1975) conducted two experiments in which they manipulated more peripheral cues. First, they varied the forcefulness of the speech. Whether or not speakers expressed high confidence in their opinions made no difference. Second, Schneider and Miller examined the impact of the speakers' enthusiasm. Whereas the enthusiastic speaker read out the essay by relying on heavy eye contact as well as on hand gestures, the unenthusiastic speaker not only spoke in a monotone fashion but also minimized gestures. Still, the original OAB pattern held. In sum, even though subjects bias their judgement, they are sensitive to the quality of the available information. You may posit that the essay's quality helps to anchor the judgement.

Relative ambiguity of the behaviour and of the situation

For adjustment to take place, a person must first identify the anchor. Still, we know that environmental stimuli are, more often than not, quite ambiguous. Fortunately, Trope (1986) recently clarified the role of ambiguity in the attribution process in general and in the anchoring step in particular. As a point of departure, his model assumes that two kinds of information, behaviour and situation, are processed in an identification stage. This leads to situational categorization or behavioural categorization. Then comes a second, inferential, stage culminating in the personality disposition.

Imagine that you see someone weeping who has just heard that a friend has terminal cancer. The weeping behaviour influences, of course, your behavioural categorization, which is also affected by the situational information. It is definitively not joy that makes the person cry. Conversely, the situational as well as the behavioural information helps you to identify the situational categorization: it is a sad event. The result of the identification sets the stage for the dispositional inference. The higher the magnitude of the situational categorization, the less the 'sad' disposition. In other words, the terminal cancer information helps the subject to decide that the person is in a sad state and not intrinsically emotional. In contrast, the higher the behavioural categorization, the higher the 'sad' disposition. If the person wept and stayed in bed for several weeks, you do not need much of the situational information to infer that this person is chronically depressed and not just sad. While most past efforts stressed the inferential stage, Trope's innovation is to insist on the identification stage and to show that situational information, for instance, intervenes several times in the process, and, sometimes, in different ways.

This returns us to the controversy between Taylor et al. (1978) and Oakes and Turner (1986) on the role of salience. Like Oakes and Turner, Trope defends the idea that information is contextual; it is both bottom-up and top-down. For him, the higher the ambiguity of the correspondent stimuli, the more pronounced the contextual effects will be. For example, you may think that tears are more ambiguous than big laughs and therefore their categorization depends more on the situation – it is an excellent joke that brings tears. It follows from the model that if the joke helped to identify the tears as joy, its influence is subtracted for the attributional inference: 'it is not an especially joyful person because I needed to know the situation he was in to be sure what he was feeling' (Trope, 1986; Trope, Cohen & Maoz, 1988). In contrast, when the situation is ambiguous – many people are laughing but the target has a poker-face – it has a greater impact on the disposition – 'this man is really not a bon vivant because he could at least smile' (Trope & Cohen, 1989). Of course, people do not always need such reasoning. Given that the identification processes are highly practised and closely related to the properties of the stimulus information, people are likely to perform them unconsciously and spontaneously. This may also be true for the inference stage, although probably to a lesser extent.

One of the verifications of the model resembles the overattribution paradigm (Trope, Cohen & Alfieri, 1991). Subjects are informed that managers who participated in a seminar on interpersonal communication had to describe a person either as persistent and serious (a positive description) or as stubborn and grim (a negative description). One of these descriptions is distributed to subjects. Its content is either positive, negative or ambiguous. The subjects must evaluate both the description and the real attitude of the manager towards the person. The description is perceived according to its content except when it is ambiguous. In that case, ambiguity is interpreted in line with the instructions – positive or negative – given to the participants of the seminar. As far as the real attitude of those giving an unambiguous description is concerned, the predictions are less extreme when the descriptions are consistent with the instructions than when they are not. For instance, a manager expected to describe a person negatively, but whose description is positive, is perceived as having a nicer personality than someone who has complied with the negative instruction. However, when the descriptions are ambiguous, the hypothesized attitude does not correspond to the positive or negative instructions. Thus, ambiguity in the descriptions confers a greater role to the context, the instructions for the identification, but substracts that impact for the attribution of a disposition.

Adjusting the judgement

The cognitive resources

Daniel Gilbert proposed an attributional model that elegantly accounts for the impact of cognitive resources upon attribution (Gilbert el al., 1988). We call it the 3 Cs model: it consists of the three stages of categorization, characterization and correction. Categorization corresponds to the extensive sense of perception: 'the bride is crying'. Characterization is the equivalent of anchoring: 'the bride is oversensitive'. Correction, finally, coincides with the adjustment stage: 'the bride is maybe not oversensitive, because the situation lends itself to crying, but she is definitively sensitive'. An essential notion in Gilbert's approach is the decreasing automaticity involved along the different steps. As automaticity is replaced by control, people need cognitive resources. Categorization is mostly automatic and its price is not exorbitant in terms of cognitive processing. Although essentially spontaneous, characterization costs more as far as cognitive resources are concerned. You should be able to make the inference between crying and emotionality. By definition, correction is the least automatic stage. It is the most demanding moment for awareness when all kinds of decision rules can be taken, from simple heuristics to rigorous procedures. This hierarchy of control explains the underemployment of the situational information – necessary for the correction – when the subjects are cognitively busy. Thus, it can also account for the OAB.

Subjects participating in one of Gilbert's experiments (Gilbert, Pelham & Krull, 1988, expt 2) heard another person reading an assigned essay. The essay was either pro- or anti-abortion. Experimenters told half the subjects that: 'You will have to use all your skills and intuitions as a person perceiver to figure out what he really believes.' The other half were also warned that after their diagnosis, they would themselves write a speech on an assigned topic. The results are presented on Figure 8.2. As can be seen,

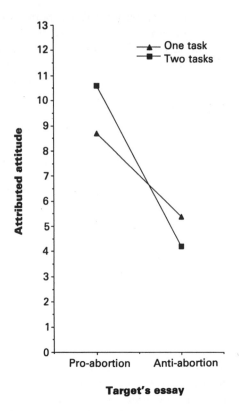

Figure 8.2 *Subjects' perceptions of target's attitude towards abortion as a function of essay direction and number of tasks (Gilbert, Pelham & Krull, 1988)*

there is indeed an overattribution to the writer's disposition in the 'normal' condition, and, as expected, the overattribution is inflated in the 'busyness' condition.

This is only one of the many ingenious studies imagined by Gilbert and his associates. Other experiments varied the material and the cognitive tasks, always with the same result: cognitive subjects are unable to make the correction. Imagine the following situation: you are invited to participate in a psychology study and the experimenter informs you that you will watch a video of two short excerpts of a get-acquainted conversation between two female students. Given the position of the camera, only one of the students is visible on the screen. You are warned that, after the clips, you will have to estimate the anxious personality of that student. The experimenter explains to you the difference between the deep trait of anxiety and a state of momentary anxiety. Your task is to report the state of anxiety during the clips by continuously adjusting the position of a pointer on an electronic slide with one pole labelled calm and the other anxious. You are finally told that in order to protect the privacy of the discussants, the soundtrack has been removed but a subtitle indicates the topic of the clips. As the movement on your potentiometer shows, the girl is pretty anxious during her get-acquainted conversation. This is not too surprising since the topics are not those a person would want to discuss with a stranger. The subtitle for one clip reads 'sexual fantasies' and the other 'greatest public humiliation'. What if the target exhibits the same nervous behaviour when the subtitles are 'hobbies' and 'ideal vacation'? This time the topics are no excuse for the nervousness; anxiety is part of the girl's personality.

This is how the subjects in one of the Gilbert and Osborne (1989, expt 1) studies reacted. More trait anxiety was attributed in the innocuous situations than in the embarrassing ones. There were two other conditions in this study in which the subjects were kept cognitively busy. In addition to watching the clips with either one or the other kind of subtitles, they had to keep in mind an eight-digit number. The results are startling and quite different from those of the non-busy subjects. The subtitles no longer make a difference. In both cases the target is rated as anxious. This happens despite the fact that the busy subjects traced the momentary state of anxiety as well as the non-busy observers.

In the study that we just summarized, Gilbert and Osborne also tried to undo the bias. Immediately after their initial rating of the anxiety of the discussant, the busy subjects were asked to report their eight-digit number. These no longer busy subjects then had five minutes to write what they thought about the target. Finally, they were asked to rate her anxiety because 'some people like to change their ratings after being given time to think about the woman, and others become even more sure of their previous ratings' (1989, p. 942). The impact of this 'cure' is that all the responses reveal a difference between the embarrassing and innocuous situations. Thus, once no longer busy, subjects are able to discount situational factors. One should not be too optimistic, however, in light of this latter result. A subsequent study (Gilbert & Osborne, 1989, expt 2) suggests that 'misperceptions are metastatic in that they influence other psychological processes, and when this happens, a shot of corrective thinking may purge the original misperception but fail to undo the subsidiary changes that this misperception has brought' (Gilbert & Osborne, 1989, p. 946). Apparently, Gilbert is preparing a 4 Cs model, but we will have to wait to find out whether the fourth C stands for cure or terminal cancer.

The range of latitude

When people try to adjust their perceptions, they may stop too soon. In terms of Kruglanski's model (1990, see Chapter 6), this early 'freezing' in the search for a solution happens because, usually, subjects are urged to give a response and the accuracy of this response is not vital for them. According to Tversky and Kahneman (1974), subjects take as an anchor whatever salient information is available (e.g. an arbitrary number on a wheel of fortune) and adjust insufficiently when confronted with a following task involving a number (e.g. the number of African countries in the United Nations). There is a difference, however, between the situation of Tversky and Kahneman's subjects having to guess the number of African nations involved in the United Nations and those who have to judge the real attitude of the essay writer. The first have only one salient piece of information available: an arbitrary number given to them by the experimenter. The second subjects have much more detailed pieces of information: the direction of the essay, their own opinion on the topic, and a decent guess about the range of opinions in the population.

According to Jones and Davis' (1965) correspondent inference theory, people should rely on category-based expectations when judging an author who is forced to take a particular stand. This means that they should disregard the content of the essay as non-diagnostic. Instead, readers should examine the kind of positions likely to be found in the group the author is a member of. This information should provide the main base for valid attributional judgements. In recent experiments, Quattrone and B. Sherman (described in Jones, 1990) have shown that subjects take this information into consideration but stop the process as soon as they hit the range of plausible positions for the judgement at hand. This means that the greater this range of latitude in the population of reference, the sooner the subjects freeze the process, and, thus, the greater the OAB is. For instance, Quattrone and Sherman found that Stanford undergraduates had a greater range of values concerning capital punishment than co-ed dormitories. They also felt prey to the OAB more in the former case than in the latter.

The effect of accountability

As seen earlier, the OAB is influenced by the amount of cognitive resources available. At a general level, however, recent research in social cognition indicates that both cognitive and motivational forces are important factors influencing the social judgement process. Previous chapters revealed that people can be motivated or stimulated to process information in complex, effort-demanding ways. This motivation can profoundly affect strategies that people use to process social information.

Tetlock (1985), for instance, applied accountability (see previous chapters) to the OAB paradigm. He operationalized accountability by asking his subjects to justify their impression of the essay writer to an associate of the experimenter. This warning was given before the subjects read the essay or after; another third of the subjects did not receive the accountability instructions. The essay concerned affirmative actions in colleges. It was written under high or low choice and took either a favourable or an unfavourable stand towards affirmative action. Overall, the OAB was replicated, as can be seen in Figures 8.3(a) and 8.3(b).

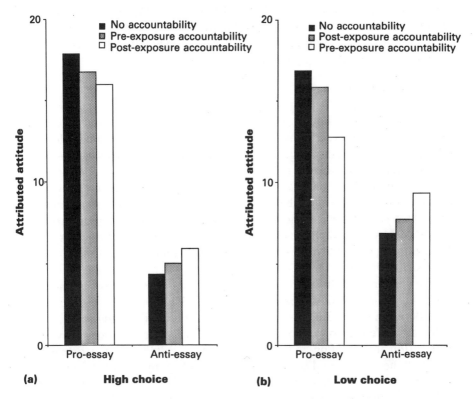

Figures 8.3(a) and (b)   *Subjects' perceptions of target's attitude as a function of choice, essay direction, and accountability (Tetlock, 1985)*

Moreover, in the high choice conditions, the accountability variable didn't have any effect whereas it did in the low choice conditions. Also, subjects who were warned beforehand that they would have to justify their impression polarized their judgements less than did the others. That is, they were less susceptible to the OAB. The difference in the timing of the accountability pressure is interesting. When researchers delivered the accountability instructions after subjects read the essay, the OAB was as strong as it usually is. This latter finding suggests that the OAB is reduced by the processing – encoding – of the information (see also Tetlock, 1983a and b), and not by the type of judgement the subjects are willing or feel required to express. In other words, accountability cannot be interpreted as a social desirability manipulation. The difference obtained in the timing of the accountability also suggests that 'belief perseverance and the fundamental attribution error [. . .] may be the product of highly over-learned or automatic processing sequences that, once enacted, people have a very hard time retrieving or reporting' (Tetlock, 1985, p. 233).

This research provides evidence for the multiple outcomes of accountability. Not only does accountability emphasize the accuracy goal (Chapter 6), and not only does it accentuate the dilution bias (Chapter 7), but it also suppresses the OAB – probably because cognition and motivation warrant a sufficient adjustment.

Summary

One very important line of research on dispositional attribution followed Jones' suggestion concerning the underlying mechanisms responsible for the OAB. Essentially, psychologists regarded the OAB as a direct consequence of a two-step faulty cognitive strategy. First people anchor their judgement and they then adjust it insufficiently. The quality of the essay and the ambiguity of the behavioural and situational information are important factors for the anchoring step. The adjustment step, in turn, is influenced by such factors as the availability of cognitive resources, the motivation guiding the observer, and the range of latitude in the observer's pre-existing beliefs.

The anchoring–adjustment heuristic implies a linear process. Its starting point is the dispositional explanation. The situational factors are only considered in terms of a possible correction of the initial judgement. The research reviewed so far does not question the basic hierarchy between disposition and situation, at least at the inferential stage; the person comes first and the situation adds. First, is this the only path possible? As will be seen soon, a few studies indicate that it is not: people are capable of building upon the situation instead of the person. Second, what determines the path taken? In our opinion, the extent to which people look at the situation and/or at the person heavily depends upon the theories they entertain about the judgements. On the one hand, the way they conceive of the particular observed behaviour, i.e. the theories they have about the behaviour under scrutiny, greatly influences their path. On the other hand, the very instructions they are explicitly or implicitly provided with in the judgement context, i.e. the task they are given, also plays a role.

In our view, the OAB is not only a trade-off between person and situation. It is also an equilibrium between judging and not judging. In other words, the combination of the experimental context and the theories about the behaviour determines the extent to which people feel entitled to judge. As such, the research that follows extends the judgeability studies presented earlier. This time, however, the adequacy level is no longer the cultural one, but the theoretical one. Subjects who fall prey to the OAB are not necessarily cognitive misers. On the contrary, they may be very active intellectually. We suggest that they creatively try to find an explanation that best fits their representation of the task. We propose that the best explanation in their eyes is the one they think is coherent in the context (Murphy & Medin, 1985). We contend that the materials as well as the instructions and the dependent variables orient the participants towards certain explanations. In that respect, this context also gives indications as to how the judgement should be performed, or if it may be performed. In other words, explicit and implicit instructions may moderate the extent to which perceivers start the explanation with the person or the situation.

People trust what they already know

People probably rely on prior knowledge that has already been used and proved useful. This assumption partly accounts for the well-known phenomenon of belief perseverance. This idea was taken over by Kulik (1983). At the core Kulik argues that the consistency of the target behaviour and the prior information about the actor are important influences on judgements. He notes that in the traditional studies on the OAB, researchers stress the differential information about the situation. One implication of this focus is that perception of situations is not supposed to vary whereas perception of targets is. It is as if the situation represents a physical reality that can only be depicted in one way by all subjects, even if this reality has to be discounted later on. Meanwhile the target can induce different perceptions. If you remember the Belgian presentation of the Castro experiment, you certainly noticed how much the teacher has to insist on the United States' peculiar situation. It is indeed not at all obvious for Belgian students that people are against Castro. Thus, the teacher must create a category-based expectation.

Kulik is interested in target-based rather than category-based expectations. He hypothesizes that an actor who behaves according to the judges' expectations will be perceived as dispositionally driven, even when situational pressures may be responsible for the consistency over time. Conversely, if the target behaves inconsistently, his or her behaviour will be attributed to situational forces even though these worked in a direction opposite to the inconsistent behaviour. Thus, once people have formed a schema about a person, they try to maintain it, sometimes by distorting the perception of the situation. The data obtained by Kulik support the hypothesis whether the targets are alien to the subjects (Kulik, 1983) or are the subjects themselves (Kulik & Mahler, 1986; Kulik, Sledge & Mahler, 1986). In light of these results, it would appear that category-based expectations lead to different outcomes than target-based expectancies. When an individual does not behave in accordance with his group membership, people believe he has a 'special' personality responsible for his deviance, even when circumstantial factors provide plausible explanations. Now, if someone doesn't act as expected, people rely on situational explanations even though pressures oppose the inconsistent behaviour. What is important, however, is that in both cases the process of attribution preserves the existing beliefs.

People pay attention to the situation

Even according to the classical paradigm, people are not inherently insensitive to situational elements. Snyder (a student of Jones) and Frankel, in 1976, provided initial support for situational attention. Snyder wanted to avoid a criticism voiced by Kelley (1971) against the OAB paradigm. According to the criticism, everything depended on whether the emphasis was put on the essay's content or on the situational constraints. In other words, a focus on the content would lessen the impact of the situation. Instead, Snyder imagined an experiment where the bias of attribution would be present only if people pay attention to the situation. To this aim, he set up the paradigm used years later by Gilbert (another of Jones' students).

Male college students watched two videotapes with no soundtracks. Each video presented the interview of a female undergraduate who behaved rather ambiguously. Either before or after watching the video-tape, the male students were informed about the questions asked of each target. One target was interviewed about sexual matters (e.g. 'Do you think partners should experiment with various sexual behaviours for the sake of trying everything at least once?') and the other one about a much less embarrassing topic, politics. One dependent variable tapped the temporary emotional state of the interviewees and showed that only the information given before the videotape had an influence. The under-graduate interviewed about sex was perceived as more anxious during the conversation than the one talking about politics. The other dependent variable measured the emotional disposition of the interviewee. The topic of the interview made a difference in both presentations, but the ambiguous behaviour of the interviewee was perceived in opposite ways depending on whether the information about the topic was given before or after the subjects watched the video. When the subjects were warned beforehand, ambiguity led to augmenting or 'engulfing'. The person interviewed about sex was viewed as having a more anxious personality than the one discussing politics. These results may indicate that subjects confirm their first hypothesis: she should be anxious and she is, she shouldn't be anxious and she isn't. In contrast, discounting took place when the information was given at the end of the interview. This time, the person interviewed about politics appeared more dispositionally anxious than the one who answered questions concerning sexual behaviour. Again, this can be seen as hypothesis confirmation: she was somewhat anxious and it is understandable, or she was somewhat anxious and she shouldn't have been. (Another interpretation looks at contextualization. This experiment is indeed a typical example quoted as evidence for Trope's [1986] model.)

Quattrone (1982), still another student of Jones, provided evidence that subjects actually overestimate the situational factors if they first link them to the behaviour rather than to the actor. According to Quattrone, the judges' attention in the traditional attitude attribution paradigm focuses upon the personal attributes of the author because of the experimental set-up. The instructions ('Try to determine the real attitude of the essay's author'), the fact that people usually write in accordance with their beliefs, the proximity between the author and the content (e.g. reading aloud while on video), and the similarity in the dimensions used to evaluate both the author and the content all contribute to the immediate focus of the subjects on the act–actor unit.

In two studies, Quattrone induces his subjects to pay particular attention to the situation. For this, he alerts subjects that, sometimes, invalid data are obtained because of experimental demands. He asks them to determine to what extent the scenario of the study they will read was contaminated by such experimental (situational) demands. In one of Quattrone's studies, subjects then receive some background information about a typical North Carolina student who was completely free to write an essay either in favour of or against the legalization of marijuana. In half of the cases, the author showed evidence that he has no opinion about the issue, whereas in the other half he has strong feelings that are reflected in the essay. Quattrone's subjects then read the essay. In half of the conditions, it is a strong demonstration for legalization; in the other half, it is a very severe opposition to legalization (the material was already used by Jones et al., 1971). The task of the subjects is to evaluate the degree to which the content of the essay is due to experimental demands.

According to Quattrone, subjects will concentrate on the situational demand to compose a pro- or anti-legalization essay, and then adjust their judgements. The question now is: adjustment relative to what? The adjustment has to be done relative to what subjects know about the author, and the only difference in the various scenarios is the author's opinion about the legalization. Thus, when subjects know that the author has a strong opinion, mirrored in the essay, they should adjust and estimate that the situational demands didn't play a role in the direction and extremity of the essay. In agreement with the insufficiency of adjustment hypothesis, this did not happen. Even though the subjects knew that the authors completely endorsed the content of the essay, they still invoked situational demands because they concentrated on those first. Of course, when the author's opinion was known, they did not invoke the situational pressures as much as when the essay writer had no opinion about the issue. Thus, subjects took the opinion of the author into account but insufficiently. In another experiment, the same induction is used with another material – nuclear energy – and this time observers are compared to the writers themselves. As expected, observers judge the situational demands to be stronger and they adjust less than do the writers.

The above examples attest that subjects in experiments do not turn their backs on the information, not even the information concerning the situation. As Quattrone's (1982) and Snyder and Frankel's (1976) results demonstrate, it is possible to direct subject's attention to the situational determinants of behaviour (see also Webster, 1993). Once such a perspective is induced among perceivers, they use the situation as an initial anchor.

The principle of cooperativeness

One explanation for the OAB is the fact that participants comply with the principle of cooperativeness in conversation (Grice, 1975). In other words, subjects assume that whatever information the experimenter presents them with, this is sufficient, truthful, relevant and clear. Without this principle of cooperativeness, it would be extremely difficult to hold a conversation. Each encounter would resemble a chess tournament or a diplomatic negotiation rather than a real exchange (see also Chapter 7).

What happens when subjects believe that they don't have relevant information? Wright and Wells (1988) conducted an experiment to answer that precise question. They ran half the subjects within the traditional procedure. The other half were further told that:

> Each participant in this study is being asked to respond to a set of questionnaire items that have been selected randomly from a larger pool of questions. Consequently, many of the questions you may be asked might seem poorly matched to the information you have received. That is, you may be asked to make judgments for which the information you were given is either irrelevant or insufficient for making that judgment. You should, therefore, not assume that the information you have received is directly relevant to each specific question you are asked. Nevertheless we would like you to make your best attempt at answering all the questions provided.

Results were clear-cut. The traditional procedure led to a huge OAB. Although the bias was substantially reduced when subjects suspected they might not have received the relevant information, it was not totally absent. The authors concluded that 'the bias is a genuine phenomenon. Nevertheless, the magnitude of the bias effect obtained with the traditional attitude-attribution paradigm has probably been exaggerated by the violation of the cooperativeness rule' (Wright & Wells, 1988, p. 188).

The influence of the principle of cooperativeness may explain why attributionally complex subjects are more prone to the OAB than less complex participants. Attributional complexity is a measure of social intelligence that taps both ability and motivation to process information about people (Fletcher, Danilovics, Fernandez, Peterson & Reeder, 1986). Therefore, complex subjects may try to cooperate more with the experimenter by giving meaning to what s/he presents. The link between the OAB and measures of social competence is not an isolated finding. In a somewhat different context, Block and Funder (1986) found that adolescents most prone to the fundamental attribution error, far from being disadvantaged in social judgement, tended to be more socially engaged and competent as well as emotionally well adjusted.

A suspicious personality

Earlier, we alluded to the discrepancy between the OAB pattern and the results found by Jones et al. (1961). Interestingly, in the paradigm used by Jones and Harris (1967), the particular behaviour is the writing of an essay. In our opinion as well as in Quattrone's (1982), such a behaviour emphasizes the dispositional causes because, in the case of controversial issues, people usually write what they believe. In the job interview situation used by Jones et al. (1961), however, a target's behaviour is readily accounted for in terms of non-enduring dispositional characteristics. The candidate who gets interviewed most probably wants the interviewer to hire him or her. If this reasoning is correct, then people have spontaneous interpretations of many behaviours. Still, it should be possible to direct subjects' attention to non-spontaneously invoked determinants of behaviours by altering the context surrounding these behaviours. For instance, the implicit view that people write what they truly believe may be questioned by modifying the reasons for the writing and therefore the interpretation given to the behaviour.

Fein, Hilton and Miller (1990; see also Hilton, Fein & Miller, 1993) provided nice evidence along these lines. In two experiments, they told half of their subjects that a student had been assigned to write an essay in a certain direction. They found the classical OAB. The remaining half of the subjects were presented with an author who was free to choose the stand but probably chose a particular stand in order to ingratiate him- or herself with an important person or to avoid an unwanted job. There was no OAB at all for the suspicious subjects. In a third experiment, Fein et al. (1990) showed that an ulterior motive (ingratiation, displeasure avoidance) does not lead the suspicious judges to block every processing of information concerning the actor. Actually, the suspicion of an ulterior motive makes the information ambiguous. This is exactly how Jones et al. (1961) interpreted their findings: you can't really trust someone who is interviewed to get a job.

The available information gives meaning to the task

We saw that people come to the experiment with pre-existing beliefs that they tend to confirm. For instance, they neglect situational pressures if the behaviour corresponds to what they expect from the target. This does not mean that people always underestimate the importance of situations and concentrate upon the persons. The actual focus depends very much on the instructions and the intake of information. Also, people assume that the experimenter tells them something relevant for their task. They therefore try to extract as much meaning as possible from the situation they are in. The instructions may be such that one usual interpretation of the behaviour is replaced by another. For instance, the content of an essay reveals not a true but a devious personality.

What happens if the presentation of the experiment is, as much as possible, devoid of information that could trigger pre-existing beliefs? Such a situation was imagined by Ajzen, Dalto and Blyth (1979) for half of their subjects. The presentation of the experiment went as follows: 'Peter G. is a student at Hamsphire College.' As a class assignment, he wrote an essay favouring or opposing abortion on demand. Either the instructor left the decision of the stand to Peter or the stand was imposed upon him. The essay was not circulated among the subjects who had to decide about the true attitude of the writer. Figures 8.4(a) and 8.4(b) show the results. The ratings are strongly polarized in the direction of the stand when Peter was free to take a stand. The data are quite different when there is no choice. The results for the two essays are not different from each other. One could say that subjects didn't really take a position but chose the middle of the scale. Here, the adjustment or correction is complete. For the other half of their subjects, Ajzen et al. distributed a non-diagnostic personality profile of Peter. A few paragraphs described Peter's personality as relatively independent, relatively insecure of his image, relatively flexible, etc. – information that young adults easily accept (Ulrich, Stachnik & Stainton, 1963) and that, from our point of view, may be considered ambiguous. When only the origin of the essay is given, subjects report, on average, a 59.5 per cent chance in favour of abortion to Peter. When the personality is added, the percentage becomes 57 per cent. It can be concluded that Peter's personality profile is non-diagnostic about his stand on abortion. A look at Figures 8.4(a) and 8.4(b) shows, however, that the personality sketch, compared to the control conditions, has a great influence upon the results. The usual OAB is equally obtained when the somewhat independent, insecure and flexible Peter is forced and when the choice is free. In other words, relative to the conditions where information about the author was absent, the presence of the personality profile polarized the results in the forced choice conditions and depolarized them in the freedom conditions.

How do Ajzen and his colleagues explain these results? In the absence of any information other than whether the opinion of the essay was free or constrained, people assume that what is written is completely diagnostic of the writer's essay. When subjects only know that the stand is forced upon Peter, however, this information becomes particularly salient. Subjects do not take the content of the essay into account and rely instead on base-rates. When experimenters provide non-diagnostic information – the omnibus personality profile – to the subjects, they use it diagnostically and revise their anchors accordingly. Both directions are possible because the information was purposefully ambiguous. According to Ajzen et al. (1979), people in the no-choice condition use the ambiguous information to confirm their hypothesis. This leads to a polarization away from the middle point of the scale. Apparently, also, some points in the personality

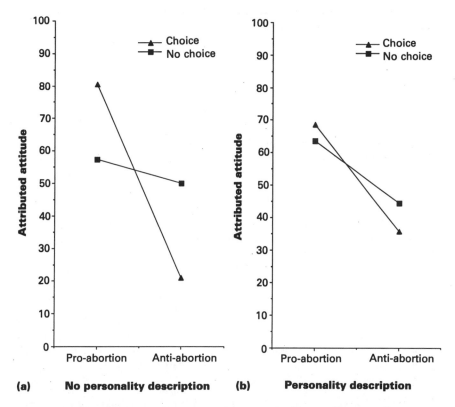

Figures 8.4(a) and (b)   *Estimated pro-abortion attitudes as a function of availability of personality description, essay direction, and choice (Ajzen, Dalto & Blyth, 1979)*

profile may seem inconsistent with the hypothesis. These are responsible for the depolarization in the choice conditions.

We believe a different explanation can better account for the available data. Half of the subjects in Ajzen et al.'s experiment are in exactly the same situation as (Belgian) students who hear about the study. Like Ajzen's subjects, they don't read an essay and the only thing they know about the author is that he is free or forced to take a stand. In both cases, participants and students do not fall prey to the OAB. One possible explanation is that without the essay subjects do not have an anchor. Interestingly, when people learn of Peter's personality, they overattribute in spite of the absence of an anchor provided by the content of the essay. We argue that the personality information supplies subjects with a specific reading of the judgement situation: 'This experiment is about personality and this is why I am asked to guess the true belief of the writer; the correct answer is to be found in the personality of the writer.'

Let us have a look at the original Jones and Harris' (1967, expt 1) experiment to see if it emphasized personality. Personality may have been stressed much more than the researchers realized.

Telling more than we think

The presentation of the study reads as follows:

> Each subject was handed a mimeographed pamphlet that contained an essay on Castro's Cuba, a prior statement manipulating the choice variable, and a final questionnaire. The experimenter then explained the purpose of the experiment as 'an attempt to determine if people can make valid judgments of another's *personality* and attitudes on the basis of very limited information'. The subjects were led to believe that a variety of *personal* materials written by the same undergraduate student were distributed among them. They were told, 'Some of you have an excerpt from the person's *autobiography*, which was originally written to accompany his college application. Others have in your pamphlet a short essay prepared for a creative writing course. The essay deals with conflicting values in contemporary society. [. . .] The remainder of you have an answer from a political science hour exam.' The subjects were then told to glance at the material to identify their condition. They were led to believe that the conditions would be compared to see which kind of written material produced the most valid *impression*, as measured by 'a lot of additional information that you do not know about'. The experimenter went on to state that other target persons would be *evaluated* by other subjects. Actually, each subject was in the 'political science exam' condition. His task was to read the examination answer and attempt to judge the true attitude of the 'target person' toward the topic. The experimenter concluded his orienting overview with some brief remarks *identifying the author of the materials as a student at the University of North Carolina, a resident of the state, and the son of an automobile salesman.* The mimeographed material began with a reproduction of the exam question [to allow the manipulation of choice and direction]. Although the essay was typed, there were occasional spelling errors, false starts, and cross-outs. The experimenter explained that this would provide information about the 'style and approach' of the target person. [. . .] The essay was followed in the booklet by *(a) a 12-item semantic differential scale for rating various personal qualities* of the target person. (Jones & Harris, 1967, pp. 4–5; emphasis ours)

We will let you judge if the emphasis is on personality. Assuredly, not all the subsequent studies have stressed the personality of the writer to that extent (nor did they use such unanimous topic as Castro). Nevertheless, all these studies present subjects with the task of making judgements for which, implicitly or explicitly, subjects have to use their clinical skills.

The selection of controversial issues (Castro, segregation, legalization of marijuana, marriage of homosexuals, nuclear power, capital punishment, abortion on demand, etc.) may also induce the idea that personality is the explanatory factor of the adopted side. If so, then there will be an adequate connection between the theory activated by the instructions and the behaviour of the writer. If there is adequacy, subjects will not refrain from judging, and, hence, they will bias their judgement in the direction of an overattribution.

OAB and naïve theories about the world

We suggest that judgements need to have an explanatory value. They must serve as a theory for explaining other people's behaviours, personality traits and physical appearances. If people do not possess an adequate theory, they will refrain from making polarized judgements. This view corresponds to the psychological essentialism presumed to underlie natural (Medin, 1989) and social categories (Rothbart & Taylor, 1992). To say that Charles is a Mediterranean, and therefore boisterous, rather than a raucous man, a vociferous physician or an obstreperous pyknic makes sense only if ethnicity has some kind of explanatory value, i.e. if it evokes some theoretical underlying personality structure. Because attribution is a special type of social judgement, we propose that the overattribution bias also relies on an adequate naïve theory in the subjects' minds.

Specifically, in the case of the OAB, we argue that the experimental instructions activate an explanatory theory among participants and that the combination of the instructions with the choice of the controversial issue makes the theory adequate for a judgement or not. If this hypothesis is true, it means that previous research capitalized on an unforeseen match between the explanatory theories elicited by the instructions and those deemed adequate by subjects. More precisely, previous research has consistently activated explanatory theories about personality, personological theories in other words, and employed attitudes issues that are adequately explained by those theories (e.g. attitudes towards abortion, homosexuality, etc.).

To test this general hypothesis, it was necessary first to establish that several controversial issues, especially those issues used in past research within the attitude attribution paradigm, were explained by personological theories and that other issues are explainable by theories other than personological ones. Leyens, Yzerbyt, Corneille, Vilain and Gonçalves (1994, expt 1) asked students to rate the extent to which a large range of controversial issues were explainable in terms of personality, social background and formal education. The results indicate that subjects' naïve theories about the world are personological for many – but not all – issues. This 'psychologization' may explain why the so-called fundamental error is so frequent (Leyens, Aspeel & Marques, 1987; Ross, 1977). Also, the issues used in past research on the overattribution bias have a systematic and privileged link with personality.

In subsequent studies, Leyens, Yzerbyt, Corneille, Vilain and Gonçalves (1994) activated either an adequate theory or an inadequate one, and they had a control condition where no theory at all was activated. The activation of the theory was done via instructions focusing, for example, on personality, social background or formal education. The adequacy of the activated theory was manipulated by the link between these instructions and the particular controversial issue. In one study (Leyens, Yzerbyt, Corneille, Vilain & Gonçalves, 1994, expt 2), the essay dealt with euthanasia, an issue explained in terms of personality. When the instructions activated a personological theory, this theory was adequate. The theory was inadequate when the instructions focused on formal education. In another study (Leyens, Yzerbyt, Corneille, Vilain & Gonçalves, 1994, expt. 3), the essay concerned the closing of mines in the UK, an issue explained in terms of social background. When the instructions stressed a sociological view, it was an adequate theory; however, when the instructions activated a personological theory, it was inadequate. Information provided by the essay can sometimes overrule the influence of adequate naïve theories. For instance, if the essays are extremely brilliant or poor, people will probably express a polarized judgement regardless of the naïve theory activated by the instructions and regardless of the theory's adequacy with the topic of the essay. To show the potency of adequate naïve theories and eliminate other factors, no essay was distributed to the subjects (as in Ajzen et al., 1979).

To a third of the subjects, the experiment was presented as a decision-making study. The essay was written in the course of an exam (no theory condition). To another third of subjects, the study was also described as a decision-making task but the author supposedly wrote the essay during an admission examination, or during a survey for a doctoral thesis in sociology. A sheet was circulated with items relevant to formal education (e.g. number of years and type of secondary school, higher education) or to social background (e.g. whether the target had a job, the income of the family, the background of the parents). The final third of the subjects were told that the experiment concerned social perception and that the author had passed a personality exam. Again, a sheet was distributed with standard personality items, supposedly part of a personality questionnaire. Contrary to what happened in Ajzen et al.'s experiment, responses were not provided so that no information about the author's personality was available. When the issue was euthanasia, the target was either free or forced to write the essay. Only the forced conditions were run with the closing of mines as the controversial issue.

Figures 8.5(a) and 8.5(b) give the results for the forced conditions in both studies. They show that the activation of an adequate theory for the task at hand is sufficient for the emergence of the OAB. This theory is often a personological one, and it was presumably so in the classical studies of the OAB. To the extent that the instructions and topics in the attitude attribution paradigm highlight personality factors, we may conjecture that subjects will have good reasons to infer that personality is important and constitutes an adequate theory. Thus, the typical OAB may depend on the framing of the experimental situation. Conversely, the present data suggest that overattribution may be more avoidable than is usually thought. To the same extent that no attribution is made when personality is relevant but supposedly deceitful (Hilton, Fein & Miller, 1993), Leyens et al.'s results show that an OAB may take place when another adequate theory than personality is available. This study is not the first one within the attitude

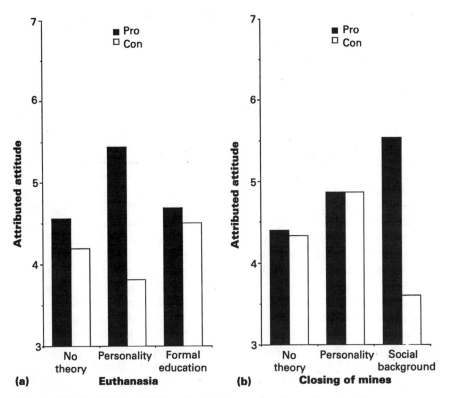

Figures 8.5(a) and (b)   *Estimated attitude as a function of essay topic, activated theory, and essay direction (Leyens, Yzerbyt, Corneille, Vilain & Gonçalves, 1994)*

attribution paradigm that shows the role of a naïve theory other than personality. Remember that Quattrone (1982; see also Krull, 1993; Webster, 1993) wanted to show the insufficiency of the actor's salience to account for the OAB. Reeder, Fletcher and Furman (1989, expt 2), on the other hand, demonstrated the fact that subjects entertain schematic assumptions about the link between behaviour and attitudes. More precisely, the writers are expected to compose an essay falling within a range of possible positions depending on their personal attitude. In contrast to these authors, we propose that subjects come to the laboratory with a set of naïve theories about the world and that they select the most appropriate one for the context. If no adequate explanatory theory is available for some reason, they will not assume that there is, for instance, a link between attitude and behaviour. Instead, they will refrain from polarizing their judgement.

In another study (Leyens, Yzerbyt, Corneille, Vilain and Gonçalves, 1994, expt 4), the non-circulated essay dealt with either euthanasia or the closing of mines. The experiment was presented in a personality or sociology frame and subjects were or were not made accountable. Results replicate the previous studies when subjects were not accountable. The OAB is present when the issue is consistent with the frame, that is, when the theory is adequate. It is absent when the theory is inadequate. As expected, when subjects are accountable, no OAB emerges regardless of the adequacy of the activated theory. It was indeed predicted that accountability would weaken the basis for the adequacy of the theory by leading subjects to realize that they have no relevant information to which to apply their theory. It should be noted that all these results are compatible with the anchoring–insufficient adjustment model or its more recent variations. However, they show that a preliminary step – the priming of an adequate theory – is important for the anchoring to occur in the first place. This observation is consistent with a result obtained by Gilbert and Hixon (1991). These authors found that cognitively busy subjects gave stereotypical answers only to the extent that the stereotype was activated beforehand. When subjects were always cognitively busy, the stereotype was neither activated nor used.

The importance of theory for the expression of social judgements is in line with a pragmatic perspective (Fiske, 1992, 1993). Social perception is essentially an action and social judgements should not be restricted to the intellectual problem-solving task of balancing categorial and individuating information in order to mirror reality. To be useful in interactions, social judgements need social validity. To meet this social validity, people often come to express judgements about others only when they feel entitled to judge, that is, when they deem the target judgeable. This view is also consistent with the thesis defended by Rothbart and Taylor (1992). These authors brilliantly argued that people infuse some kind of essence into otherwise arbitrary social categories. This essence corresponds to some naïve theory about the world and is not restricted to natural categories (Medin, 1989). In conclusion, the important role of adequate explanatory theories for the emergence of the OAB indicates the activity, rather than the passivity, of social perceivers. Far from being simply 'cognitive misers', these social perceivers, or social agents, try to selectively account for what happens around them in terms of accumulated knowledge that has often proved useful in the past.

Conclusions

Not innocently, we started this chapter by presenting the ultimate attribution error. As shown by Hewstone (1990), Pettigrew's (1979) intuitions are well established. However, ethnocentric attributions are not universal but depend upon the ideology or naïve theories of the subjects. Most of the chapter was then devoted to the OAB singled out by Jones and Harris in 1967. This phenomenon is usually explained by a heuristic of anchoring and insufficient adjustment. We reviewed different factors proposed to account for both the anchoring and the adjustment. We suggested that participants are very active in the attitude attribution paradigm. Also, they rely upon prior knowledge when it is available. They look for cooperation with the experimenter and assume that he or she provides them with sufficient, true, clear and relevant material. They are very responsive to the intake of information and to the presentation of the instructions. They try, sometimes very hard, to find meaning in the information and in the experimental situation.

It happens that, without being aware of it, researchers generally induced the idea that personality is the key factor that introduces meaning in the situation. They did it by their instructions, by the general presentation of the experiment – which deals with social perception or perspicacity – and by the choice of the controversial issue. Personality does not need to be the heart of the paradigm, but people are more prone to embrace personality than other factors – biological or sociological, for instance – to explain the divergences in other people's views. This unusual weight given to personality may explain the frequency of the OAB. Generally, it is very effective to believe that personality is responsible for behaviour.

This chapter has obviously been intended to illustrate the theoretical level of adequacy of judgement. People do not only rely on data and theories about data. They also need theories about their judgements. These theories about judgments are produced by a given culture for the sake of efficient interactions, and they necessitate that judgements themselves are 'theories', theoretical explanations of the world. Judgements, such as stereotypes, provide meaning to the social world. If people can't come up with this meaning, this essence, they just do not judge.

Conclusion

To judge is to unite what is diverse. . . . It is not making it singular.

De L'Esprit, P. Ricoeur

When we say that our colleague is creative and that our neighbour is generous, this is no *strictu senso* perception. There is no such thing called generosity or creativity that would be sensed by our retina. When social psychologists speak of social perception, they are referring to the knowledge about others that is expressed through social judgements. These judgements are themselves correspondences between behaviours enacted in specific situations and social categories. In the Introduction to this book, we implied that the number of categories is greater than the possible number of behaviours. Here, we dare to go further and suggest that the number of social categories is infinite whereas the number of behaviours and of situations is finite. There is a limit to behaviours and circumstances, which do not change much with eras and cultures. However, there is no limit to social categories, most of which are arbitrary. As a category, Czechoslovaks existed only between 1918 and 1993. The category 'Jew' has known several definitions through history. The notion of 'mad person' varies through cultures. Homer never said that Paris was attractive and that Hector was courageous at war; he said that Paris looked like a god (*theoeidés*) and that Hector's helmet was vibrating (*koruthaiolos*); in other words, Homer used fewer personality traits than we do.

Flexibility and perseverance

Fundamentally, the human being is an ambiguous entity to try to perceive and to know. The same behaviours may have different meanings depending on the context, different behaviours may have the same meaning, meanings may change in the course of interactions, partners of interactions may deceive each other about what their respective behaviours really mean, and people may not know what they mean while behaving, etc. There is more than ambiguity, however, in social perception. There is indetermination. The imbalance between the finite number of behaviours and situations or circumstances on the one hand, and the infinite number of mostly arbitrary categories, on the other hand, makes social perception intrinsically and ultimately indeterminate. There is not one true perception of others. From a pragmatic viewpoint, however, people must act as if such true perception existed, as if there was no ultimate indetermination. Stated otherwise, efficient interactions cannot and do not rest upon absolute relativism; they take into account the different constraints imposed by the data, theories about data and theories about judgements.

Ambiguity, indetermination and pragmatic concerns explain the flexibility as well as perseverance in social perception. Given the luxury of individuating information and the arbitrariness of most social categories, perception of others must be flexible. Similarly, it is easy for a social perception to be persistent since no solution imposes itself: objections are always possible, if not legitimate.

To better understand flexibility of perception, consider Milgram's famous experiments on obedience to authority. Usually, when people know nothing about these experiments, they believe that only a few individuals will obey until the end and send 450 volts to a partner. Remember, for instance, that Milgram (1974) asked psychiatrists to estimate the number of persons who would be completely obedient in a given experimental condition. Psychiatrists guessed that one out of one thousand subjects would obey up to 450 volts. Shafer (1980) showed his students Milgram's movie *Obedience*, where 65 per cent of subjects go to the end in this classical condition. One week later, he told his students about another condition of Milgram's experiments: subjects were free to select the shock intensities themselves and were not pressured by the experimenter. When asked to estimate the mean shock intensity delivered in this condition, Shafer's students answered an average of 119 volts, with an increase of intensity going from 43 volts for the first trial to 174 volts for the last trial. These estimates contrast with those obtained from naïve subjects who did not see the movie. These uninformed students predicted an average of 84 volts, which is not far from the real behaviours of Milgram's subjects, who delivered, in general, shocks from 45 to 60 volts. These results suggest that Shafer's students went from the naïve theory, according to which 'human beings are fundamentally good and reasonable', to the naïve theory that 'homo homini lupus' ('man is a wolf to man'). Proverbs are supposed to reflect popular wisdom; they also show flexibility, and it is rare not to find a proverb that contradicts another, for instance, 'opposites attract' but 'birds of the same feather flock together'. Proverbs themselves are not fooled by their flexibility, however, since one also says 'Menteur comme un proverbe' ('Liar, like a proverb') (Leyens, 1983).

Flexibility is often intertwined with perseverance, as the following examples show. The authors of this book consider themselves anti-military pacifists who were opposed to the American threat of intervention before the Gulf War. However, very early on 18 January 1991, when they heard on CNN that the war was over with an American victory, they shamefully thought that, all things considered, the American intervention was OK. In the evening, however, they had returned to their original opinion when hearing that the war was not finished after all. In the morning, everything looked as if American adults had spanked a naughty child; in the evening, American warriors were abusing children. Two years after the war, Di Giacomo (1993) showed to first-year students at the University of Lille the televised testimony of a Kuwaiti woman who reported that the Iraqis had stopped incubators in maternity hospitals, causing the death of many children. This testimony produced important polarizations in the students' attitudes towards the Gulf War. Surprisingly, when they saw another TV programme explaining that the testimony was a complete fake, students did not depolarize their judgements. These latter results are very akin to those obtained by Loftus (1979). This author showed that a witness retains his or her impact upon the jury even when he or she is discredited. Ross, Lepper and Hubbard (1975) conducted an experiment that is even more illustrative for our purpose. They led some subjects to think that they were good at detecting false from authentic suicide notes. Other subjects were induced to believe that they were poor at the task. Even after subjects heard that the feedback concerning their performance had been given at random, they continued to believe that they were either good or bad at that type of task. In a similar experiment, Anderson, Lepper and Ross (1980) provided their subjects with information concerning a successful and cautious firefighter, or concerning a successful and audacious firefighter. Subjects then wrote a sketch explaining the relation between success as a firefighter and caution or risk. Afterwards, when the experimenters explained that the relation provided with the information had been given at random, subjects continued to believe in the relationship they had developed in their sketch. These results show perseverance and flexibility of beliefs: people are ready to take one position or another and they persist in their opinion.

This perseverance is most likely due to the fact that people succeed in finding an explanation for the data and that they are reluctant to change this plausible explanation. 'Maybe the feedback was random, but it nevertheless applied to the case I received.' When told that you are good at detecting authentic suicide notes, you may tell yourself: 'No wonder, I am a psychology student. I usually empathize with others.' When told you are bad, you probably reason that: 'No wonder, I have never known a person who committed suicide. I never thought of committing suicide. How could I be good at detecting fake and authentic notes?' Both lines of reasoning plausibly support the information the subject was randomly given – he or she is good/bad at detecting authentic suicide notes. However, the conditions favouring flexibility or perseverance are still a matter of intense investigation (e.g. Leyens & Van Duüren, 1994; Schul & Manzury, 1990).

Accuracy and directional goals

The preceding reasoning implies that the reality level of adequacy is both important and insufficient for social judgements. It is important because people must behave as if it was sufficient, as if there was an objective reality out there providing a true response. However, there is no 'objective reality out there' that informs people correctly. The reality level is thus insufficient and the social judgement should not merely be considered an intellectual problem-solving task. Instead, social perception is an action that is based on previous knowledge and that brings in new knowledge to accomplish further action. Because of the insufficiency of the reality level, we insisted on a multiplicity of adequacy levels. Besides the reality level, the social judgeability levels must also be taken into account. Integrity of the self and of the ingroup, social rules and naïve theories partially determine conditions under which people feel entitled to express a valid judgement. Valid means here socially valid, as opposed to epistemologically valid.

From a pragmatic viewpoint, it is also important to distinguish between two types of goals in social perception. One is the accuracy goal and the other could be called the directional goals. The accuracy goal aims at discovering the 'true' perception. It is the goal pursued, for instance, by professional psychologists who have to render a diagnosis about their clients. The directional goals aim at finding a more circumscribed 'truth' such as that needed for forming perceptions of new neighbours, of colleagues, etc. As these examples illustrate, we deal more often with directional goals than the accuracy goal in everyday life. Different levels of adequacy apply to both types of goals. It would be a mistake to identify, for example, the reality level with the accuracy goal and the directional goals with the integrity of the self and of the group. All levels of adequacy play a role in both kinds of goals, but their emphasis is different as is the use of cognitive and motivational factors.

The professional psychologist who has to diagnose someone is directed by the accuracy goal. He will, therefore, pay special attention to the data, the reality level. Nevertheless, he will also be sensitive to the integrity of the self or of the group. According to his theoretical orientation, he may, consciously or not, process information in a way that does not undermine the orientation to which he belongs. Social rules are also important; the psychologist will certainly not make a judgement based only on categorial information. This psychologist will also work according to theories. The nature of these theories probably depends upon his psychological training, and he would not call them naïve, although they could be more naïve than he thinks. Even the greatest efforts at respecting the different levels of adequacy do not guarantee that the judgment will be correct. We have already said that there is no ultimate truth. Also, as Tetlock and Boettger, 1989 have showed, the pressure to be accurate may increase biases such as the dilution effect. In the case of accuracy-oriented perception, an individuated rather than a categorial judgement is often the task. However, individuation is not synonymous with accuracy and a categorial judgement is sometimes more accurate than an individuated one. When driven by an accuracy goal, people are more concerned to get to know persons than to get along with those persons (Snyder, 1992). This emphasis, however, does not prevent social perception from being essentially an action that immediately bears upon further actions and further knowledge.

Situations that induce directional goals are probably more common than circumstances requiring accuracy goals. In everyday life, we do not have the time to test every possible hypothesis about the person we meet. Were we to do so, we would not be able to interact with many people. However, the reality level is as important for directional goals as are the social judgeability levels. Someone who wants to be promoted in a company should get an idea of what her boss is like. This idea will not be as elaborate as a professional psychological diagnosis, but it is to the candidate's advantage that her idea be realistic.

Stereotypes as expressions of naïve theories

Classically, stereotypes are viewed as judgements that are rigid, oversimplifying and erroneous because they are overgeneralizations. We do not share this view. If stereotypes are considered part of social perception, they should be flexible as well as rigid. Stereotypes are not only lists of attributes that apply to social categories. They function also, and mainly, as theoretical naïve explanations of the world. To the same extent that a person does not change theories all the time, stereotypes should be rigid. Assume for a moment that people have elaborated a theory about the Germans that is based on their 'scientific mind' and their 'hard-working personality'. Will people change their stereotypes of Germans when they hear that Germans, more than other Europeans, are more likely to go on vacations to exotic places having nothing to do with science or culture? Probably not. What they will most likely do is to fit the need for vacation in relaxing places with the necessity of the 'scientific mind' to get distracted in order to renew itself. Remember the wolf in Aesop's and La Fontaine's fable who blames the sheep for drinking in the same river as he does. He is obliged to invent all kinds of wrong-doings on the part of the sheep because no blame stands by itself and Aesop concludes that there is no defence against people who are committed to injustice. However, remember that stereotypes are also flexible. Many examples of this flexibility have been provided throughout this book and even in this Conclusion; this is the fable of the fox suddenly realizing that the grapes are too green.

Stereotypes certainly simplify reality, but they do not necessarily result from intellectual laziness. Aesop's wolf goes to great lengths to justify his illegitimate appetite for the sheep. As we have already said, stereotypes are a means of shorthand for a vast amount of data, but also a means of extrapolating from a little information. At the same time that categorization simplifies, it also brings in extra meanings. If only categories of Croats, Serbs and Bosnians existed, with no overlap between these categories (such as ex-Yugoslavians), it would probably be difficult to understand what is happening between members of these different categories. It would even be harder if no category existed at all! Thus, to the same extent that stereotypes are both flexible and rigid, they simplify past knowledge and create new knowledge. Also, as in the case of Croats, Serbs and Bosnians, people often define themselves as members of a category and behave accordingly. For them, categories are not simplifying devices. Categories are reservoirs of meanings.

Stereotypes are, by definition, generalizations. This does not mean that the process of stereotyping is in some way pathological. On the contrary, stereotyping is a normal and reasonable process. By using stereotypes, it is said, one does not respect the person's individuality. What does that mean? We feel sorry for the person who would be comparable to no one else, completely distinctive. In fact, stereotypes would probably not be attacked if they were positive instead of negative. The attacks are directed at the content of stereotypes rather than at their generalizing component. This generalization aspect does not bother us much. It is fortunate that people can generalize, and it would be even more fortunate if they knew that they generalize. This book has provided evidence that people are quick to interpret categorial information as individuating information, but also that they are often capable of recognizing the difference.

The generalization of negative personality traits bothers us less than the kinds of naïve theories underlying the expression of positive and negative stereotypes. Medin (1989) argued that people tend to infuse some kind of essence into categories of natural objects to explain their coherence. Rothbart and Taylor (1992) defended the same idea for social categories. We agree with them. We believe that stereotypes are gestalts whose elements, or attributes, are glued together by a naïve theory. Often, but not always, the naïve theory is a personological one. Assume that a person has a naïve personological theory about the category 'Jews'. Most likely, this theory has several levels. At a superficial level, the theory will explain why Jews are both bright (a positive trait) and sly (a negative trait). At more elaborate levels, this theory will also explain facts that do not seem to fit with brightness and slyness. Why, for instance, did Jews not recognize earlier the Nazi threat and why did they remain apparently so passive during the years preceding the Second World War? We fear that, at the highest level of the theory, a person might think that Jewish genes explain why Jews are both bright and sly. This genetic theory will transform the understanding (comprehension) of an action into the cause of an event. Bright behaviours, therefore, would seem to result only from a gene which caused, for example, the discovery of relativity. Of course, not everybody who entertains personological theories adheres to genetic determinism, but it is a serious threat when one says, for instance, that French are intrinsically cultivated and that Scots are intrinsically penny-pinching.

'One is not a person', says a Latin proverb. A Robinson Crusoe having lived his entire life on an isolated island would not be a human being, only a biological magma. 'The' unique individual is an abstraction and stereo-types are efficient devices to deal with concrete everyday life. This is the meaning conveyed by the quotation from the French philosopher, Paul Ricoeur, at the beginning of this Conclusion. Stereotypes may be stupid judgements and they may show bad taste. However, they are useful and inescapable. Debunking their underlying naïve theories and showing the role of these theories in their use would have a greater positive impact than pretending they should not exist. By doing so, researchers will view stereotypes as explanatory meanings rather than as erroneous pieces of information.

References

Aboud, F.E. (1988). *Children and prejudice*. Oxford: Blackwell.

Abrams, D. & Hogg, M.A. (1988). Comments on the motivational status of self-esteem in social identity and intergroup discrimination. *European Journal of Social Psychology, 18,* 317–334.

Abrams, D., Wetherell, M.S., Cochrane, S., Hogg, M.A. & Turner, J.C. (1990). Knowing what to think by knowing who you are: Self-categorization and the nature of norm formation, conformity, and group polarization. *British Journal of Social Psychology, 29,* 97–119.

Adorno, T.W. (1951). Freudian theory and the pattern of fascist propaganda. In G. Roheim (Ed.), *Psychoanalysis and social science*. New York: International University Press.

Adorno, T.W., Frenkel-Brunswik, E., Levinson, D.J. & Sanford, R.N. (1950). *The authoritarian personality*. New York: Harper & Row.

Ajzen, I. (1977). Intuitive theories of events and the effects of base-rate information on prediction. *Journal of Personality and Social Psychology, 35,* 303–314.

Ajzen, I., Dalto, C.A. & Blyth, D.P. (1979). Consistency and bias in the attribution of attitudes. *Journal of Personality and Social Psychology, 37,* 1871–1876.

Allport, G.W. (1954). *The nature of prejudice*. Reading, MA: Addison-Wesley.

Allport, G.W. & Kramer, B.M. (1946). Some roots of prejudice. *Journal of Psychology, 22,* 9–39.

Allport, G.W. & Postman, L. (1965). *The psychology of rumor*. New York: Russel.

Amancio, L. (1991, September). Stereotypes or ideologies: The case of gender stereotypes. Conference presented at the Small Group Meeting of the European Association of Experimental Social Psychology.

Amir, Y. (1969). Contact hypothesis in ethnic relations. *Psychological Bulletin, 71,* 319–342.

Andersen, S.M. & Klatzky, R.L. (1987). Traits and social stereotypes: Levels of categorization in person perception. *Journal of Personality and Social Psychology, 53,* 235–246.

Andersen, S.M., Klatzky, R.L. & Murray, J. (1990). Traits and social stereotypes: Efficiency differences in social information-processing. *Journal of Experimental Social Psychology, 59,* 192–201.

Anderson, C.A. & Sedikides, C. (1991). Thinking about people: Contributions of a typological alternative to associationistic and dimensional models of person perception. *Journal of Personality and Social Psychology, 60,* 203–217.

Anderson, C.A., Lepper, M.R. & Ross, L. (1980). Perseverence of social attribution: The role of explanation in the persistence of discredited information. *Journal of Personality and Social Psychology, 39,* 1037–1049.

Anderson, N.H. (1974). Cognitive algebra: Integration theory applied to social attribution. In L. Berkowitz (Ed.), *Advances in experimental social psychology* (Vol. 7). New York: Academic Press.

Anderson, N.H. (1981). *Foundations of information integration theory*. New York: Academic Press.

Anderson, N.H. & Hubert, S. (1963). Effects of concomitant verbal recall on order effects in personality impression formation. *Journal of Verbal Learning and Verbal Behavior, 2,* 379–391.

Arcuri, L. (1982). Three patterns of social categorization in attribution memory. *European Journal of Social Psychology, 12,* 271–282.

Asch, S.E. (1946). Forming impressions of personality. *Journal of Abnormal and Social Psychology, 41*, 258–290.

Asch, S.E. (1952). *Social psychology.* Englewood Cliffs, NJ: Prentice Hall.

Asch, S.E. & Zukier, H. (1984). Thinking about persons. *Journal of Personality and Social Psychology, 46*, 1230–1240.

Ashmore, R.D. (1981). Sex stereotypes and implicit personality theory. In D.L. Hamilton (Ed.), *Cognitive processes in stereotyping and intergroup behavior* (pp. 37–81). Hillsdale, NJ: Erlbaum.

Ashmore, R.D. & Del Boca, F.K. (1981). Conceptual approaches to stereotypes and stereotyping. In D. Hamilton (Ed.), *Cognitive processes in stereotyping and intergroup behavior* (pp. 1–35). Hillsdale, NJ: Erlbaum.

Azzi, A. (1994). Modes de resolution des conflits intergroupes. In R. Bourhis & J.-P. Leyens (Eds.), *Perceptions et relations intergroupes.* Brussels: Mardaga.

Bakan, D. (1966). *The duality of human existence: An essay on psychology and religion.* Chicago: Rand McNally.

Banaji, M.R., Hardin, C. & Rothman, A.J. (1993). *Implicit stereotyping in person judgment.* Unpublished manuscript, University of Yale.

Bargh, J.A. (1984). Automatic and conscious processing of social information. In R.S. Wyer & T.K. Srull (Eds.), *Handbook of social cognition* (pp. 1–43). Hillsdale, NJ: Erlbaum.

Bargh, J.A. (1989). Conditional automaticity: Varieties of automatic influence in social perception and cognition. In J.S. Uleman & J.A. Bargh (Eds.), *Unintended thought: Limits of awareness, intention, and control* (pp. 3–51). New York: Guilford.

Bargh, J.A., Bond, R.N., Lombardi, W.J. & Tota, M.E. (1986). The additive nature of chronic and temporary sources of construct accessibility. *Journal of Personality and Social Psychology, 50*, 869–878.

Bargh, J.A., Lombardi, W.J. & Higgins, E.T. (1988). Automaticity of chronically accessible constructs in Person × Situation effects on person perception: It's just a matter of time. *Journal of Personality and Social Psychology, 55*, 599–605.

Bargh, J.A. & Pietromonaco, P. (1982). Automatic information processing and social perception: The influence of trait information presented outside of conscious awareness on impression formation. *Journal of Personality and Social Psychology, 43*, 437–449.

Bargh, J.A. & Thein, R.D. (1985). Individual construct accessibility, person memory, and the recall–judgment link: The case of information overload. *Journal of Personality and Social Psychology, 49*, 1129–1146.

Bar-Hillel, M. (1980). The base-rate fallacy in probability judgments. *Acta Psychologica, 44*, 211–233.

Bartlett, F.C. (1932). *Remembering: A study in experimental and social psychology.* Cambridge: Cambridge University Press.

Bassili, J.N. & Smith, M.C. (1986). On the spontaneity of trait attribution: Converging evidence for the role of cognitive strategy. *Journal of Personality and Social Psychology, 50*, 239–245.

Beauvois, J.-L. (1984). *La psychologie quotidienne.* Paris: PUF.

Ben-Ari, R. & Amir, Y. (1988). Intergroup contact, cultural information, and change in ethnic attitudes. In W. Stroebe, A.W. Kruglanski, D. Bar-Tal & M. Hewstone (Eds.), *The social psychology of intergroup conflict* (pp. 151–165). Berlin: Springer.

Berkowitz, L. (1972). Frustrations, comparisons, and other sources of emotion arousal as contributors to social unrest. *Journal of Social Issues, 28*, 77–91.

Berkowitz, L. (1993). *Aggression: Its causes, consequences, and control.* New York: McGraw-Hill.

Billig, M. (1976). *Social psychology and intergroup relations.* London: Academic Press.

Billig, M. & Tajfel, H. (1973). Social categorization and similarity in intergroup behavior. *European Journal of Social Psychology, 3*, 27–52.

Blake, R.R. & Mouton, J.S. (1962). Overevaluation of own group's product in intergroup competition. *Journal of Abnormal and Social Psychology, 64*, 237–238.

Blaney, P.H. (1986). Affect and memory. *American Psychologist, 36*, 129–148.

Bless, H., Bohner, G., Schwarz, N. & Strack, F. (1990). Mood and persuasion: A cognitive response analysis. *Personality and Social Psychology Bulletin, 16*, 331–345.

Block, J. & Funder, D.C. (1986). Social roles and social perception: Individual differences in attribution and error. *Journal of Personality and Social Psychology, 51*, 1200–1207.

Blondel, M. (1962). Pragmatisme. In A. Lalande (Ed.), *Vocabulaire technique et critique de la philosophie* (9th ed.). Paris: PUF. (Original work published 1902.)

Bodenhausen, G.V. (1990). Stereotypes as judgmental heuristics: Evidence of circadian variations in discrimination. *Psychological Science, 1*, 319–322.

Bodenhausen, G.V. (1993). Emotions, arousal, and stereotypic judgments: A heuristic mode of affect and stereotyping. In D.M. Mackie & D.L. Hamilton (Eds.), *Affect, cognition, and stereotyping: Interactive processes in group perception* (pp. 13–37). San Diego, CA: Academic Press.

Bodenhausen, G.V. & Kramer, G.P. (1990a). *Affective states and the heuristic use of stereotypes in social judgment.* Unpublished manuscript, Michigan State University, East Lansing.

Bodenhausen, G.V. & Kramer, G.P. (1990b). *Affective states trigger stereotypic judgments.* Paper presented at the annual convention of the American Psychological Society, Dallas.

Bogardus, E.S. (1925). Measuring social distances. *Journal of Applied Sociology, 9*, 299–308.

Borgida, E. (1978). Scientific deduction – Evidence is not necessarily informative: A reply to Wells and Harvey. *Journal of Personality and Social Psychology, 36*, 477–482.

Bornstein, G., Crum, L., Wittenbraker, J., Harring, K., Insko, C.A. & Thibaut, J. (1983). On the measurement of social orientations in the minimal group paradigm. *European Journal of Social Psychology, 13*, 321–350.

Bourhis, R.Y. & Leyens, J.-P. (Eds.). (1994). *Stéréotypes, discriminations et relations intergroupes.* Brussels: Mardaga.

Bourhis, R.Y., Sachdev, I. & Gagnon, A. (1994). Conducting research with the Tajfel matrices: Some methodological notes. In M.P. Zanna & J. Olson (Eds.), *The Ontario Symposium: The psychology of prejudice* (Vol. 7, pp. 209–232). Hillsdale, NJ: Erlbaum.

Bower, G.H. (1981). Emotional mood and memory. *American Psychologist, 36*, 129–148.

Bower, G.H. (1991). Mood congruity of social judgments. In J.P. Forgas (Ed.), *Emotion and social judgments.* (pp. 31–53). Oxford: Pergamon.

Boyd, W. (1985). *Stars and bars.* Harmondsworth: Penguin.

Brand, E.S., Ruiz, R.A. & Padilla, A.M. (1974). Ethnic identification and preference: A review. *Psychological Bulletin, 81*, 860–890.

Branscombe, N.R., Wann, D.L., Noel, J.G. & Coleman, J. (1993). In-group or out-group extremity: Importance of threatened social identity. *Personality and Social Psychology Bulletin, 19*, 381–388.

Brewer, M.B. (1979). Ingroup bias and the minimal group paradigm: A cognitive-motivational analysis. *Psychological Bulletin, 86*, 307–324.

Brewer, M.B. (1988). A dual process of impression formation. In T.K. Srull & R.S. Wyer (Eds.), *Advances in social cognition* (Vol. 1, pp. 1–36). Hillsdale, NJ: Erlbaum.

Brewer, M.B. (1991). The social self: On being the same and different at the same time. *Personality and Social Psychology Bulletin, 17*, 475–482.

Brewer, M.B., Dull, V. & Lui, L. (1981). Perception of the elderly: Stereotypes as prototypes. *Journal of Personality and Social Psychology, 41*, 656–670.

Brewer, M.B. & Lui, L. (1985). Categorization of the elderly by the elderly: Effects of perceiver category membership. *Personality and Social Psychology Bulletin, 10*, 585–595.

Brewer, M.B. & Lui, L. (1989). The primacy of age and sex in the structure of person categories. *Social Cognition, 7*, 262–274.

Brewer, M.B. & Miller, N.E. (1988). Contact and cooperation: When do they work? In P. Katz & D. Taylor (Eds.), *Eliminating racism: Profiles in controversy* (pp. 315–326). New York: Plenum Press.

Brigham, J.C. (1971). Ethnic stereotypes. *Psychological Bulletin, 76*, 15–38.

Brigham, J.C. (1986). Race and eyewitness identification. In S. Worchel & W.G. Austin (Eds.), *Psychology of intergroup relations* (pp. 260–282). Chicago: Nelson-Hall.

Brown, R. (1965). *Social psychology*. New York: Free Press.

Brown, R. (1986). *Social psychology: The second edition*. New York: Free Press.

Brown, R.J. (1984). The effects of intergroup similarity and cooperative vs competitive orientation on intergroup discrimination. *British Journal of Social Psychology, 23*, 21–33.

Brown, R.J. & Wade, G.S. (1987). Superordinate goals and intergroup behaviours: The effects of role ambiguity and status on intergroup attitudes and task performance. *European Journal of Social Psychology, 17*, 131–142.

Bruner, J.S. (1957). On perceptual readiness. *Psychological Review, 64*, 123–151.

Bruner, J.S. & Potter, M.C. (1964). Interference in visual recognition. *Science, 44*, 424–425.

Bruner, J.S., Goodnow, J.J. & Austin, G.A. (1956). *A study of thinking*. New York: Wiley.

Bruner, J.S. & Tagiuri, R. (1954). The perception of people. In G. Lindzey (Ed.), *Handbook of social psychology* (Vol. 2, pp. 634–654). Reading, MA: Addison-Wesley.

Caddick, B. (1982). Perceived illegitimacy and intergroup relations. In H. Tajfel (Ed.), *Social identity and intergroup relations* (pp. 137–154). Cambridge: Cambridge University Press.

Caetano, A. (1993, September). *Social judgeability and status*. Paper presented at the 10th General meeting of the European Association of Experimental Social Psychology, Lisbon, Portugal.

Campbell, D.T. (1958). Common fate, similarity, and other indices of the status of aggregates of persons as social entities. *Behavioural Sciences, 3*, 14–25.

Campbell, D.T. (1965). Ethnocentric and other altruistic motives. In D. Levine (Ed.), *Nebraska Symposium on Motivation* (Vol. 13, pp. 283–311). Lincoln: University of Nebraska Press.

Cantor, N. & Mischel, W. (1977). Traits as prototypes: Effects on recognition memory. *Journal of Personality and Social Psychology, 35*, 38–48.

Cantor, N. & Mischel, W. (1979). Prototypes in person perception. In L. Berkowitz (Ed.), *Advances in experimental social psychology* (Vol. 12, pp. 3–52). New York: Academic Press.

Capozza, D. (1994). In R.Y. Bourhis & J.-P. Leyens (Eds.), *Perceptions et relations intergroupes*, Brussels: Mardaga.

Carter, L.F. (1948). The identification of 'racial membership'. *Journal of Abnormal and Social Psychology, 43*, 279–286.

Chaiken, S. (1980). Heuristic versus systematic information processing and the use of message versus message cues in persuasion. *Journal of Personality and Social Psychology, 39*, 752–766.

Chaiken, S. (1987). The heuristic model of persuasion. In M.P. Zanna, J.M. Olson & C.P. Herman (Eds.), *Social influence: The Ontario Symposium* (Vol. 5, pp. 3–39). Hillsdale, NJ: Erlbaum.

Chapman, L.J. & Chapman, J.P. (1967). Genesis of popular but erroneous diagnostic observations. *Journal of Abnormal Psychology, 72*, 193–204.

Chapman, L.J. & Chapman, J.P. (1969). Illusory correlation as an obstacle to the use of valid psychodiagnostic signs. *Journal of Abnormal Psychology, 74*, 271–280.

Claeys, W. (1990). On the spontaneity of behavior categorization and its implications for personality measurement. *European Journal of Personality, 4*, 173–186.

Clark, M.S. & Isen, A.M. (1982). Toward understanding the relationship between feeling states and social behavior. In A. Hastorf & A. Isen (Eds.), *Cognitive social psychology* (pp. 73–108). New York: Elsevier North Holland.

Cohen, C.E. (1981). Goals and schemas in person perception: Making sense out of the stream of behavior. In N. Cantor & J. Kihlstrom (Eds.), *Personality, cognition, and social behavior*. Hillsdale, NJ: Erlbaum.

Condor, S. (1990). Social stereotypes and social identity. In D. Abrams & M.A. Hogg (Eds.), *Social identity theory: Constructive and critical advances* (pp. 230–249). Hemel Hempstead: Harvester Wheatsheaf.

Cook, S.W. (1979). Social science and school desegregation: Did we mislead the Supreme Court? *Personality and Social Psychology Bulletin, 5*, 420–437.

Cook, S.W. (1984). The 1954 social science statement and school desegregation: A reply to Gerard. *American Psychologist, 39*, 819–832.

Crocker, J., Thompson, L.J., McGraw, K.M. & Ingerman, C. (1987). Downward comparison, prejudice, and evaluations of others: Effects of self-esteem and threat. *Journal of Personality and and Social Psychology, 52*, 907–917.

Crosby, F. (1976). A model of egoistic relative deprivation. *Psychological Review, 83*, 85–113.

Crosby, F. (1982). *Relative deprivation and working women.* New York: Oxford University Press.

Czapinski, J. (1985). Negativity bias in psychology: An analysis of Polish publications. *Polish Psychological Bulletin, 16*, 27–44.

Dardenne, B. & Leyens, J.-P. (in press). Confirmation bias as a social skill. *Personality and Social Psychology Bulletin.*

Darley, J.M. & Gross, P.H. (1983). A hypothesis-confirming bias in labeling effects. *Journal of Personality and Social Psychology, 44*, 20–33.

Darley, J.M. & Latané, B. (1968). Bystander intervention in emergencies: Diffusion of responsibility. *Journal of Personality and Social Psychology, 8*, 377–383.

Davis, J.A. (1959). A formal interpretation of the theory of relative deprivation. *Sociometry, 22*, 280–296.

Davis, J.C. (Ed.) (1971). *When men revolt and why: A reader in political violence and revolution.* New York: Free Press.

Dawes, R.M. & Smith, T.L. (1985). Attitude and opinion measurement. In G. Lindzey & E. Aronson (Eds.), *The handbook of social psychology* (3rd ed.; Vol. 1, pp. 509–566). New York: Random House.

Deaux, K. & Lewis, L.L. (1984). Structure of gender stereotypes: Interrelationships among components and gender label. *Journal of Personality and Social Psychology, 46*, 991–1004.

Deaux, K., Winton, W., Crowley, M. & Lewis, L.L. (1985). Level of categorization and content of gender stereotypes. *Social Cognition, 3*, 145–167.

Deboeck, P. (1978). On the evaluative factor in the trait scales of Peabody's study of trait inferences. *Journal of Personality and Social Psychology, 36*, 619–621.

Denhaerinck, P., Leyens, J.-P. & Yzerbyt, V.Y. (1989). The dilution effect and group membership: An instance of the pervasive impact of out-group homogeneity. *European Journal of Social Psychology, 19*, 243–250.

Dépret, E.F. & Fiske, S.T. (1993). Social cognition and power: Some cognitive consequences of social structure as a source of control deprivation. Unpublished manuscript. University of Massachusetts.

Deschamps, J.-C. (1973–1974). L'attribution, la catégorisation sociale et les relations intergroupes. *Bulletin de Psychologie, 27*, 710–721.

Deutsch, M. & Krauss, R.M. (1965). *Theories in social psychology.* New York: Basic Books.

Devine, P.G. (1989). Stereotypes and prejudice: Their automatic and controlled components. *Journal of Personality and Social Psychology, 56*, 5–18.

Devine, P.G., Hamilton, D.L. & Ostrom, T.M. (Eds.). (1994). *Social cognition: Contributions to classic issues in social psychology.* New York: Springer.

Devine, P.G. & Ostrom, T.M. (1988). Dimensional versus information-processing approaches to social knowledge: The case of inconsistency management. In D. Bar-Tal & A. Kruglanski (Eds.), *The social psychology of knowledge* (pp. 231–261). Cambridge: Cambridge University Press.

Diab, L.N. (1970). A study of intra-group and intergroup relations among experimentally produced small groups. *Genetic Psychology Monographs, 82*, 49–82.

Di Giacomo, J.P. (1980). Intergroup alliances and rejections within a protest movement: Analysis of the social representations. *European Journal of Social Psychology, 10*, 329–344.

Di Giacomo, J.P. (1993). Belief perseverance: When discredited evidence fails to alter established attitudes. Unpublished manuscript, University of Lille, France.

Dijker, A.J.M. (1987). Emotional reactions to ethnic minorities. *European Journal of Social Psychology, 17*, 305–325.

Ditto, P.H. & Lopez, D.F. (1992). Motivated skepticism: Use of differential decision criteria for preferred and nonpreferred conclusions. *Journal of Personality and Social Psychology*, *63*, 568–584.

Dollard, J., Doob, L.W., Miller, N.E., Mowrer, O.H. & Sears, R.R. (1939). *Frustration and aggression*. New Haven. CT: Yale University Press.

Dorfman, D.D., Keeve, S. & Saslow, C. (1971). Ethnic identification: A signal detection analysis. *Journal of Personality and Social Psychology*, *18*, 373–379.

Dubois, N. (1987). *La psychologie du contrôle*. Grenoble: Presses Universitaries de Grenoble.

Duncan, B. (1976). Differential social perception and attribution of intergroup violence: Testing the lower limits of stereotyping Blacks. *Journal of Personality and Social Psychology*, *34*, 590–598.

Eagly, A.H. (1987) *Sex differences in social behavior: A social-role interpretation*. Hillsdale, NJ: Erlbaum.

Eagly, A.H. & Kite, M.E. (1987). Are stereotypes of nationalities applied to both women and men? *Journal of Personality and Social Psychology*, *53*, 451–462.

Eagly, A.H. & Steffen, V.J. (1984). Gender stereotypes stem from the distribution of men and women into social roles. *Journal of Personality and Social Psychology*, *46*, 735–754.

Eagly, A.H. & Wood, W. (1991). Explaining sex differences in social behavior: a meta-analytic perspective. *Personality and Social Psychology Bulletin*, *17*, 306–315.

Eiser, J.R. (1990). *Social judgment*. Buckingham: Open University Press.

Elliott, D.N. & Wittenberg, B.H. (1955). Accuracy of identification of Jewish and non-Jewish photographs. *Journal of Abnormal and Social Psychology*, *51*, 339–341.

Erber, R. & Fiske, S.T. (1984). Outcome dependency and attention to inconsistent information about others. *Journal of Personality and Social Psychology*, *47*, 709–726.

Fazio, R.H., Effrein, E.A. & Falender, J.J. (1981). Self-perceptions following social interaction. *Journal of Personality and Social Psychology*, *41*, 232–242.

Fein, S., Hilton J.L. & Miller, D.T. (1990). Suspicion of ulterior motivation and the correspondence bias. *Journal of Personality and Social Psychology*, *58*, 753–764.

Ferguson, C.K. & Kelley, H.H. (1964). Significant factors in over-evaluation of own groups' products. *Journal of Abnormal and Social Psychology*, *69*, 223–228.

Festinger, L. (1954). A theory of social comparison processes. *Human Relations*, *7*, 117–140.

Festinger, L. (1957). *A theory of cognitive dissonance*. Stanford, CA: Stanford University Press.

Fiedler, K. (1990). Mood-dependent selectivity in cognition. *European Review of Social Psychology 1*, 1–32.

Fiedler, K. (1991a). On the task, the measures, and the mood: Research on affect and social cognition. In J.P. Forgas (Ed.), *Emotion and social judgments* (pp. 83–104). Oxford: Pergamon.

Fiedler, K. (1991b). The tricky nature of skewed frequency tables: An information loss account of distinctiveness-based illusory correlations. *Journal of Personality and Social Psychology*, *60*, 24–36.

Fiedler, K., Asbeck, J. & Nickel, S. (1991). Mood and constructive memory effects on social judgement. *Cognition and Emotion*, *5*, 363–378.

Fiedler, K. & Forgas, J. (1988). *Affect, cognition, and social behavior*. Toronto: Hogrefe.

Fiske, S.T. (1988). Compare and contrast: Brewer's dual process model and Fiske et al.'s continuum model. In T.K. Srull & R.S. Wyer (Eds.), *Advances in social cognition* (Vol. 1, pp. 65–76). Hillsdale, NJ: Erlbaum.

Fiske, S.T. (1989). Examining the role of intent: Toward understanding its role in stereotyping and prejudice. In J.S. Uleman and J.A. Bargh (Eds.), *Unintended thought: Limits of awareness, intention, and control* (pp. 253–283). New York: Guilford Press.

Fiske, S.T. (1992). Thinking is for doing: Portraits of social cognition from daguerreotype to laserphoto. *Journal of Personality and Social Psychology*, *63*, 887–889.

Fiske, S.T. (1993). Social cognition and social perception. *Annual Review of Psychology*, *44*.

Fiske, S.T. & H.M. Hendy von (1992). Personality feedback and situational norms can control stereotyping processes. *Journal of Personality and Social Psychology, 62*, 577–596.

Fiske, S.T. & Linville, P.W. (1980). What does the schema concept buy us? *Personality and Social Psychology Bulletin, 6*, 543–557.

Fiske, S.T. & Neuberg, S.L. (1990). A continuum of impression formation from category-based to individuating processes: Influences of information and motivation on attention and interpretation. In M.P. Zanna (Ed.), *Advances in Experimental Social Psychology* (Vol. 23, pp. 1–74). New York: Academic Press.

Fiske, S.T. & Pavelchak, M. (1986). Category-based versus piecemeal-based affective responses: Developments in schema-triggered effect. In R.M. Sorrentino & E.T. Higgins (Eds.), *Handbook of motivation and cognition: Foundations of social behavior* (Vol. 1, pp. 167–202). New York: Guilford Press.

Fiske, S.T. & Rusher, J.B. (1993). Negative interdependence and prejudice: Whence the affect? In D.M. Mackie & D.L. Hamilton (Eds.), *Affect, cognition, and stereotyping: Interactive processes in group perception* (pp. 239–268). San Diego, CA: Academic Press.

Fiske, S.T. & Taylor, S.E. (1984). *Social cognition.* Reading, MA: Addison-Wesley.

Fiske, S.T. & Taylor, S.E. (1991). *Social cognition: Second edition.* New York: McGraw-Hill.

Fletcher, G.J.O., Danilovics, P., Fernandez, G., Peterson, D. & Reefer, G.D. (1986). Attributional complexity: An individual differences measure. *Journal of Personality and Social Psychology, 51*, 875–884.

Forgas, J.P. (1983). The effects of prototypicality and cultural salience on perceptions of people. *Journal of Research in Personality, 17*, 153–173.

Forgas, J.P. (1992). Affect and social perception: Research evidence and an integrative theory. *European Review of Social Psychology, 3*, 183–223.

Forgas, J.P. & Moylan, S.J. (1991). Affective influences on stereotype judgments. *Cognition and Emotion, 5*, 379–395.

Fosterling, F. (1989). Models of covariation and attribution: How do they relate to the analogy of analysis of variance? *Journal of Personality and Social Psychology, 57*, 615–625.

Funder, D.C. (1987). Errors and mistakes: Evaluating the accuracy of social judgment. *Psychological Bulletin, 101*, 75–90.

Gaertner, S., Dovidio, J., Anastasio, A., Bachman, B. & Rust, M. (1993). The common ingroup identity: Recategorization and the reduction of intergroup bias. *European Review of Social Psychology, 4*, 1–26.

Gagnon, A. (1993) Les effets du pouvoir et de l'identité sociale sur les polerisation collective de la discrimination intergroupe, Thèse de doctorat, Université du Québec à Montréal.

Gardner, R.C., Lalonde, R.N., Nero, A.M. & Young, M.Y. (1988). Ethnic stereotypes: Implications of measurement techniques. *Social Cognition, 6*, 40–60.

Gardner, R.C., Wonnacott, E.J. & Taylor, D.M. (1968). Ethnic stereotypes: A factor analysis investigation. *Canadian Journal of Psychology, 22*, 35–44.

Gerard, H.B. (1983). School desegregation: The social science role. *American Psychologist, 38*, 869–877.

Gigerenzer, G. (1991). How to make cognitive illusions disappear: Beyond 'heuristics and biases'. *European Review of Social Psychology, 2*, 83–115.

Gilbert, D.T. & Hixon, J.G. (1991). The trouble of thinking: Activation and application of stereotypic beliefs. *Journal of Experimental Social Psychology, 60*, 509–517.

Gilbert, D.T. & Osborne, R.E. (1989). Thinking backward: Some curable and incurable consequences of cognitive busyness. *Journal of Personality and Social Psychology, 57*, 940–949.

Gilbert, D.T., Pelham, B.W. & Krull, D.S. (1988). On cognitive busyness: When person perceivers meet persons perceived. *Journal of Personality and Social Psychology, 54*, 733–740.

Gilbert, G.M. (1951). Stereotype persistence and change among college students. *Journal of Abnormal and Social Psychology, 46*, 245–254.

Ginossar, Z. & Trope, Y. (1980). The effects of base-rates and individuating information on judgments about another person. *Journal of Experimental Social Psychology, 16*, 228–242.

Ginossar, Z. & Trope, Y. (1987). Problem-solving in judgment under uncertainty. *Journal of Personality and Social Psychology*, *52*, 464–474.

Golding, W. (1954). *Lord of the flies*. London: Faber & Faber.

Gould, S.J. (1983). *The mismeasure of man*. New York: W.W. Norton & Company.

Grice, H.P. (1975). Logic and conversation. In P. Cole & J.L. Morgan (Eds.), *Syntax and semantics: Speech acts* (Vol. 3, pp. 41–58). Orlando, FL: Academic Press.

Guimond, S. & Dubé-Simard, L. (1983). Relative deprivation theory and the Quebec movement: The cognition–emotion distinction and the person–group deprivation issue. *Journal of Personality and Social Psychology*, *44*, 526–535.

Guimond, S. & Tougas, F. (1994). Sentiments d'injustice et actions collectives. In R.Y. Bourhis & J.-P. Leyens (Eds.), *Perceptions et relations intergroupes*. Brussels: Mardaga.

Gurr, T.R. (1970). *Why men rebel*. Princeton, NJ: Princeton University Press.

Hamilton, D.L. (1979). A cognitive-attributional analysis of stereotyping. In L. Berkowitz (Ed.), *Advances in Experimental Social Psychology* (Vol. 12, pp. 53–84). New York: Academic Press.

Hamilton, D.L. (1981). Cognitive representations of persons. In E.T. Higgins, C.P. Herman & M.P. Zanna (Eds.), *Social cognition: The Ontario Symposium* (Vol. 1, pp. 135–159). Hillsdale, N.J.: Erlbaum.

Hamilton, D.L. (1988). Causal attribution viewed from an information processing perspective. In D. Bar-Tal & A.W. Kruglanski (Eds.), *The social psychology of knowledge* (pp. 359–385). Cambridge: Cambridge University Press.

Hamilton, D.L. & Bishop, G.D. (1976). Attitudinal and behavioral effects of initial integration of white suburban neighborhoods. *Journal of Social Issues*, *32*, 47–67.

Hamilton, D.L., Driscoll, D.M. & Worth, L.T. (1989). Cognitive organization of impressions: Effects of incongruency in complex representations. *Journal of Personality and Social Psychology*, *56*, 925–939.

Hamilton, D.L., Dugan, P.M. & Trolier, T.K. (1985). The formation of stereotypic beliefs: Further evidence for distinctiveness-based illusory correlations. *Journal of Experimental Social Psychology*, *48*, 5–17.

Hamilton, D.L. & Gifford, R.K. (1976). Illusory correlation in interpersonal perception: A cognitive basis of stereotype judgments. *Journal of Experimental Social Psychology*, *12*, 392–407.

Hamilton, D.L., Katz, L.B. & Leirer, V.O. (1980a). Cognitive representations of personality impressions? Organizational processes in first impression formation. *Journal of Personality and Social Psychology*, *39*, 1050–1063.

Hamilton, D.L., Katz, L.B. & Leirer, V.O. (1980b). Organizational processes in impression formation. In R. Hastie, T.M. Ostrom, E.B. Ebbesen, R.S. Wyer Jr., D.L. Hamilton & D.E. Carlston (Eds.), *Person memory: The cognitive basis of social perception* (pp, 121–153). Hillsdale, NJ: Erlbaum.

Hamilton, D.L. & Rose, T.L. (1980). Illusory correlation and the maintenance of stereotypic beliefs. *Journal of Personality and Social Psychology*, *39*, 832–845.

Hamilton, D.L. & Sherman, S.J. (1989). Illusory correlations: Implications for stereotype theory and research. In D. Bar-Tal, C.F. Graumann, A.W. Kruglanski & W. Stroebe (Eds.), *Stereotyping and prejudice: Changing conceptions* (pp. 59–82). New York: Springer.

Hamilton, D.M., Stoessner, S.J. & Mackie, D.M. (1993). The influence of affect on stereotyping: The case of illusory correlations, In D.M. Mackie & D.L. Hamilton (Eds.), *Affect, cognition, and stereotyping: Interactive processes in group perception* (pp. 39–61). San Diego, CA: Academic Press.

Hartley, E.L. (1946). *Problems in prejudice*. New York: King's Crown Press.

Haslam, S.A. & Turner, J.C. (1992). Context-dependent variation in social stereotyping 2: The relationship between frame of reference, self-categorization and accentuation. *European Journal of Social Psychology*, *22*, 251–278.

Haslam, S.A., Turner, J.C., Oakes, P.J., McGarty, C. & Hayes, B.K. (1992). Context-dependent variation in social stereotyping 1: The effects of intergroup relations as mediated by social change and frame of reference. *European Journal of Social Psychology*, *22*, 3–20.

Hastie, R. (1980). Memory for behavioral information that confirms or contradicts a personality impression. In R. Hastie, T.M. Ostrom, E.B. Ebbesen, R.S. Wyer Jr., D.L. Hamilton & D.E. Carlson (Eds.), *Person memory: The cognitive basis of perception* (pp. 155–177). Hillsdale, NJ: Earlbaum.

Hastie, R. & Kumar, P.A. (1979). Person memory: Personality traits as organizing principles in memory for behaviors. *Journal of Personality and Social Psychology*, *37*, 28–38.

Hastie, R. & Park, B. (1986). The relationship between memory and judgment depends on whether the judgment task is memory-based or on-line. *Psychological Review*, *93*, 258–268.

Hastie, R., Park, B. & Weber, R. (1984). Social memory. In R.S. Wyer & T.K. Srull (Eds.), *Handbook of social cognition* (Vol. 2, pp. 151–212). Hillsdale, NJ: Erlbaum.

Hastie, R. & Razinski, K.A. (1988). The concept of accuracy in social judgment. In D. Bar-Tal & A.W. Kruglanski (Eds.), *The social psychology of knowledge* (pp. 193–208). Cambridge: Cambridge University Press.

Haye, A.-M. de la (1989). La mémoire des personnes: I. Les fondements mémoriels de la construction du jugement. *Année Psychologique*, *89*, 585–613.

Haye, A.-M. de la (1990). La mémoire des personnes: II. Construction cognitive des individus et des groupes. *Année Psychologique*, *90*, 93–108.

Haye, A.-M. de la & Lauvergeon, G. (1991). Processus de mémoire dans la formation des corrélations illusoires. *Psychologie Française*, *36*, 67–77.

Heider, F. (1944). Social perception and phenomenal causality. *Psychological Review*, *51*, 358–374.

Heider, F. (1958). *The psychology of interpersonal relationships*. New York: Wiley.

Heider, F. & Simmel, M. (1944). An experimental study of apparent behavior. *American Journal of Psychology*, *57*, 243–259.

Herr, P.M. (1986). Consequences of priming: Judgment and behavior. *Journal of Personality and Social Psychology*, *51*, 1106–1115.

Hewstone, M. (1989). *Causal attribution: From cognitive processes to collective beliefs*. Oxford and Cambridge, MA: Blackwell.

Hewstone, M. (1990). The ultimate attribution error: A review of the literature on intergroup causal attribution. *European Journal of Social Psychology*, *20*, 311–355.

Hewstone, M. & Brown, R.J. (1986). Contact is not enough: An intergroup perspective on the contact hypothesis. In M. Hewstone & R.J. Brown (Eds.), *Contact and conflict in intergroup discrimination* (pp. 1–44). Oxford: Blackwell.

Hewstone, M., Gale, L. & Purkhardt, N. (1990). *Intergroup attributions for success and failure: Group-serving bias and group-serving causal schemata*. Unpublished manuscript, University of Bristol.

Hewstone, M., Hantzi, A. & Johnston, L. (1991). Social categorization and person memory: The pervasiveness of race as an organizing principle. *European Journal of Social Psychology*, *21*, 517–528.

Hewstone, M. & Ward, C. (1985). Ethnocentrism and causal attribution in Southeast Asia. *Journal of Personality and Social Psychology*, *48*, 614–623.

Higgins, E.T. & Bargh, J.A. (1987). Social cognition and social perception. *Annual Review of Psychology*, *38*, 369–425.

Higgins, E.T., King, G. & Mavin, G.H. (1982). Individual construct accessibility and subjective impressions and recall. *Journal of Personality and Social Psychology*, *43*, 35–47.

Higgins, E.T., Rholes, W.S. & Jones, C.R. (1977). Category accessibility and impression formation. *Journal of Experimental Social Psychology*, *13*, 141–154.

Higgins, E.T. & Sorrentino, R.M. (Eds.). (1990). *Handbook of motivation and cognition: Foundations of social behavior* (Vol. 2). New York: Guilford.

Hilton, D.J. (1990). Conversational processes and causal explanation. *Psychological Bulletin*, *107*, 65–81.

Hilton, D.J. & Slugoski, B.R. (1986). Knowledge-based causal attribution: The abnormal conditions focus model. *Psychological Review*, *93*, 75–88.

Hilton, J.L. & Darley, J.M. (1989). The effect of interaction goals on person perception. In

M.P. Zamma (Ed.) *Advances in experimental social psychology* (Vol. 24, pp. 235–267). San Diego, CA: Academic Press.

Hilton, J.L. & Fein, S. (1989). The role of typical diagnosticity in stereotype-based judgments. *Journal of Personality and Social Psychology, 57,* 201–211.

Hilton, J.L., Fein, S. & Miller, D.T. (1993). Suspicion and dispositional influence. *Personality and Social Psychology Bulletin, 19,* 501–512.

Himmelfarb, S. (1966). Studies in the perception of ethnic group members: I. Accuracy, response bias, and anti-semitism. *Journal of Personality and Social Psychology, 4,* 347–355.

Himmelfarb, S. (1993). The measurement of attitudes. In A.H. Eagly & S. Chaiken (Eds.), *The psychology of attitudes* (pp. 23–87). Fort Worth: Harcourt Brace.

Hinsz, V.B., Tindale, R.S., Nagao, D.H., Davis, J.H. & Robertson, B.A. (1988) The influence of the accuracy of individuating information on the use of base rate information in probability judgments. *Journal of Experimental Social Psychology, 24,* 127–145.

Hoffman, C. & Hurst, N. (1990). Gender stereotypes: Perception or rationalization? *Journal of Personality and Social Psychology, 58,* 197–208.

Hogg, M.A. (1992). *The social psychology of group cohesiveness: From attraction to social identity.* London: Harvester Wheatsheaf.

Hogg, M.A. & Abrams, D. (1988). *Social identification: A social psychology of intergroup relations and group processes.* London: Routledge.

Horwitz, M. & Rabbie, J.M. (1982). Individuality and membership in the intergroup system. In H. Tajfel (Ed.), *Social identity and intergroup relations* (pp. 241–274). Cambridge: Cambridge University Press.

Horwitz, M. & Rabbie, J.M. (1989). Stereotypes of groups, group members, and individuals in categories: A differential analysis of different phenomena. In D. Bar-Tal, C.F. Graumann, A.W. Kruglanski & W. Stroebe (Eds.), *Stereotyping and prejudice: Changing conceptions* (pp. 105–129). New York: Springer.

Huddy, L. and Virtanen, S. (1993). Exclusive ingroup boundaries among subgroups of Latinos as a function of familiarity and positive distinctiveness. Unpublished manuscript, University of New York at Starry Brook.

Huici, C. (1984). The individual and social functions of sex stereotypes. In H. Tajfel (Ed.), *The social dimension: European developments in social psychology* (Vol. 2, pp. 579–602). Cambridge: Cambridge University Press.

Ibáñez, T. (1994) Ideologie et relations intergroupes. In R.Y. Bourhis & J.-P. Leyens (Eds.), *Perceptions et relations intergroupes.* Brussels: Mardega.

Institut für Sozialforschung (1936). *Studien über Autorität und Familie.* Paris: ALCAN.

Isen, A.M. (1984). Toward understanding the role of affect in cognition. In R.S. Wyer, Jr. & T.K. Srull (Eds.), *Handbook of social cognition* (Vol. 3, pp. 179–236). Hillsdale, NJ: Erlbaum.

Isen, A.M. (1987). Positive affect, cognitive processes, and social behavior. In L. Berkowitz (Ed.), *Advances in experimental social psychology* (Vol. 20). New York, Academic Press.

Islam, M.R. & Hewstone, M. (1993). Intergroup attributions and affective consequences in majority and minority groups. *Journal of Personality and Social Psychology, 64,* 936–950.

Jackson, L.A., Sullivan, L.A. & Hodge, C.N. (1993). Stereotype effects on attributions, predictions, and evaluations: No two social judgments are quite alike. *Journal of Personality and Social Psychology, 65,* 69–84.

Jaspars, J.M.F. (1983). The process of causal attribution in common sense. In M. Hewstone (Ed.), *Attribution theory: Social and functional extensions* (pp. 28–44). Oxford: Blackwell.

Jay, M. (1973). *The dialectical imagination: A history of the Frankfurt School and the Institute of Social Research, 1923–1950.* London: Heinemann.

Johnson, M.K. & Raye, C.L. (1981). Reality monitoring. *Psychological Review, 88,* 67–85.

Johnston, L. & Hewstone, M. (1992). Cognitive models of stereotype change, 3: Subtyping and the perceived typicality of disconfirming groups' members. *Journal of Experimental Social Psychology, 28,* 360–386.

Jones, E.E. (1979). The rocky road from acts to dispositions. *American Psychologist, 34,* 104–117.

Jones, E.E. (1990). *Interpersonal perception.* New York: Freeman.

Jones, E.E. & Davis, K.E. (1965). From acts to disposition: The attribution process in person perception. In L. Berkowitz (Ed.), *Advances in Experimental Social Psychology* (Vol. 2, pp. 219–266). New York: Academic Press.

Jones, E.E., Davis, K.E. & Gergen, K.J. (1961). Role playing variations and their informational value for person perception. *Journal of Abnormal and Social Psychology, 63,* 302–310.

Jones, E.E. & Harris, V.A. (1967). The attribution of attitudes. *Journal of Experimental Social Psychology, 3,* 1–24.

Jones, E.E. & Nisbett, R. (1972). The actor and the observer: Divergent perceptions of the causes of behavior. In E.E. Jones, D.E. Kanouse, H.H. Kelley, R.E. Nisbett, S. Valins & B. Weiner (Eds.), *Attribution: Perceiving the causes of behavior* (pp. 79–94). Morristown, NJ: General Learning.

Jones, E.E. & Thibaut, J.W. (1958). Interaction goals as bases of human inference in interpersonal perception. In R. Tagiuri & L. Petrullo (Eds.), *Person perception and interpersonal behavior* (pp. 151–178), Stanford, CA: Stanford University Press.

Jones, E.E., Wood, G.C. & Quattrone, G. (1981). Perceived variability of personal characteristics in in-groups and out-groups: The role of knowledge and evaluation. *Personality and Social Psychology Bulletin, 7,* 523–528.

Jones, E.E., Worchel, S., Goethals, G.R. & Grumet, J.F. (1971). Prior expectancy and behavioral extremity as determinants of attitude attribution. *Journal of Experimental Social Psychology, 7,* 59–80.

Judd, C.M. & Park, B. (1988). Out-group homogeneity: Judgments of variability at the individual and group levels. *Journal of Personality and Social Psychology, 54,* 778–788.

Jussim, L. (1991). Social perception and social reality: A reflection–construction model. *Psychological Review, 98,* 54–73.

Jussim, L., Coleman, L.M. & Lerch, L. (1987). The nature of stereotypes: A comparison and integration of three theories. *Journal of Personality and Social Psychology, 52,* 536–546.

Kahneman, D. & Tversky, A. (1973). On the psychology of prediction. *Psychological Review, 80,* 237–251.

Karlins, M. Coffman, T.L. & Walters, G. (1969). On the fading of social stereotypes: Studies in three generations of college students. *Journal of Personality and Social Psychology, 13,* 1–16.

Katz, D. & Braly, K.W. (1933). Racial stereotypes in one hundred college students. *Journal of Abnormal and Social Psychology, 28,* 280–290.

Katz, D. & Braly, K.W. (1935). Racial prejudice and racial stereotypes. *Journal of Abnormal and Social Psychology, 30,* 175–193.

Kelley, H.H. (1967). Attribution theory in social psychology. In D. Levine (Ed.), *Nebraska Symposium on Motivation* (Vol. 15, pp. 192–238). Lincoln: University of Nebraska Press.

Kelley, H.H. (1971). Attribution in social interaction. In E.E. Jones, D.E. Kanouse, H.H. Kelley, R.E. Nisbett, S. Valins & B. Weiner (Eds.), *Attribution: Perceiving the causes of behavior* (pp. 1–26). Morristown, NJ: General Learning.

Kelley, H.H. (1972). The process of causal attribution. *American Psychologist, 28,* 107–128.

Kelly, G.A. (1955). *The psychology of interpersonal constructs.* New York: Norton & Company.

Kenny, D.A. & Albright, L. (1987). Accuracy in interpersonal perception: A social relations analysis. *Psychological Bulletin, 102,* 390–402.

Kim, H.S. & Baron, R.A. (1988). Exercise and the illusory correlation: Does arousal heighten stereotypic processing? *Journal of Experimental Social Psychology, 24,* 366–380.

Krosnick, J.A., Li, F. & Lehman, D.R. (1990). Conversational conventions, order of information acquisition, and the effect of base-rates and individuating information on social judgment. *Journal of Personality and Social Psychology, 59,* 1140–1152.

Kruglanski, A.W. (1989). The psychology of being 'right': The problem of accuracy in social perception and cognition. *Psychological Bulletin, 106,* 395–409.

Kruglanski, A.W. (1990). Motivations for judging and knowing: Implications for causal attribution. In E.T. Higgins & R.M. Sorrentino (Eds.), *Handbook of motivation and cognition: Foundations of social behavior* (Vol. 2, pp. 13–37). New York: Guilford Press.

Kruglanski, A.W. & Ajzen, I. (1983). Bias and error in human judgment. *European Journal of Social Psychology, 13*, 1–44.

Kruglanski, A.W. & Freund, T. (1983). The freezing and unfreezing of lay-inferences: Effects of impressional primacy, ethnic stereotyping and numerical anchoring. *Journal of Experimental Social Psychology, 19*, 448–468.

Kruglanski, A.W. & Klar, Y. (1987). A view from a bridge: Synthetizing the consistency and attribution paradigms from the lay epistemic perspective. *European Journal of Social Psychology, 17*, 211–241.

Kruglanski, A.W. & Mayseless, O. (1988). Contextual effects in hypothesis testing: The role of competing alternatives and epistemic motivations. *Social Cognition, 6*, 1–20.

Krull, D.S. (1993). Does the grill change the mill? The effect of the perceiver's inferential goal on the process of social inference. *Personality and Social Psychology Bulletin, 19*, 340–348.

Kulik, J.A. (1983). Confirmatory attribution and the perpetuation of social beliefs. *Journal of Personality and Social Psychology, 44*, 1171–1181.

Kulik, J.A. & Mahler, H.I.M. (1986). Self-confirmatory effects of delay on perceived contribution to a joint activity. *Personality and Social Psychology Bulletin, 12*, 344–352.

Kulik, J.A., Sledge, P. & Mahler, H.I.M. (1986). Self-confirmatory attribution, egocentrism, and the perpetuation of self-beliefs. *Journal of Personality and Social Psychology, 50*, 587–594.

Kunda, Z. (1990). The case for motivated reasoning. *Psychological Bulletin, 108*, 480–498.

Lemyre, L. & Smith, P.M. (1985). Intergroup discrimination and self-esteem in the minimal group paradigm. *Journal of Personality and Social Psychology, 49*, 660–670.

LeVine, R.A. & Campbell, D.T. (1972). *Ethnocentrism: Theories of conflict, ethnic attitudes, and group behavior*. New York: Wiley.

Levine, R.V., West, L.J. & Reis, H.T. (1980). Perceptions of time and punctuality in the United States and Brazil. *Journal of Personality and Social Psychology, 38*, 541–550.

Lewicka, M. (1988). On objective and subjective anchoring of cognitive acts: How behavioral valence modifies reasoning schemata. In W.J. Baker, L.P. Mos, H.V. Rappard & H.J. Stam (Eds.), *Recent trends in theoretical psychology* (pp. 285–301). New York: Springer.

Lewin, K. (1948). *Resolving social conflicts*. New York: Harper & Row.

Leyens, J.-P. (1983). *Sommes-nous tous des psychologues? Approche psychosociale des théories implicites de personnalité*. Brussels: Mardaga.

Leyens, J.-P. (1989). Another look at confirmatory strategies during a real interview. *European Journal of Social Psychology, 19*, 255–262.

Leyens, J.-P. (1990). Intuitive personality testing: A social approach. In J. Extra, A. van Knippenberg, J. van der Pligt & M. Poppe (Eds.), *Fundamentele sociale psychologie* (Vol. 4, pp. 3–20). Tilburg: Tilburg University Press.

Leyens, J.-P, Aspeel, S. & Marques, J.M. (1987). Cognitions sociales et pratiques psychologiques. In J.L. Beauvois, R.V. Joule & J.M. Monteil (Eds.), *Perspectives cognitives et conduites sociales: Théories implicites et conflits cognitifs* (Vol. 1, pp. 63–84). Cousset: Delval.

Leyens, J.-P., Dardenne, B. & Fiske, S. (1994). *Is there a useful bias in hypothesis confirmation?* Unpublished manuscript, University of Louvain at Louvain-la-Neuve.

Leyens, J.-P. & Fiske, S.T. (1994). Impression formation: Something old, something new, and even something borrowed. In P.G. Devine, D.L. Hamilton & T.M. Ostrom (Eds.), *Social cognition: Contributions to classic issues in social psychology*. New York: Springer.

Leyens, J.-P. & Maric, M.L. (1990). Intuitive personality testing: Goals and types of questions makes the difference in interviews. *Revue Internationale de Psychologie Sociale, 2*, 425–440.

Leyens, J.-P. & Van Duüren, F. (1990). The discredited eyewitness: The impact of a prior judgment, the nature and the direction of the discrediting testimony. Unpublished manuscript, University of Louvain, Louvain-la-Neuve.

Leyens, J.-P. & Van Duüren, F. (1994). Conflicting eyewitness testimonies: The impact of a prior judgement, the nature and the direction of the conflicting information. *International Review of Social Psychology*, in press.

Leyens, J.-P. & Yzerbyt, V.Y. (1992). The ingroup overexclusion effect: Impact of valence and confirmation on stereotypical information search. *European Journal of Social Psychology*, *22*, 549–570.

Leyens, J.-P., Yzerbyt, V.Y., Corneille, O., Vilain, D., Gonçalves, G. (1994) The role of naïve theories in the production of the over attribution bias. Unpublished manuscript, University of Louvain, Louvain-la-Neuve.

Leyens, J.-P., Yzerbyt, V.Y. & Schadron, G. (1992). The social judgeability approach to stereotypes. *European Review of Social Psychology*, *3*, 91–120.

Lindzey, G. & Rogolsky, S. (1950). Prejudice and identification of minority group membership. *Journal of Abnormal and Social Psychology*, *45*, 37–53.

Linville, P.W. (1982). The complexity–extremity effect and age-based stereotyping. *Journal of Personality and Social Psychology*, *42*, 193–211.

Linville, P.W., Fisher, G.W. & Salovey, P. (1989). Perceived distributions of the characteristics of in-group and out-group members: Empirical evidence and a computer simulation. *Journal of Personality and Social Psychology*, *57*, 165–188.

Linville, P.W. & Jones, E.E. (1980). Polarized appraisals of out-group members. *Journal of Personality and Social Psychology*, *38*, 689–703.

Linville, P.W., Salovey, P. & Fisher, G.W. (1986). Stereotyping and perceived distributions of social characteristics. In J.F. Dovidio & S.L. Gaertner (Eds.), *Prejudice, discrimination, and racism* (pp. 165–208). Orlando, FL: Academic Press.

Lipe, M.G. (1991). Counterfactual reasoning as a framework for attribution theories. *Psychological Bulletin*, *109*, 456–471.

Lippmann, W. (1922). *Public opinion*. New York: Harcourt & Brace.

Locksley, A., Borgida, E., Brekke, N.C. & Hepburn, C. (1980). Sex stereotypes and social judgment. *Journal of Personality and Social Psychology*, *39*, 821–831.

Locksley, A., Hepburn, C. & Ortiz, V. (1982). Social stereotypes and judgments of individuals: An instance of the base-rate fallacy. *Journal of Experimental Social Psychology*, *18*, 23–42.

Loftus E.F. (1974). *Eyewitness testimony*. Cambridge, MA: Harvard University Press.

Lombardi, W.J., Higgins, E.T. & Bargh, J.A. (1987). The role of consciousness in priming effects on categorization: Assimilation versus contrast as a function of awareness of priming task. *Personality and Social Psychology Bulletin*, *13*, 411–429.

Lorenzi-Cioldi, F. (1988). *Individus dominants et groupes dominés*. Grenoble: Presses Universitaires de Grenoble.

Lorenzi-Cioldi, F. (1993). They all look alike but so do we . . . sometimes: Perceptions of in-group and out-group homogeneity as a function of sex and context. *British Journal of Social Psychology*, *32*, 111–124.

Lyon, D. & Slovic, P. (1976). Dominance of accuracy information and neglect of base-rates in probability estimation. *Acta Psychologica*, *40*, 287–298.

Maass, A. & Schaller, M. (1991). Intergroup biases and the cognitive dynamics of stereotype formation. *European Review of Social Psychology*, *2*, 189–209.

McArthur, L.Z. (1972). The how and what of why: Some determinants and consequences of causal attribution. *Journal of Personality and Social Psychology*, *22*, 171–193.

McArthur, L.Z. & Friedman, S.A. (1980). Illusory correlation in impression formation: Variations in the shared distinctiveness effect as a function of the distinctive person's age, race, and sex. *Personality and Social Psychology Bulletin*, *7*, 615–624.

McCauley, C. & Stitt, C.L. (1978). An individual and quantitative measure of stereotypes. *Journal of Personality and Social Psychology*, *39*, 929–940.

McCauley, C., Stitt, C.L. & Segal, M. (1980). Stereotyping: From prejudice to prediction. *Psychological Bulletin*, *87*, 195–208.

McGarty, C., Haslam, S.A., Turner, J.C. & Oakes, P.J. (1993). Illusory correlation as accentuation of actual intercategory difference: Evidence for the effect with minimal stimulus information. *European Journal of Social Psychology*, *23*, 391–410.

McGill, A.L. (1989). Context effects in judgments of causation. *Journal of Personality and Social Psychology*, *57*, 189–200.

Mackie, D.M. & Worth, L.T. (1989). Processing deficits and the mediation of positive affect in persuasion. *Journal of Personality and Social Psychology*, *57*, 27–40.

Mackie, D.M. & Worth, L.T. (1991). 'Feeling good but not thinking straight': Positive mood and persuasion. In J.P. Forgas (Ed.), *Emotion and social judgments* (pp. 201–220). Oxford: Pergamon.

Macrae, C.N., Hewstone, M. & Griffiths, R.J. (1993). Processing load and memory for stereotype-based information. *European Journal of Social Psychology*, *23*, 77–87.

Macrae, C.N., Milne & Bodenhausen, G.V. (1994). Stereotypes as energy-saving devices. *Journal of Personality and Social Psychology*, *64*, 37–47.

Maquet, J.J. (1961). *The premise of inequality in Rwanda: A study of political relations in a central African community*. London: Oxford University Press.

Markus, H., Smith, J. & Moreland, R.L. (1985). Role of the self-concept in the perception of others. *Journal of Personality and Social Psychology*, *49*, 1494–1512.

Markus, H. & Zajonc, R. (1985). The cognitive perspective in social psychology. In G. Lindzey & E. Aronson (Eds.), *Handbook of social psychology* (Vol. 1, pp. 137–230). New York: Random House.

Marques, J.M. (1990). The black-sheep effect: Outgroup homogeneity in social comparison settings. In D. Abrams & M.A. Hogg (Eds.), *Social identity theory: Constructive and critical advances* (pp. 131–151). Hemel Hempstead: Harvester Wheatsheaf.

Marques, J.M. & Yzerbyt, V.Y. (1988). The black-sheep effect: Judgmental extremity towards ingroup members in inter- and intra-group situations. *European Journal of Social Psychology*, *18*, 287–292.

Marques, J.M., Yzerbyt, V.Y. & Leyens, J.-Ph. (1988). Extremity of judgments towards ingroup members as a function of ingroup identification. *European Journal of Social Psychology*, *18*, 1–16.

Martin, L.L. (1986). Set/reset: The use and disuse of concepts in impression formation. *Journal of Personality and Social Psychology*, *51*, 493–504.

Martin, L.L., Seta, J.J. & Crelia, R.A. (1990). Assimilation and contrast as a function of people's willingness and ability to expend effort in forming an impression. *Journal of Personality and Social Psychology*, *57*, 27–37.

Medcof, J.W. (1990). PEAT: An integrative model of attribution processes. In M.P. Zanna (Ed.), *Advances in experimental social psychology* (Vol. 23, pp. 111–210). New York: Academic Press.

Medin, D.L. (1988). Social categorization: Structures, processes and purposes. In T.K. Srull & R.S. Wyer (Eds.), *Advances in social cognition* (Vol. 1, pp. 119–126). Hillsdale, NJ: Erlbaum.

Medin, D.L. (1989). Concepts and conceptual structure. *American Psychologist*, *44*, 1469–1481.

Messick, D.M. & Mackie, D.M. (1989). Intergroup relations. *Annual Review of Psychology*, *40*.

Michotte, A. (1946). *La perception de la causalité*. Louvain: Presses Universitaires de Louvain.

Milgram, S. (1974) *Obedience to authority*. New York: Harper & Row.

Miller, A.G. (1976). Constraint and target effects in the attribution of attitude. *Journal of Experimental Social Psychology*, *12*, 325–339.

Miller, A.G. (1982). *In the eye of the beholder: Contemporary issues in stereotyping*. New York: Praeger.

Miller, A.G., Ashton, W. & Mishal, M. (1990). Beliefs concerning the features of constrained behavior: A basis for the fundamental attribution error. *Journal of Personality and Social Psychology*, *59*, 635–650.

Miller, N.E. & Brewer, M.B. (Eds.). (1984). *Groups in contact: The psychology of desegregation*. Orlando, FL: Academic Press.

Minard, R.D. (1952). Race relationships in the Pocahontas coal field. *Journal of Social Issues*, *8*, 408–420.

Mlicki, P. (1993). *Intergroup relations in the minimal group paradigm: Social identity theory or interdependence hypothesis.* Unpublished manuscript, University of Utrecht, the Netherlands.

Monteil, J.M. (1991). Social regulation and individual cognitive function: Effects of individuation on cognitive performance. *European Journal of Social Psychology, 21,* 225–238.

Moscovici, S. (1982). The coming era of social representations. In J.-P. Codol & J.-P. Leyens (Eds.), *Cognitive analysis of social behavior* (pp. 115–150). The Hague: Martinus Nijhoff.

Moskowitz, G.B. & Uleman, J.S. (1987). The facilitation and inhibition of spontaneous trait inferences. Unpublished manuscript, New York University.

Mullen, B. & Hu, L. (1989). Perceptions of ingroup and outgroup variability: A meta-analytic integration. *Basic and Applied Social Psychology, 10,* 233–252.

Mummendey, A. (1993). Positive distinctiveness and social discrimination: An old couple living in divorce? Tajfel lecture of the European Association of Experimental Social Psychology, Lisbon, Portugal.

Mummendey, A. & Schreiber, H.-J. (1983). 'Different' just means 'better': Some obvious and some hidden pathways to in-group favouritism. *British Journal of Social Psychology, 23,* 363–368.

Mummendey, A. & Schreiber, H.-J. (1984). Social comparison, similarity and ingroup favouritism – A replication. *European Journal of Social Psychology, 14,* 231–233.

Mummendey, A. & Simon, B. (1989). Better or just different? III: The impact of importance of comparison dimension and relative in-group size upon intergroup discrimination. *British Journal of Social Psychology, 28,* 1–16.

Mummendey, A., Simon, B., Dietze, C., Gruenert, M., Haeger, G., Kesser, S., Lettgen, S. & Schaeferhoff, S. (1992). Categorization is not enough: Intergroup discrimination in negative outcome allocations. *Journal of Experimental Social Psychology, 28,* 125–144.

Murphy, G.L. & Medin, D.L. (1985). The role of theories in conceptual coherence. *Psychological Review, 92,* 289–316.

Murphy, G., Murphy, L.B. & Newcomb, T.M. (1937). *Experimental social psychology,* New York: Harper.

Myers, A. (1962). Team competition, success and the adjustment of group members. *Journal of Abnormal and Social Psychology, 65,* 297–303.

Neuberg, S.L. (1989). The goal of forming accurate impressions during social interactions: Attenuating the impact of negative expectancies. *Journal of Personality and Social Psychology, 56,* 374–386.

Neuberg, S.L. & Fiske, S.T. (1987). Motivational influences on impression formation: Outcome dependency, accuracy-driven attention, and individuating processes. *Journal of Personality and Social Psychology, 53,* 431–444.

Newcomb, T.M. (1947). Attitude development as a function of reference groups: The Bennington study. In E.E. Maccoby, T.M. Newcomb & E.L. Hartley (Eds.), *Readings in social psychology* (pp. 265–275). New York: Holt, Rinehart & Winston.

Newman, L.S. (1991). Why are traits inferred spontaneously? A developmental approach. *Social Cognition, 9,* 221–253.

Newman, L.S. & Uleman, J.S. (1989). Spontaneous trait inference. In J.S. Uleman & J.A. Bargh (Eds.), *Unintended thought: Limits of awareness, intention, and control* (pp. 155–188). New York: Guilford Press.

Newman, L.S. & Uleman, J.S. (1990). Assimilation and contrast effects in spontaneous trait inference. *Personality and Social Psychology Bulletin, 16,* 224–240.

Newman, L.S. & Uleman, J.S. (1993). When are you what you did? Behaviour identification and dispositional inference in person memory attribution and social judgment. *Personality and Social Psychology Bulletin, 19,* 513–525.

Nisbett, R.E. & Borgida, E. (1975). Attribution and the psychology of prediction. *Journal of Personality and Social Psychology, 32,* 932–943.

Nisbett, R.E. & Ross, L. (1980). *Human inference: Strategies and shortcomings of social judgment.* Englewood Cliffs, NJ: Prentice Hall.

Nisbett, R.E. & Wilson, T.D. (1977). Telling more than we can know: Verbal reports on mental processes. *Psychological Review, 84,* 231–259.

Nisbett, R.E., Zukier, H. & Lemley, R.E. (1981). The dilution effect: Non-diagnostic information weakens the implications of diagnostic information. *Cognitive Psychology, 13,* 248–277.

Oakes, P.J. (1987). The salience of social categories. In J.C. Turner, M.A. Hogg, P.J. Oakes, S.D. Reicher & M. Wetherell, *Rediscovering the social group: A self-categorization theory* (pp. 117–171). Oxford: Blackwell.

Oakes, P.J. & Turner, J.C. (1980). Social categorization and intergroup behavior: Does minimal intergroup discrimination make social identity more positive? *European Journal of Social Psychology, 10,* 295–301.

Oakes, P.J. & Turner, J.C. (1986). Distinctiveness and the salience of social category memberships: Is there an automatic perceptual bias towards novelty? *European Journal of Social Psychology, 16,* 325–344.

Oakes, P.J. & Turner, J.C. (1990). Is limited information processing capacity the cause of social stereotyping? *European Review of Social Psychology, 1,* 111–137.

Oakes, P.J., Haslam, S.A. & Turner, J.C. (1994). *Stereotyping and social reality.* Oxford: Blackwell.

Osgood, C.E. (1960). *Graduated reciprocation in tension-reduction: A key to initiative in foreign policy.* Urbana: Institute of Communications Research, University of Illinois.

Osgood, C.E., Suci, G.J. & Tannenbaum, P.H. (1957). *The measurement of meaning.* Urbana: University of Illinois Press.

Ostrom, T.M. (1977). Between-theory and within-theory conflict in explaining context effects in impression formation. *Journal of Experimental Social Psychology, 13,* 492–503.

Ostrom, T.M. (1984). The sovereignty of social cognition. In R.S. Wyer & T.K. Srull (Eds.), *Handbook of social cognition* (Vol. 1, pp. 1–38). Hillsdale, NJ: Erlbaum.

Ostrom, T.M., Pryor, J.B. & Simpson, D. D. (1981). The organization of social information. In E.T. Higgins, C.P. Herman, & M.P. Zanna (Eds.), *Social cognition: The Ontario Symposium* (Vol. 1, pp. 3–38). Hillsdale, NJ: Erlbaum.

Ostrom, T.M. & Sedikides, C. (1992). Out-group homogeneity effect in natural and minimal groups. *Psychological Bulletin, 112,* 536–552.

Park, B. & Hastie, R. (1987). Perception of variability in category development: Instance-versus abstraction-based stereotypes. *Journal of Personality and Social Psychology, 53,* 621–635.

Park, B. & Judd, C.M. (1990). Measures and model of perceived group variability. *Journal of Personality and Social Psychology, 59,* 173–191.

Park, B. & Rothbart, M. (1982). Perception of outgroup homogeneity and levels of social categorization: Memory for the subordinate attributes of ingroup and outgroup members. *Journal of Personality and Social Psychology, 42,* 1051–1068.

Peabody, D. (1967). Trait inferences: Evaluative and descriptive aspects. *Journal of Personality and Social Psychology,* Monograph 7 (Whole No. 644).

Peeters, G. (1992, May). *Self–other anchored evaluations of national stereotypes.* Paper presented at the Annual Meeting of the Belgian Psychological Society, Gent, Belgium.

Peeters, G. & Czapinski, J. (1990). Positive–negative asymmetry in evaluations: The distinction between affective and informational negativity effects. *European Review of Social Psychology, 1,* 33–60.

Pettigrew, T.F. (1958). Personality and socio-cultural factors in intergroup attitudes: A cross-national comparison. *Journal of Conflict Resolution, 2,* 29–42.

Pettigrew, T.F. (1978). Three issues in ethnicity: Boundaries, deprivations, and perceptions. In J.M. Yinger & S.J. Cutler (Eds.), *Major social issues: A multidisciplinary view* (pp. 25–49). New York: Free Press.

Pettigrew, T.F. (1979). The ultimate attribution error: Extending Allport's cognitive analysis of prejudice. *Personality and Social Psychology Bulletin, 5,* 461–476.

Pettigrew, T.F. (1981). Extending the stereotype concept. In D.L. Hamilton (Ed.), *Cognitive processes in stereotyping and intergroup behavior* (pp. 303–331). Hillsdale, NJ: Erlbaum.

Pettigrew, T.F., Allport, G.W. & Barnett, E.O. (1958). Binocular resolution and perception of race in South Africa. *British Journal of Psychology*, *49*, 265–278.

Petty, R.E. & Cacioppo, J.T. (1981). *Attitudes and persuasion*. Dubuque, IA: Brown.

Petty, R.E. & Cacioppo, J.T. (1986). *Communication and persuasion: Central and peripheral routes to attitude change*. New York: Springer.

Petty, R.E. & Wegener, D.T. (1993). Flexible correction processes in social judgment: Correcting for context-induced contrast. *Journal of Experimental Social Psychology*, *29*, 137–165.

Pietromonaco, P. & Nisbett, R.E. (1982). Swimming upstream against the fundamental attribution error: Subjects' weak generalizations from the Darley and Batson Study. *Social Behaviour and Personality*, *10*, 1–4.

Pryor, J.B. (1986). The influence of different encoding sets upon the formation of illusory correlation and group impression. *Personality and Social Psychology Bulletin*, *12*, 216–226.

Pryor, J.B., Simpson, D.D., Mitchell, M., Ostrom, T.M. & Lydon, J. (1982). Structural selectivity in the retrieval of social information. *Social Cognition*, *4*, 336–337.

Pulos, L. & Spilka, B. (1961). Perceptual selectivity, memory and anti-semitism. *Journal of Abnormal and Social Psychology*, *62*, 690–692.

Pyszczynski, T.A. & Greenberg, J. (1987). Toward an integration of cognitive and motivational perspectives on social inference: A biased hypothesis-testing model. In L. Berkowitz (Ed.), *Advances in Experimental Social Psychology* (Vol. 21, pp. 297–340). New York: Academic Press.

Quanty, M.B., Keats, J.A. & Harkins, S.G. (1975). Prejudice and criteria for identification of ethnic photographs. *Journal of Personality and Social Psychology*, *32*, 449–454.

Quattrone, G.A. (1982). Overattribution and unit formation: When behavior engulfs the person. *Journal of Personality and Social Psychology*, *42*, 593–607.

Quattrone, G.A. (1986). On the perception of a group's variability. In S. Worchel & W.G. Austin (Eds.), *Psychology of intergroup relations*. Chicago: Nelson-Hall.

Quattrone, G.A. & Jones, E.E. (1980). The perception of variability within in groups and out-groups: Implications for the law of small numbers. *Journal of Personality and Social Psychology*, *38*, 141–152.

Rabbie, J.M. (1966, December). *Ingroup–outgroup differentiation under minimal social conditions*. Paper presented to the Second European Conference of Experimental Social Psychology, Sorrento, Italy.

Rabbie, J.M. (1991). *Conference*. Leuven, Belgium.

Rabbie, J.M. & Horwitz, M. (1969). The arousal of ingroup outgroup bias by a chance win or loss. *Journal of Personality and Social Psychology*, *13*, 269–277.

Rabbie, J.M. & Horwitz, M. (1988). Categories versus groups as explanatory concepts in intergroup relations. *European Journal of Social Psychology*, *18*, 117–123.

Rabbie, J.M., Schot, J.C. & Visser, L. (1989). Social identity theory: A conceptual and empirical critique from the perspective of a behavioral interaction model. *European Journal of Social Psychology*, *19*, 171–202.

Rabbie, J.M. & Wilkens, G. (1971). Ingroup competition and its effect on intragroup relations. *European Journal of Social Psychology*, *1*, 215–234.

Rajecki, D.W. (1990). *Attitudes: Second edition*. Sunderland, MA: Sinauer Associates.

Reeder, G.D. & Brewer, M.B. (1979). A schematic model of dispositional attribution in interpersonal perception. *Psychological Review*, *86*, 61–79.

Reeder, G.D., Fletcher, G.J.O. & Furman, K. (1989). The role of observers' expectations in attitude attribution. *Journal of Experimental Social Psychology*, *25*, 168–188.

Reeder, G.D., Messick, D.M. & Van Avermaet, E. (1977). Dimensional asymmetry in attributional inference. *Journal of Experimental Social Psychology*, *13*, 46–57.

Regan, D.T. & Crawley, D.M. (1984, August). Illusory correlation and stereotype: Replication and extension. Paper presented at the 86th Annual Convention of the APA. Toronto, Ontario, Canada.

Rice, S.A. (1926–1927). Stereotypes, a source of error in judging human character. *Journal of Personnel Research*, *5*, 267–276.

Rijsman, J.R. (1983). The dynamics of social comparison in personal and categorical comparison situations. In W. Doise & S. Moscovici (Eds.), *Current issues in European social psychology* (Vol. 1, pp. 279–312). Cambridge: Cambridge University Press.

Rojahn, K. & Pettigrew, T.F. (1992). Memory for schema-relevant information: A meta-analytic resolution. *British Journal of Social Psychology, 31*, 81–109.

Rokeach, M. (1960). *The open and closed mind.* New York: Basic Books.

Rosch, E. (1978). Principles of categorization. In E. Rosch & B. Lloyd (Eds.), *Cognition and categorization* (pp. 28–49). Hillsdale, NJ: Erlbaum.

Rosenberg, S. (1988). Self and others: Studies in social personality and autobiography. In L. Berkowitz (Ed.), *Advances in Experimental Social Psychology* (Vol. 21, pp. 57–96). New York: Academic Press.

Rosenberg, S. & Jones, R. (1972). A method for investigating a person's implicit theory of personality: Theodore Dreiser's view of people. *Journal of Personality and Social Psychology, 22*, 372–386.

Rosenberg, S. & Sedlak, A. (1972) Structural representations of implicit personality theory. In L. Berkowitz (Ed.), *Advances in Experimental Social Psychology* (Vol 6, pp. 235–297). New York: Academic Press.

Rosenberg, S., Nelson, C. & Vivekanathan, P.S. (1968). A multidimensional approach to the structure of personality impressions. *Journal of Personality and Social Psychology, 9*, 283–294.

Rosnow, R.L. (1991). Inside rumor: A personal journey. *American Psychologist, 46*, 484–496.

Ross, L. (1977). The intuitive psychologists and his shortcomings: Distortions in the attribution process. In L. Berkowitz (Ed.), *Advances in Experimental Social Psychology* (Vol. 10, pp. 173–220). New York: Academic Press.

Ross, L., Lepper, M.R. & Hubbard, M. (1975). Perseverence in self perception and social perception: Shared attributional processes in the debriefing paradigm. *Journal of Personality and Social Psychology, 32*, 880–892.

Rothbart, M. (1981). Memory and social beliefs. In D.L. Hamilton (Ed.), *Cognitive processes in stereotyping and intergroup behavior* (pp. 145–181). Hillsdale, NJ: Erlbaum.

Rothbart, M., Evans, M. & Fulero, S. (1979). Recall for confirming events: Memory process and the maintenance of social stereotypes. *Journal of Personality and Social Psychology, 15*, 343–355.

Rothbart, M. & Taylor, M. (1992). Category labels and social reality: Do we view social categories as natural kinds? In G. Semin and K. Fiedler (Eds.), *Language, interaction and social cognition* (pp. 11–36). London: Sage.

Runciman, W.G. (1966). *Relative deprivation and social justice.* Berkeley: University of California Press.

Rusher, J.B. & Fiske, S.T. (1990). Interpersonal competition can cause individuating impression formation. *Journal of Personality and Social Psychology, 58*, 832–843.

Sagar, H.A. & Schofield, J.W. (1980). Racial and behavioral cues in black and white children's perceptions of ambiguously agressive acts. *Journal of Personality and Social Psychology, 39*, 590–598.

St Claire, L. & Turner, J.C. (1982). The role of demand characteristics in the social categorization paradigm. *European Journal of Social Psychology, 12*, 307–314.

Saint-Exupéry, A. de (1944). *Lettre à un otage.* Paris: Gallimard.

Sanbonmatsu, D.M., Shavitt, S., Sherman, S.J. & Roskos-Ewoldsen, D.R. (1987). Illusory correlation in the perception of performance by self or a salient other. *Journal of Experimental Social Psychology, 23*, 518–543.

Sanbonmatsu, D.M., Sherman, S.J. & Hamilton, D.L. (1987). Illusory correlation in the perception of individuals and groups. *Social Cognition, 5*, 1–25.

Sanford, N. (1973). The roots of prejudice: Emotional dynamics. In P. Watson (Ed.), *Psychology and race.* Harmondsworth: Penguin.

Sanitioso, R., Kunda, Z. & Fong, G.T. (1990). Motivated recruitment of autobiographical memory. *Journal of Personality and Social Psychology, 59*, 229–241.

Schadron, G. (1991). *L'impact des stéréotypes sur le jugement social: L'approche de la jugeabilité sociale.* Unpublished doctoral dissertation, Catholic University of Louvain, Louvain-la-Neuve, Belgium.

Schadron, G. & Yzerbyt, V.Y. (1991). Social judgeability: Another framework for the study of social inference. *Cahiers de Psychologie Cognitive/European Bulletin of Cognitive Psychology, 11,* 229–258.

Schadron, G. & Yzerbyt, V.Y. (1993). Les stéréotypes et l'approche de la jugeabilité sociale: Un impact des stéréotypes sur le jugement indépendant de leur contenu. In J.L. Beauvois, R.V. Joule & J.M. Monteil (Eds.), *Perspectives cognitives et conduites sociales* (Vol. 3, pp. 15–35). Neuchâtel: Delachaux et Niestlé.

Schadron, G., Yzerbyt, V.Y., Leyens, J.-P. & Rocher, S. (in press) Jugeabilité sociale et stéréotypes: L'estimation de l'origine d'une impression comme déterminant de l'impact des stéréotypes dans le jugement social. *Revue Internationale de Psychologie Sociale.*

Schaller, M. & Maass, A. (1989). Illusory correlation and social categorization: Toward an integration of motivational and cognitive factors in stereotype formation. *Journal of Personality and Social Psychology, 56,* 709–721.

Schneider, D.J., Hastorf, A.H. & Ellsworth, P. (1979). *Person perception.* Reading, MA: Addison-Wesley.

Schneider, D.J. & Miller, R.S. (1975). The effect of enthusiasm and quality of arguments on outside attribution. *Journal of Personality, 43,* 693–708.

Schoenfeld, W.N. (1942). An experimental study of some problems relating to stereotypes. *Archives of Psychology, 270.*

Schul, Y. & Burnstein, E. (1988). On Greeks and horses: Impression formation with social and nonsocial objects. In T.K. Srull & R.S. Wyer (Eds.), *Advances in social cognition* (Vol. 1, pp. 145–155). Hillsdale, NJ: Erlbaum.

Schul, Y. & Manzury, F. (1990). The effects of type of encoding and strength of discounting appeal on the success of ignoring an invalid testimony. *European Journal of Social Psychology, 20,* 327–349.

Schwarz, N. (1990). Feeling as information: Informational and motivational functions of affective states. In E.T. Higgins & R. Sorrentino (Eds.), *Handbook of motivation and cognition* (Vol. 2, pp. 527–561). New York: Guilford.

Schwarz, N. & Bless, H. (1991). Happy and mindless, but sad and smart? The impact of affective states on analytic reasoning. In J.P. Forgas (Ed.), *Emotion and social judgments* (pp. 55–71), Oxford: Pergamon.

Schwarz, N. & Bless, H. (1992). Constructing reality and its alternatives: An inclusion/exclusion model of assimilation and contrast effects in social judgment. In L. Martin & A. Tesser (Eds.), *The construction of social judgment* (pp. 217–245). Hillsdale, NJ: Erlbaum.

Schwarz, N. & Clore, G.L. (1983). Mood, misattribution, and judgments of well-being: Informative and directive functions of affective states. *Journal of Personality and Social Psychology, 45,* 513–523.

Schwarz, N. & Clore, G.L. (1988). How do I feel about it? Informative functions of affective states. In K. Fiedler & J. Forgas (Eds.), *Affect, cognition, and social behavior* (pp. 44–62). Toronto: Hogrefe.

Schwarz, N., Strack, F., Hilton, D. & Naderer, G. (1991). Base-rates, representativeness, and the logic of conversation: The contextual relevance of 'irrelevant' information. *Social Cognition, 9,* 67–84.

Schwarzwald, J. & Amir, Y. (1984). Interethnic relations and education: An Israeli perspective. In N.E. Miller & M.B. Brewer (eds.), *Groups in contact: The psychology of desegregation* (pp. 53–76). Orlando, FL: Academic Press.

Scodel, A. & Austrin, H. (1956). The perception of Jewish photographs by non-Jews and Jews. *Journal of Abnormal and Social Psychology, 54,* 278–280.

Secord, P.F. & Backman, C.W. (1974). *Social Psychology.* New York: McGraw-Hill.

Secord, P.F. & Saumer, E. (1960). Identifying Jewish names: Does prejudice increase accuracy? *Journal of Abnormal and Social Psychology. 61,* 144–145.

Semin, G.R. & Strack, F. (1980). The plausibility of the implausible: A critique of Snyder and Swann (1978). *European Journal of Social Psychology, 10*, 379–388.

Shafer, M.A. (1980). Attributing evil to the subject, not the situation: Student reaction to Milgram's film on obedience. *Personality and Social Psychology Bulletin, 6*, 205–209.

Sherif, M. (1966). *In common predicament: Social psychology of intergroup conflict and cooperation*. Boston: Houghton-Mifflin.

Sherif, M. (1979). Superordinate goals in the reduction of intergroup conflict: An experimental evaluation. In W.G. Austin & S. Worchel (Eds.), *The social psychology of intergroup relations* (pp. 257–261). Monterey, CA: Brooks/Cole.

Sherif, M., Harvey, O.J., White, B.J., Hood, W.R. & Sherif, C.W. (1961). *Intergroup conflict and cooperation: The Robbers' Cave experiment*. Norman: University of Oklahoma Book Exchange.

Sherman, S.J. & Corty, E. (1984). Cognitive heuristics. In R.S. Wyer & T.K. Srull (Eds.), *Handbook of social cognition* (Vol. 1, pp. 189–286). Hillsdale, NJ: Erlbaum.

Sherman, S.J., Hamilton, D.L. & Roskos-Ewoldsen, D.R. (1989). Attenuation of illusory correlation. *Personality and Social Psychology Bulletin, 15*, 559–571.

Sherman, S.J., Zehner, K.S., Johnson, J. & Hirt, E.R. (1983). Social explanations: The role of timing, set, and recall on subjective likelihood estimates. *Journal of Experimental Social Psychology, 17*, 142–158.

Shiffrin, R.M. (1988). Attention. In R.C. Atkinson, R.J. Herrnstein, G. Lindzey & R.D. Luce (Eds.). *Steven's handbook of experimental psychology* (2nd ed., pp. 739–831). New York: Wiley.

Shweder, R.A. (1980). *Fallible judgment in behavioral research: New directions for methodology of social and behavioral science* (Vol. 4). San Francisco: Jossey-Bass.

Sigall, H.H. & Page, R. (1971). Current stereotypes: A little fading, a little faking. *Journal of Personality and Social Psychology, 18*, 247–255.

Simon, B. (1992). The perception of ingroup and outgroup homogeneity: Reintroducing the intergroup context. *European Review of Social Psychology, 3*, 1–30.

Simon, B. & Brown, R. (1987). Perceived intragroup homogeneity in minority–majority contexts. *Journal of Personality and Social Psychology, 53*, 703–711.

Simon, B. & Pettigrew, T.F. (1990). Social identity and perceived group homogeneity: Evidence for the ingroup homogeneity effect. *European Journal of Social Psychology, 20*, 269–286.

Singer, J.A. & Salovey, P. (1988). Mood and memory: Evaluating the network theory of affect. *Clinical Psychological Review, 8*, 211–251.

Skov, R.B. & Sherman, S.J. (1986). Information-gathering processes: Diagnosticity, hypothesis-confirmatory strategies and perceived hypothesis confirmation. *Journal of Experimental Social Psychology, 22*, 93–121.

Slusher, M.P. & Anderson, C.A. (1987). When reality monitoring fails: The role of imagination in stereotype maintenance. *Journal of Personality and Social Psychology, 52*, 653–662.

Smith, E.R. (1989). Procedural efficiency and on-line social judgments. In J.N. Bassili (Ed.), *On-line cognition in person perception* (pp. 19–37). Hillsdale, NJ: Erlbaum.

Smith, E.R. (1991). Illusory correlation in a simulated exemplar-based memory. *Journal of Experimental Social Psychology, 27*, 107–123.

Smith, E.R. (1993). Social identity and social emotions: Toward new conceptualizations of prejudice. In D.M. Mackie & D.L. Hamiton (Eds.), *Affect, cognition, and stereotyping: Interactive processes in group perception* (pp. 297–315). San Diego, CA: Academic Press.

Smith, E.R. & Miller, F.D. (1983). Mediation among attributional inferences and comprehension processes: Initial findings and a general method. *Journal of Personality and Social Psychology, 44*, 492–505.

Snyder, M. (1984). When belief creates reality. In L. Berkowitz (Ed.), *Advances in experimental social psychology* (Vol. 18, pp. 248–306). New York: Academic Press.

Snyder, M. (1992). Motivational foundations of behavioral confirmation. In M.P. Zanna

(Ed.), *Advances in experimental social psychology* (Vol. 25, pp. 67–114). San Diego, CA: Academic Press.

Snyder, M. & Gangestad, S. (1981). Hypothesis-testing processes. In J.H. Harvey, W.J. Ickes & R.F. Kidd (Eds.), *New directions in attribution research* (Vol. 3, pp. 171–198). Hillsdale, NJ: Erlbaum.

Snyder, M. & Swann, W.B. (1978). Hypothesis-testing processes in social interaction. *Journal of Personality and Social Psychology, 36,* 1202–1212.

Snyder, M. & Uranowitz, S.W. (1978). Reconstructing the past: Some cognitive consequences of person perception. *Journal of Personality and Social Psychology, 36,* 941–950.

Snyder, M.L. & Frankel, A. (1976). Observer bias: A stringent test of behavior engulfing the field. *Journal of Personality and Social Psychology, 34,* 857–864.

Snyder, M.L. & Jones, E.E. (1974). Attitude attribution when behavior is constrained. *Journal of Experimental Social Psychology, 10,* 585–600.

Sorrentino, R.M. & Higgins, E.T. (Eds.). (1986). *Handbook of motivation and cognition* (Vol. 1). New York: Guilford Press.

Sousa, E. & Leyens, J.-P. (1987). A priori vs spontaneous models of attribution: The case of gender and achievement. *British Journal of Social Psychology, 26,* 281–292.

Spears, R., van der Plight, J. & Eiser, J.R. (1985). Illusory correlation in the perception of group attitudes. *Journal of Personality and Social Psychology, 48,* 863–875.

Spears, R., van der Pligt, J. & Eiser, J.R. (1986). Generalizing the illusory correlation effect. *Journal of Personality and Social Psychology, 51,* 1127–1134.

Srull, T.K. (1981). Person memory: Some tests of associative storage and retrieval models. *Journal of Experimental Psychology: Human Learning and Memory, 7,* 440–463.

Srull, T.K., Lichtenstein, M. & Rothbart, M. (1985). Associative storage and retrieval processes in person memory. *Journal of Experimental Psychology: Learning, Memory and Cognition, 11,* 316–345.

Srull, T.K. & Wyer, R.S. (1979). The role of category accessibility in the interpretation of information about persons: Some determinants and implications. *Journal of Personality and Social Psychology, 37,* 1660–1672.

Srull, T.K. & Wyer, R.S. (1980). Category accessibility and social perception: Some implications for the study of person memory and interpersonal judgment. *Journal of Personality and Social Psychology, 38,* 841–856.

Srull, T.K. & Wyer, R.S. (1989). Person memory and judgment. *Psychological Review, 96,* 58–83.

Stangor, C. (1988). Stereotype accessibility and information processing. *Personality and Social Psychology Bulletin, 14,* 694–708.

Stangor, C. & Duan, C. (1991). Effects of multiple tasks demands upon memory for information about social groups. *Journal of Experimental Social Psychology, 27,* 357–378.

Stangor, C. & McMillan, D. (1992). Memory for expectancy-consistent and expectancy-inconsistent social information: A meta-analytic review of the social psychological and social developmental literatures. *Psychological Bulletin, 111,* 42–61.

Stephan, W.G. (1985). Intergroup relations. In G. Lindzey & E. Aronson (Eds.), *Handbook of social psychology* (Vol. 2, pp. 599–658). New York: Random House.

Stephan, W.G. & Stephan, C.W. (1985). Intergroup anxiety. *Journal of Social Issues, 41,* 157–175.

Stern, L.D., Marrs, S.S., Millar, M.G. & Cole, E. (1984). Processing time and the recall of inconsistent behaviors of individuals and groups. *Journal of Personality and Social Psychology, 47,* 253–262.

Strack, F. (1992). The different routes to social judgments: Experiential versus informational strategies. In L.L. Martin & A. Tesser (Eds.), *The construction of social judgment.* Hillsdale, NJ: Erlbaum.

Stroebe, W. & Insko, C.A. (1989). Stereotypes, prejudice, and discrimination. Changing conceptions in theory and research. In D. Bar-Tal, C.F. Grauman, A.W. Kruglanski & W. Stroebe (Eds.), *Stereotypes and prejudice: Changing conceptions* (pp. 3–34). New York: Springer.

Stroebe, W., Lenkert, A. & Jonas, K. (1988). Familiarity may breed contempt: The impact of student exchange on national stereotypes and attitudes. In W. Stroebe, A.W. Kruglanski, D. Bar-Tal & M. Hewstone (Eds.), *The social psychology of intergroup conflict* (pp. 167–187). Berlin: Springer.

Sumner, W.G. (1906). *Folkways*. New York: Ginn.

Tajfel, H. (1957). Value and the perceptual judgment of magnitude. *Psychological Review, 64*, 192–204.

Tajfel, H. (1959). Quantitative judgements in social perception. *British Journal of Psychology, 50*, 16–29.

Tajfel, H. (1968). Social and cultural factors in perception. In G. Lindzey & E. Aronson (Eds.), *Handbook of social psychology* (2nd ed.; Vol. 3, pp. 315–394). Reading, MA: Addison-Wesley.

Tajfel, H. (1969). The cognitive aspect of prejudice. *Journal of Social Issues, 25*, 79–97.

Tajfel, H. (1972a). La catégorisation sociale. In S. Moscovici (Ed.), *Introduction à la psychologie sociale* (Vol. 1, pp. 272–302). Paris: Larousse.

Tajfel, H. (1972b). Experiments in a vacuum. In J. Israel & H. Tajfel (Eds.), *The context of social psychology: A critical assessment* (pp. 69–119). London: Academic Press.

Tajfel, H. (1981). *Human groups and social categories*. Cambridge: Cambridge University Press.

Tajfel, H. (1982). Social psychology of intergroup relations. *Annual Review of Psychology, 33*, 1–39.

Tajfel, H., Billig, M., Bundy, R. & Flament, C. (1971). Social categorization and intergroup behaviour. *European Journal of Social Psychology, 1*, 149–178.

Tajfel, H. & Turner, J.C. (1979). An integrative theory of intergroup relations. In W.G. Austin & S. Worchel (Eds.), *The psychology of intergroup relations* (pp. 33–47). Monterey, CA: Brooks-Cole.

Tajfel, H. & Turner, J.C. (1986). An integrative theory of intergroup relations. In S. Worchel & W.G. Austin (Eds.), *Psychology of intergroup relations* (pp. 7–24). Chicago: Nelson-Hall.

Tajfel, H. & Wilkes, A.L. (1963). Classification and quantitative judgment. *British Journal of Psychology, 54*, 101–114.

Taylor, S.E. (1981). A categorization approach to stereotyping. In D.L. Hamilton (Ed.), *Cognitive processes in stereotyping and intergroup behavior* (pp. 88–114). Hillsdale, NJ: Erlbaum.

Taylor, S.E. & Crocker, J. (1981). Schematic basis of social information processing. In E.T. Higgins, C.P. Herman & M.P. Zanna (Eds.), *Social cognition: The Ontario Symposium* (Vol. 1, pp. 89–134). Hillsdale, NJ: Erlbaum.

Taylor, S.E. & Fiske, S.T. (1978). Salience, attention, and attribution: Top of the head phenomena. In L. Berkowitz (Ed.), *Advances in Experimental Social Psychology* (Vol. 11, pp. 250–289). New York: Academic Press.

Taylor, S.E., Fiske, S.T., Etcoff, N.L. & Ruderman, A.J. (1978). Categorical bases of person memory and stereotyping. *Journal of Personality and Social Psychology, 36*, 778–793.

Tetlock, P.E. (1983a). Accountability and the complexity of thought. *Journal of Personality and Social Psychology, 45*, 74–83.

Tetlock, P.E. (1983b). Accountability and the perseverance of first impressions. *Social Psychology Quarterly, 46*, 285–292.

Tetlock, P.E. (1985). Accountability: A social check on the fundamental attribution error. *Social Psychology Quarterly, 48*, 227–236.

Tetlock, P.E. & Boettger, R. (1989). Accountability: A social magnifier of the dilution effect. *Journal of Personality and Social Psychology, 57*, 388–398.

Tetlock, P.E. & Kim, J. (1987). Accountability and judgment processes in a personality prediction task. *Journal of Personality and Social Psychology, 52*, 700–709.

Trope, Y. (1986). Identification and inferential processes in dispositional attribution. *Psychological Review, 93*, 239–257.

Trope, Y. & Bassok, M. (1982). Confirmatory and diagnosing strategies in social information gathering. *Journal of Personality and Social Psychology, 43*, 22–34.

Trope, Y. & Bassok, M. (1983). Information gathering strategies in hypothesis testing. *Journal of Experimental Social Psychology, 19*, 560–576.

Trope, Y., Bassok, M. & Alon, E. (1984). The questions lay interviewers ask. *Journal of Personality, 52*, 90–106.

Trope, Y. & Cohen, O. (1989). Perceptual and inferential determinants of behavior-correspondent attributions. *Journal of Experimental Social Psychology, 25*, 142–158.

Trope, Y., Cohen, O. & Alfieri, T. (1991). Behaviour identification as a mediator of dispositional inference. *Journal of Personality and Social Psychology, 16*, 873–883.

Trope, Y., Cohen, O. & Maoz, Y. (1988). The perceptual and inferential effects of situational inducements on dispositional attribution. *Journal of Personality and Social Psychology, 55*, 165–177.

Tulving, E. & Thomson, D.M. (1973). Encoding specificity and retrieval processes in episodic memory. *Psychological Review, 80*, 352–373.

Turner, C.W., Cole, A.M. & Cerro, D.S. (1984). Contributions of aversive experiences to robbery and homicide: A demographic analysis. In R.M. Kaplan, V.J. Konecni & R.W. Novaco (Eds.), *Aggression in children and youth* (pp. 296–342). The Hague: Martinus Nijhof.

Turner, J.C. (1975). Social comparison and social identity: Some prospects for intergroup behaviour. *European Journal of Social Psychology, 5*, 5–34.

Turner, J.C. (1981). The experimental social psychology of intergroup behavior. In J.C. Turner & H. Giles (Eds.), *Intergroup behavior* (pp. 66–101). Oxford: Blackwell.

Turner, J.C. (1982). Towards a cognitive redefinition of the social group. In H. Tajfel (Ed.). *Social identity and intergroup relations* (pp. 15–40). Cambridge: Cambridge University Press.

Turner, J.C. (1983). Some comments on the measurement of social orientations in the minimal group paradigm. *European Journal of Social Psychology, 13*, 351–368.

Turner, J.C. (1984). Social identification and psychological group formation. In H. Tajfel (Ed.), *The social dimension: European developments in social psychology* (Vol. 2, pp. 518–538). Cambridge: Cambridge University Press.

Turner, J.C. (1985). Social categorization and the self-concept: A social cognitive theory of group behavior. In E.J. Lawler (Ed.), *Advances in group processes* (Vol. 2, pp. 77–121). Greenwich, CT: JAI Press.

Turner, J.C. (1987). *Rediscovering the social group. A self-categorization theory*. Oxford: Blackwell.

Turner, J.C. (1988). In M.A. Hogg & D. Abrams (Eds.), *Social identification: A social psychology of intergroup relations and group processes*. London: Routledge.

Turner, J.C., Hogg, M.A., Oakes, P.J. & Smith, P.M. (1984). Failure and defeat as determinants of group cohesiveness. *British Journal of Social Psychology, 23*, 97–111.

Turner, J.C., Hogg, M.A., Oakes, P.J., Reicher, S.D. & Wetherell, M. (1987). *Rediscovering the social group: A self-catagorization theory*. Oxford: Blackwell.

Tversky, A. (1977). Features of similarity. *Psychological Review, 84*, 327–352.

Tversky, A. & Kahneman, D. (1973). Availability: A heuristic for judging frequency and probability. *Cognitive Psychology, 5*, 207–232.

Tversky, A. & Kahneman, D. (1974). Judgment under uncertainty: Heuristics and biases. *Science, 185*, 1123–1131.

Uleman, J.S. (1989). A framework for thinking intentionally about unintended thought. In J.S. Uleman & J.A. Bargh (Eds.), *Unintended thought: Limits of awareness, intention, and control* (pp. 425–449). New York: Guilford Press.

Uleman, J.S. & Moskowitz, G.B. (1992). *The control and the referents of spontaneous trait inferences*. Unpublished manuscript, University of New York.

Uleman, J.S. & Moskowitz, G.B. (1994). Unintended effects of goals on unintended inferences. *Journal of Personality and Social Psychology, 66*, 490–501.

Uleman, J.S., Newman, L. & Winter, L. (1992). Can personality traits be inferred automatically? Spontaneous inferences require cognitive capacity at encoding. *Consciousness and Cognition*, *1*, 77–90.

Ulrich, R.E., Stachnik, T.J. & Stainton, N.K. (1963). Student acceptance of generalized personality interpretations. *Psychological Reports*, *13*, 831–834.

Vala, J., Leyens, J.-P. & Monteiro, M.B. (1989). Causal dimensions of interpersonal violence. *European Bulletin of Cognitive Psychology*, *7*, 393–411.

Vala, J., Monteiro, M.B. & Leyens, J.-P. (1988). Perception of violence as a function of observer's ideology and actor's group membership. *British Journal of Social Psychology*, 231–237.

Visscher, P. de (1992). *Us, avatars et métamorphoses de la dynamique de groupe: Une brève historie des groupes restreints*. Grenoble: Presses Universitaires de Grenoble.

Vivian, J., Hewstone, M. & Brown, R. (1993). *Intergroup contact: Theoretical and empirical developments*. Unpublished manuscript, University of Kent, UK.

Walker, P. & Antaki, C. (1986). Sexual orientation as a basis for categorization in recall. *British Journal of Social Psychology*, *25*, 337–339.

Weber, R. & Crocker, J. (1983). Cognitive processing in the revision of stereotypic beliefs. *Journal of Personality and Social Psychology*, *45*, 961–977.

Webster, D.M. (1993). Motivated augmentation and reduction of the overattribution bias. *Journal of Personality and Social Psychology*, *65*, 261–271.

Wells, G.L. & Harvey, J.H. (1977). Do people use consensus information in making causal attributions? *Journal of Personality and Social Psychology*, *35*, 279–293.

Wetherell, M. (1982). Cross-cultural studies of unusual groups: Implications for the social identity theory of intergroup relations. In H. Tajfel (Ed.) Social identity and intergroup relations (pp. 207–240). Cambridge: Cambridge University Press.

Wilder, D.A. (1978). Homogeneity of jurors: the majority's influence depends upon their perceived independence. *Law and Human Behaviour*, *2*, 365–376.

Wilder, D.A. & Allen, V.L. (1978). Group membership and preference for information about others. *Psychological Bulletin*, *4*, 106–110.

Wilder, D.A. & Shapiro, P.N. (1991). Facilitation of outgroup stereotypes by enhanced ingroup identity. *Journal of Experimental Social Psychology*, *27*, 431–452.

Williams, J.E. & Best, D.L. (1982). *Measuring sex stereotypes: A thirty nation study*. Beverly Hills, CA: Sage.

Winter, L. & Uleman, J.S. (1984). When are social judgments made? Evidence for spontaneousness of trait inferences. *Journal of Personality and Social Psychology*, *47*, 237–252.

Winter, L., Uleman, J.S. & Cunniff, C. (1985). How automatic are social judgments? *Journal of Personality and Social Psychology*, *49*, 904–917.

Wishner, J. (1960) Reanalysis of 'Impression of Personality'. *Psychological Review*, *67*, 97–112.

Worchel, S., Lind, E. & Kaufman, K. (1975). Evaluations of groups products as a function of expectations of group longevity, outcomes of competition, and publicity of evaluations. *Journal of Personality and Social Psychology*, *31*, 1089–1097.

Wright, E.F. & Wells, G.L. (1988). Is the attitude-attribution paradigm suitable for investigating the dispositional bias? *Personality and Social Psychology Bulletin*, *14*, 183–190.

Wyer, R.S. & Gordon, S.E. (1982). The recall of information about persons and groups. *Journal of Experimental Social Psychology*, *18*, 128–164.

Wyer, R.S. & Gordon, S.E. (1984). The cognitive representation of social information. In R.S. Wyer & T.K. Srull (Eds.), *Handbook of social cognition* (Vol. 2, pp. 73–150). Hillsdale, NJ: Erlbaum.

Young, K. (1946). *Handbook of social psychology*. London: Kegan, Trench & Trubner.

Yzerbyt, V.Y. (1990). *De l'exploitation des informations dans le jugement social: Vers une approche de la jugeabilité sociale*. Unpublished doctoral dissertation, University of Louvain, Louvain-la-Neuve, Belgium.

Yzerbyt, V.Y. & Leyens, J.-P. (1991). Requesting information to form an impression: The influence of valence and confirmatory status. *Journal of Experimental Social Psychology*, 27, 337–356.

Yzerbyt, V.Y., Leyens, J.-P. & Bellour, F. (1994). The ingroup overexclusion effect: Identity concerns in decisions about group membership. *European Journal of Social Psychology*, 24, in press.

Yzerbyt, V.Y., Leyens, J.-P., Corneille, O. & Geeraerts, B. (1994). *Do you read yourself allright? Further evidence for the role of social judgeability concerns in impression formation.* Unpublished manuscript, University of Louvain, Louvain-la-Neuve, Belgium.

Yzerbyt, V.Y., Leyens, J.-P. & Schadron, G. (1994). *Social judgeability: The impact of the mere presence of information on the dilution of stereotypes.* Unpublished manuscript, University of Louvain, Louvain-la-Neuve, Belgium.

Yzerbyt, V.Y., Schadron, G., Leyens, J.-P. & Rocher, S. (1994). Social judgeability: The impact of meta-informational cues on the use of stereotypes. *Journal of Personality and Social Psychology*, 66, 48–55.

Yzerbyt, V.Y. & Schadron, G. (1994). Stéréotypes et jugement social. In R.Y. Bourhis & J.-P. Leyens (Eds.), *Stéréotypes, discriminations et relations intergroupes* (in press). Brussels: Madaga.

Zanna, M.P. & Hamilton, D.L. (1977). Further evidence of meaning change in impression formation. *Journal of Experimental Social Psychology*, 13, 224–238.

Zebrowitz, L.A. (1990). *Social perception.* Milton Keynes: Open University Press.

Zima, P.V. (1974). *L'école de Francfort: Dialectique de la particularité.* Paris: Editions Universitaires.

Zukier, H. (1982). The dilution effect: The role of the correlation and the dispersion of predictor variables in the use of nondiagnostic information. *Journal of Personality and Social Psychology*, 43, 1163–1174.

Zukier, H. (1986). The paradigmatic and narrative modes in goal-guided inference. In R.M. Sorrentino & E.T. Higgins (Eds.), *Handbook of motivation and cognition: Foundations of social behavior* (Vol. 1, pp. 465–502). New York: Guilford.

Zukier, H. & Jennings, D.L. (1984). Nondiagnosticity and typicality effects in prediction. *Social Cognition*, 2, 187–198.

Zukier, H. & Pepitone, A. (1984). Social roles and strategies in prediction: Some determinants of the use of base-rate information. *Journal of Personality and Social Psychology*, 47, 349–360.

Index

The following abbreviations have been used in the index: OAB overattribution bias